# TREASURE IN CLAY

An electronic preacher *(Courtesy, Society for the Propagation of the Faith)*

# TREASURE
# IN
# CLAY

## THE AUTOBIOGRAPHY OF
### *Fulton J. Sheen*

IMAGE BOOKS/DOUBLEDAY
*New York   London   Toronto
Sydney   Auckland*

AN IMAGE BOOK
PUBLISHED BY DOUBLEDAY

A hardcover edition of ths book was originally published in 1980
by Doubleday.

Published in the United States by Doubleday,
an imprint of The Doubleday Publishing Group,
a division of Random House, Inc., New York.
www.doubleday.com

Book design by Jennifer Ann Daddio

Library of Congress Cataloging-in-Publication Data
Sheen, Fulton J.
Treasure in clay : the autobiography of Fulton J. Sheen.—1st
paperback ed.
p. cm.
"Originally published in 1980."
I. Sheen, Fulton J. (Fulton John), 1895–1979. 2. Catholic
Church—United States—Bishops—Biography. I. Title.
BX4705 S612A37 2008
282.092—dc22
[B]
2008006617

ISBN 978-0-385-17709-2

PRINTED IN THE UNITED STATES OF AMERICA

*Salve Regina*

*Salve Regina*

# CONTENTS

# FOREWORD

*A Prophet Suffering in Silence*

In 1957 Bishop Fulton Sheen, then the best-known Catholic in America, with an unmatched television following, began the great trial of his life. He would lose much more than the public ever realized, all over his refusal to give Cardinal Francis Spellman of New York milk money.

In the late 1950s the government donated millions of dollars worth of powdered milk to the New York Archdiocese. In turn, Cardinal Spellman handed that milk over to the Society for the Propagation of the Faith to distribute to the poor of the world. On at least one occasion he demanded that the director of the Society, Bishop Sheen, *pay* the Archdiocese for the donated milk. He wanted millions of dollars. Despite Cardinal Spellman's considerable powers of persuasion and influence in Rome, Sheen refused.

These were funds donated by the public to the missions,

funds Sheen himself had personally contributed to and raised over the airwaves. He felt an obligation to protect them, even from the itchy fingers of his own Cardinal. Undeterred, Spellman appealed the case to Pope Pius XII personally, in Sheen's presence. After examining the facts, Pope Pius sided with Sheen. His biographer, Thomas Reese, reports that Sheen was later confronted by Spellman, who said, "I will get even with you. It may take six months or ten years, but everyone will know what you are like." It took Spellman less than ten years.

By the fall of 1957, Bishop Sheen, a Catholic media fixture for nearly thirty years, "retired" from the airwaves, ending his "Life is Worth Living" program at the height of its popularity. It is widely believed that Cardinal Spellman drove Sheen off the air. (At the time the show was shuttered an estimated 30 million viewers and listeners tuned in each week.) Suddenly the illustrious preacher found himself unwelcome in the churches of New York. Spellman cancelled Sheen's annual Good Friday sermons at St. Patrick's Cathedral and discouraged clergy from befriending the Bishop. By 1966, Spellman would get Sheen reassigned to Rochester, New York, terminating his leadership at the Society for the Propagation of the Faith.

As compelling as all of this is (and it is), none of the details related to the Spellman affair nor Sheen's personal feelings about the Cardinal's actions are mentioned in this autobiography. These omissions raise an interesting point.

Somewhere in these pages Sheen writes: "The curious would like me to open healed wounds; the media in particular would relish a chapter which would pass judgment on others . . . 'We live in days of assassins'—where evil is sought in lives more than good to justify a world with a bad conscience." In the pages that follow, no scores are settled, no names named. Oh, there are the fleeting references to "trials both inside and outside the Church" (p. 360) and asides like, "I am certain that it is God who made certain people throw stones at me . . ." (p. 332). But those looking for literary payback need to look elsewhere. (Spellman is even praised!) Instead, what follows is a singular autobiography, one that is more an internal portrait of a man than an external one. And what a man Bishop Fulton Sheen was.

Pope Pius XII once referred to Sheen as "a prophet of the times." He engaged all facets of the culture in a dazzling way. An author of more than sixty books and a columnist, he used his well-trained mind to touch the common man. Explaining the Gospel with true innovation, he often appealed to poetry, philosophy, history, architecture, song, and art to drive home his message. For sixteen years as the National Director of the Society for the Propagation of the Faith he raised hundreds of millions of dollars for the world's poor, donating about 10 million dollars of his personal earnings to the missions. Sheen built churches and hospitals for poor blacks in Alabama, tirelessly preached retreats, visited the imprisoned and sick, taught convert classes, and offered Mass in parishes around the world.

But he is perhaps best known for his broadcast work. Before Mother Angelica, Pat Robertson, and Joel Osteen, there was Bishop Fulton Sheen. In his magenta cape and zucchetto he was a media trailblazer who often beat Milton Berle and Frank Sinatra in the ratings. For more than fifty years he transformed rarified theology into the idiom of the masses, using radio and then television to bring a message of hope to people of all faiths and those of none at all.

I remember being in need of a spiritual favor about sixteen years ago. Knowing that I was in television, a priest friend suggested that I "go make a deal with Archbishop Sheen." Following his advice, I knelt before the crypt at St. Patrick's in New York one afternoon and promised the Archbishop that if he interceded with God on my behalf, I would do all I could to get his program back on television. Sheen answered my prayer. It would take me several years to fulfill my part of the bargain. At this writing, Sheen's "Life is Worth Living" follows the broadcast of my program on EWTN each Friday night.

Watching the reruns today can be a jarring experience. The stylized nineteenth-century gestures, the dramatic vocal escalations, and that unfurled cape lack the naturalism we have come to expect from television personalities. But if you can get past the visuals and focus on the message, there are rich treasures there.

This autobiography would be Bishop Sheen's last treasure. It is at once an exploration of an apostle's journey and a history of the Catholic Church in the twentieth century. A participant at the Second Vatican Council, Sheen offers a stinging critique of the failure to properly interpret the Council documents. He also presents one of the most cogent and reasonable explanations of celibacy one is likely to ever read (turning to Gandhi and Dag Hammarskjöld to make his case).

The professor in Sheen can't help but use this autobiography to instruct; so as you learn about the man, you will also receive insights on the nature of the Eucharist, the papacy, and the Blessed Mother. Included here are hilarious and touching remembrances from his long life. But it is the reflective personal revelations—the spiritual lessons learned in pain—that distinguish what is here.

This book was written during a period of intense physical suffering for Sheen. Starting in 1977, he underwent a series of surgeries that sapped his strength and even made preaching difficult. He must have known that this would be his final work because one senses an urgency on these pages, an eagerness to impart these lessons, particularly those dealing with the spiritual bounty found in pain. The last chapters crackle with the same zeal and determination of his final homilies from the late 70s: they are prophetic and impassioned, free from the gilded edges of the past.

"The Three Stages of My Life," the final chapter here, is worth the sticker price. In it, the Bishop honestly admits his vanity, his fondness for "creature comforts" and says, "I had to be brought through trials, both inside and outside the Church before I could understand the full meaning of my life. It was not enough to be a priest; one also had to be a victim." In the end, Fulton Sheen became a victim. Parts of what you will read were recited from his sickbed as he clutched a crucifix. His final meditation on the cross, which concludes the book, is particularly moving.

Like all great biographies, this one furnishes us with a chance to reflect on our own lives in the afterglow of one who has gone before us. In Sheen's case, his life and example shine brighter now than when he passed away, nearly thirty years ago.

In the middle of this book, Sheen ponders some questions we should all consider: "Have I really served the Church as well as I should? Have I used the many talents the Lord has given me? Have I cast fire upon the earth as the Lord asked me to do?" I think, in Sheen's case, one must answer these questions in the affirmative. Few bishops, or laymen for that matter, have done it so well for so long, and with such panache. And the story goes on.

Sheen's cause for sainthood is now under consideration at the Vatican, which seems entirely appropriate. The media is in desperate need of a patron (particularly reality show creators and news departments), and this culture needs reminders that sanctity, not sensationalism, endures. Unlike so many of the illustrious names mentioned herein who have faded in history's advance (Clare Boothe Luce, Heywood Broun, and George Gobel, for instance), Sheen's memory remains vibrant not due to his television renown, but for the timeliness of the truth he expounded and the passion with which he did so. There is indeed a treasure in this clay: the treasure of lasting truth imparted by a true apostle.

Raymond Arroyo
Ash Wednesday, 2008
Northern Virginia

# LIST OF ILLUSTRATIONS

# TREASURE IN CLAY

## One

# IT ALL DEPENDS ON HOW YOU LOOK AT IT

When the record of any human life is set down, there are three pairs of eyes who see it in a different light. There is the life:

1. As I see it.
2. As others see it.
3. As God sees it.

Let it be said here at the beginning that this is not my real autobiography. That was written twenty-one centuries ago, published and placarded in three languages, and made available to everyone in Western civilization.

Carlyle was wrong in saying that "there is no life of a man faithfully recorded." Mine was! The ink used was blood, the parchment was skin, the pen was a spear. Over eighty chapters make up the book, each for a year of my life. Though I pick it up every day, it never reads the same. The more I lift my eyes from its pages, the more I feel the need of doing my own autobiography that all might see what I want them to see. But the more I fasten my gaze on it, the more I see that everything worthwhile in it was received as a gift from Heaven. Why then should I glory in it?

That old autobiographical volume was like the sun. The farther I walked from it, the deeper and the longer were the shadows that stretched before my eyes: regrets, remorse and fears. But as I walked toward it, the shadows fell behind me, less awesome but still reminders of what I had left undone. But when I took the book into my hands, there were no shadows either fore or aft, but the supernal joy of being bathed in light. It was like walking directly under the sun, no mirages to solicit, no phantoms to follow.

*That autobiography is the crucifix*—the inside story of my life not in the way it walks the stage of time, but how it was recorded, taped and written in the Book of Life. It is not the autobiography that I tell you, but the autobiography I *read to myself*. In the crown of thorns, I see my pride, my grasping for earthly toys in the pierced Hands, my flight from shepherding care in the pierced Feet, my wasted love in the wounded Heart, and my prurient desires in the flesh hanging from Him like purple rags. Almost every time I turn a page of that book, my heart weeps at what *eros* has done to *agape*, what the "I" has done to the "Thou," what the professed friend has done to the Beloved.

But there have been moments in that autobiography when my heart leaped with joy at being invited to His Last Supper; when I grieved when one of my own left His side to blister His lips with a kiss; when I tried falteringly to help carry His gibbet to the Hill of the Skull; when I moved a few steps closer to Mary to help draw the thrust sword from her heart; when I hoped to be now and then in life a disciple like the disciple called "Beloved"; when I rejoiced at bringing other Magdalenes to the Cross to become the love we fall just short of in all love; when I tried to emulate the centurion and press cold water to thirsty lips; when, like Peter, I ran to an empty tomb and then, at a seashore, had my heart broken a thousand times as He kept asking over and over again in my life: "Do you love Me?" These are the more edifying moments of the autobiography which can be written as a kind of second and less authentic edition than the real autobiography written two thousand years ago.

What is contained in this edition is not the whole truth—the Scars are the whole truth. My life, as I see it, is crossed up with the crucifix. Only the two of us—my Lord and I—read it, and as the years go on we spend more and more time reading it together. What it contains will be telecast to the world on the Day of Judgment.

What you read is truth nevertheless, but on a lower level: the narrative of a jewel and its setting, the treasure and its wrapping, the lily and its pond.

How, then, do I see my life? I see it as a priest. That means I am no longer my own but at every moment of existence acting in the person of Christ. As a United States ambassador in a foreign country whether at recreation or in council chambers is always being judged as a representative of our country, so too a priest is always an ambassador of Christ. But that is only one side of the coin. The priest is still a man.

That is why the title of this autobiography is *Treasure in Clay*. It is taken from a letter St. Paul wrote to the Corinthians about himself and other apostles of the Lord as being no better than "pots" of earthenware to contain the treasure. The example may have been the clay lamps in which oil was put to hold light. I have chosen this text to indicate the contrast between the nobility of the vocation to the priesthood and the frailty of the human nature which houses it. We have the awesome power to act *in Persona Christi*, that is, to forgive the grossest of sins, to transplant the Cross of Calvary to the altar, to give divine birth to thousands of children at the baptismal font, and to usher souls on deathbeds to the Kingdom of Heaven.

But, on the other hand, we look like anyone else. We have the same weaknesses as other men, some to the bottle, or a woman, or a dollar, or a desire to be a little higher in the hierarchy of power. Each priest is a man with a body of soft clay. To keep that treasure pure, he has to be stretched out on a cross of fire. Our fall can be greater than the fall of anyone else because of the height from which we tumble. Of all the bad men, bad religious men are the worst, because they were called to be closer to Christ.

That is why it is hard for one with this calling to write an autobiography, because there is enacted the frightening tension between the dignity of his calling and the corruptibility of his clay. As Cardinal Newman wrote: "I could not even bear the scrutiny of an angel; how then can I see Thee and live? I should be seared as grass, should I be exposed to the glow of Thy Countenance." But at the very white-hot center of this tension between the divinity of the mission and the poor weak human instrumentality there is always the out-pouring of the love of Christ. He never permits any of us to be tempted beyond our strength; and even in our weaknesses He loves us, for the Good Shepherd loves lost shepherds, as much as lost sheep. The tension is greatest, perhaps, for those who try to love Him with total surrender.

But the way I see my life in conformity with my vocation is different from how others might see it. That is why there are biographies as well as autobiographies. Even biographies can differ one from the other: the life of Christ that John left in his Gospel is quite different from the life that Judas would have written had he used a pen instead of a halter. Biographies generally are not written until one becomes a celebrity—or until one who is not known well enough to talk to is known well enough to talk about.

Shakespeare surmised that, in biography,

> *The evil that men do lives after them,*
> *The good is oft interred with their bones.*

But when it comes to writing about a bishop who is given the throne a few feet above the people, there is danger of seeing him in pomp and dignity. Again, appealing to Shakespeare:

> *Man, proud man*
> *Dressed in a little brief authority,*

*Most ignorant of what he's most assur'd,*
*His glossy essence, like an angry ape,*
*Plays such fantastic tricks before high heaven*
*As make the angels weep.*

When one enjoys some popularity in the world, such as the Lord has given to me in great measure, one is praised and respected even beyond desserts. As a little boy wrote to me on my eighty-fourth birthday: "I hop you have a happy birthday. I hop you will live long and I hop that one day you will be Pop."

At the end of a long life, one generally finds that there are two things said: things that are too good to be true and things that are too bad to be true. The excess is on the side of credit, which is indeed a tribute to the laity who see the priest as he is really supposed to be—"another Christ."

The Lord does not choose the best. I was not given a vocation because God, in His divine wisdom, saw that I would be better than other men. *Even God's love is blind.* I know thousands of men who are far more deserving of being a priest than I am. He often chooses weak instruments in order that His power might be manifested; otherwise it would seem that the good was done by the clay, rather than by the Spirit. The Lord came into Jerusalem on an ass. He can ride into New York and London and down the middle aisle of any cathedral in a human nature that is not much better. The Lord does not hold in great esteem those who are high in popularity polls: "Woe to you when all men speak well of you."

This might seem to put the Gospel in a repulsive light, but what our Lord meant was that we may begin to believe our newspaper clippings and to be carried away by what the world thinks of us. Generally, the more we accept popular estimates, the less time we spend on our knees examining conscience. The outer world becomes so full of limelight as to make us forget the light within. Praise often creates in us a false impression that we deserve it. Our reaction to it changes with the years: in the beginning one is embarrassed and flustered; then we love it while claiming that it runs off us like water off a duck's back—but the duck likes water! The latter stage is apt to end in cynicism as we wonder what the one who praises *really* wants.

Finally, there is my life as God sees it. Here the judgment is completely different. Man reads the face but God reads the heart. David was not chosen for his good looks, nor Elijah rejected because of his. Our Lord has a double view of us: the way He intended us to be and the way we corresponded to His grace. God took a great risk in giving us free will as parents do when they grant freedom to their children. The prophet Jeremiah offers a very beautiful story of the difference between the ideal that God has for each of us and the way we make ourselves. God writes the final epitaph—not on monuments but on hearts. I only know that those who received more talents from God will be more strictly judged. When a man has been given much, much will be expected of him; and the more a man might have had entrusted to him, the more he could be required to repay. God has given me not only a vocation, but He enriched it with opportunities and gifts, which means that He will expect me to pay a high income tax on the Final Day.

How God will judge I know not, but I trust that He will see me with mercy and compassion. I am only certain that there will be three surprises in Heaven. First of all, I will see some people there whom I never expected to see. Second, there will be a number whom I expect to be there who will not be there. And, even relying on His mercy, the biggest surprise of all may be that I will be there.

## Two

# THE MOLDING
# OF THE CLAY

Clay has to be molded, and that is done primarily in the family, which is more sacred than the state. The determining mold of my early life was the decision of my parents that each of their children should be well educated. This resolve was born not out of their own education, but their lack of it. My father never went beyond the third grade because his father felt he was needed on the farm. My mother had no more than an eighth-grade education at a time when there was one teacher for all the grades.

On my mother's side both my grandparents came from Croghan, a little village in County Roscommon, Ireland, near the town of Boyle. My father's father (whom I never knew because he died when I was quite small) was born in Ireland also. My father's mother, however, was born in Indiana. Unfortunately, she, too, died before I was old enough to know her.

My father, Newton Sheen, and my mother, Delia Fulton, owned a hardware store in El Paso, Illinois, about thirty miles east of Peoria. One day, my father sent the store's errand boy down to the basement for some merchandise. The boy—who later on became a banker in the town—saw his father enter the front door as he was coming back up the stairs. The boy was smoking a cigarette, which was almost anathema for a young boy in those days. Fearful of his father, he threw it under the stairs. It fell in a fifty-gallon can of gasoline and the whole business section of El Paso burned down! Perhaps to recoup the losses, and in order to earn his living, my father then moved to a farm which he had inherited from his father.

From earliest age I showed a distaste for anything associated with farm life, and my father often said that, as a young boy, I took a saw and destroyed one of the endgates of his best wagon. By this time, there were two sons in the family, I being the oldest and Joe next in line, following me by two years. I suppose that being poor creates in some a desire to be rich; but in any case, my parents' want of education begot in them a resolve that their children should be educated. So they moved to Peoria in order that I might be enrolled in St. Mary's, the parochial school there, and begin a Christian education.

It was at this point in my life that I was given the name of Fulton. It seems that I cried for almost the first two years of my mortal life. Later, as a boy, I was so embarrassed when visiting relatives and a family doctor would always begin the conversation to my mother: "Oh, this is the boy who never stopped crying." I became such a burden to my mother that her own mother and father would often relieve her tears. Jok-

The Archbishop's birthplace—the hardware store and apartment at 25 Front Street, El Paso, Illinois, where the Sheen family lived. Archbishop Sheen was born here, and his father ran the hardware store. *(Courtesy, Fulton J. Sheen Archives)*

ingly, relatives and friends would say to my mother: "Oh,
he's Fulton's baby." When I was enrolled in the parochial
school my grandfather Fulton was asked my name and he answered: "It's Fulton." Though I had been baptized Peter in
St. Mary's Church in El Paso, Illinois, I now was called Fulton. In the course of time, my brother Joe became a lawyer
in Chicago, and the one next to him, Tom, became a doctor
in New York, and the fourth, Al, entered industry—so the
children of Newton and Delia Sheen did receive an education. Thirty or forty years later, when I was taken to a hospital in New York after collapsing in a radio studio, my
brother the doctor discovered that as a child I had had tuber-
culosis, which produced the profuse tears, and they in turn
produced calcium, which helped cure the affliction and give
me a strong set of lungs. In any case, after taking the name
John at Confirmation, I became Fulton John Sheen.

My first-grade teacher was Sister Alexine. I stayed in contact with Sister Alexine not only through high school, but
even after Ordination and until her death. She never seemed
to age a single day. By teaching the young, she remained
young. Virtue does more to preserve youthfulness than all the
pomades in Elizabeth Arden's. She could never recall locking
me one day in the classroom closet for a few minutes because
of disobedience. I suspect she did not want to remember it!
But I remembered it very well—and the imprisonment
seemed to be years. It did me no harm.

In one of the very early grades, probably the first, I was
kept after school because I had not learned to spell *which*. I
tried spelling it a half-dozen or more ways, but to no avail.
One little girl in back of me whispered "w-h-i-c-h" in my
ear. I met her again when she was eighty-three in an old folks'

home and thanked her for furthering my education, *which* would have been much hampered without her whisper.

While still in the early grades, I recall telling my mother that I had lost first place in a spelling contest to Margaret Kennedy. I did not know how to spell *thralldom*. (Webster now gives the alternative spelling with one *l*—the way I had spelled it.) I struggled to be a leader in the class, and I would come home with holy pictures and medals, but I would never receive one word of praise from my parents. Occasionally my mother would say a word about having done well, but my fa-

Fulton J. Sheen as a schoolboy, astride his pony, Bob, which he rode like a veteran.
*(Courtesy, Fulton J. Sheen Archives)*

ther never did. I spoke once to my mother about it and asked why my father never praised me. Her answer was: "He does not wish to spoil you, but he is telling all the neighbors."

I became an altar boy when I was about eight, serving Mass in St. Mary's Cathedral, Peoria, Illinois. Early one morning, I was serving the great Bishop John L. Spalding. This particular morning, I dropped the wine cruet on the marble floor. There is no atomic explosion that can equal in intensity of decibels the noise and explosive force of a wine cruet falling on the marble floor of a cathedral in the presence of a bishop. I was frightened to death. What would the Bishop say? When Mass was over, Bishop Spalding called me and put his arms around me saying: "Young man, where are you going to school when you get big?" To an eight-year-old boy, "big" was high school. I said: "Spalding Institute," which was the high school named after him. (One has to admit it was a rather diplomatic answer, but I was not so conscious then of its diplomacy.) He tried again: "I said 'when you get big.' Did you ever hear of Louvain?" I answered: "No, Your Grace." "Very well, you go home and tell your mother that I said when you get big you are to go to Louvain, and someday you will be just as I am." I told my mother what the Bishop had said, and she explained that Louvain was one of the great universities of the world, located in Belgium.

I never thought again of the Bishop's statement until two years after Ordination when I set my foot in Louvain to attend the university. I thought, "Oh, this is the place where Bishop Spalding told me to go." Nor did I ever recall again his prophecy about being a bishop, since it was merely the priesthood I was pursuing.

The fifth grade was divided into big boys and big girls. I

Graduation from St. Mary's parochial school in Peoria, Illinois, c. 1909.
Young Fulton in middle, front row. *(Courtesy, Fulton J. Sheen Archives)*

was among the little boys and little girls. A contest in arithmetic was arranged between the Davids and the Goliaths.
One boy named Ed was chosen to represent the Goliaths
while I was chosen to represent the Davids. We were put in a
classroom with both classes attending as cheering groups.
The blackboards were at right angles to one another so we
could not copy. A Sister from the Goliath group would read
a problem, and then a Sister from the David group would do
likewise. The contest went on for about thirty minutes, and
became highly tense while the students kept on applauding
as we both finished at the same time. Then the Sister from
the Goliath group read a problem which I remembered and
I began working it out at once. Ed was waiting for the problem to be read. I had finished the problem before he had even
begun it. The Sister in the upper classroom became so angry
at one of the Davids beating her Goliath that she threw the
arithmetic book at me, but her aim was poor and it missed.

After parochial school, I enrolled in Spalding Institute, conducted by the Brothers of Mary. They were excellent teachers, given to discipline, yet much beloved. One of my classmates was Jimmy Jordan, who later on became known on radio as Fibber McGee. Just across the street in the girls' Academy of Our Lady was a young girl who later became Fibber's wife Molly on radio. One block away at Peoria High School was a boy whom neither of us knew but who later became Andy of the famous Amos and Andy team. Thus Peoria produced three famous radio personalities of those times and even a fourth, if the reader is charitable.

Every year in order to raise money for Spalding, the students presented a theatrical play. I had no theatrical ability as the tests proved, but the Brothers felt that somehow or other I had to be in the play because my father paid for the program. I still remember the only line I had, which was a line of intercession. Someone was about to kill my father in a forest and my line was: "Have pity on him for your little Angelo's sake."

In the fourth year of high school I was the valedictorian of the class, but the Brothers were never very well pleased with me as a valedictorian speaker. A trigonometry medal was given at the end of the year for the highest mark in that subject. Ralph Buechel and I were tied, each with 100 per cent for the year. To work off the tie, three problems in trigonometry were given to us in a special examination. The third problem I recalled from the trigonometry book; as soon as the Brother started reading it, I worked it out from memory. When the papers were examined, I received 66⅔ per cent and Ralph received 100 per cent and the medal. I said to the Brother afterward: "I think that third problem of

mine was right because I remember it from the manual."
"Oh," he said, "yes, it was right according to the book, but
you were not listening to me; so I changed the angle of the
flagpole and that is the reason you lost the medal."

After high school, I enrolled at St. Viator College (now
defunct, though I remember it well). Conducted by the Via-
torian Fathers, it had among notable professors Professor
Kenyon of Harvard, who gave us excellent training in Shakespeare ... Father Bergan, one of the greatest inspirations of
my life, who was Professor of Philosophy ... Father McGuire,
who came to Roman Catholicism from the Anglican min-

When Fulton was graduated from Spalding Institute in 1913 at Peoria, Illinois. *(Courtesy, Fulton J.
Sheen Archives)*

istry and was a graduate of Oxford . . . and Dr. Potter, a graduate of Wharton School of Economics.

During the scholastic year, the students would recite the Rosary every day. In fair weather, this was done on the football field; in foul weather, in the gymnasium. I was chosen by the students to lead the Rosary. This particular afternoon it was in the gymnasium, at the far end of which was a stage prepared for a debate with a college in Iowa. I was on the debating team. The thought of being on that stage that night distracted me so much that I could not finish the Rosary. I believe that all the nervousness of my whole existence must have been concentrated in those few moments, for I was never seriously nervous again in my life before an audience.

The molding of the clay was done by great sacrifices on the part of my father and my mother, who would deny themselves every personal comfort and luxury in order that their sons might be well clothed and well cared for. Our family life was simple and the atmosphere of our home Christian. Grace was said before and after each meal; when we had visitors none of us was permitted to sit at table without wearing a coat and tie; the Rosary was said every evening; the priests of the cathedral visited the home once every week; and visits of old-country cousins were very frequent.

I remember once receiving a spanking from my father. We had a horse which we kept in a barn behind the residence. He would be used for family driving during the week and on Sunday. This particular day it was my duty to feed Morgan, the horse, which I did at the appointed hour. That evening when my father came in, he asked me if I had fed the horse and I told him I had done so. Morgan must have been particularly hungry that day for apparently there was no hay left in the manger. My father thought I was lying so he gave me a spanking. He applied the palm of his hand to the seat of my pants with some dexterity. There is nothing that develops character in a young boy like a pat on the back, provided it is given often enough, hard enough and low enough. I complained later to my mother that I had fed the horse and she testified to the truth of my statement. My father said: "I'm sorry, but that will do for the next time." I never remembered the next time, for I went through the rest of my life without spankings but not without reprimands.

Looking back on those early days, I recall great differences in the economic order. My father would sell corn from his farm for fifty cents a bushel and wheat for a dollar a bushel, which was considered extreme in those days before Russia started buying our wheat. But a better indication of the difference in price index was the fact that almost every day except Friday I would be sent to the grocery store to buy thirty cents' worth of sirloin steak. The butcher would always throw in a wiener—what today is called a hot dog—with every purchase. That thirty cents fed my father, mother, grandmother and four boys, and without any skimping. Milk was five cents a gallon.

We kept a charge account at one of the grocery stores. When I was about nine, on the way to school I put on the charge account a box of Nabisco biscuits, in those days worth about ten cents. My father later on discovered this deceit and I received a short but firm lecture on honesty.

Another lesson on the same subject was learned after I stole a geranium which was exhibited in front of a grocery store. I saw these geraniums advertised for ten cents a plant. I knew that my mother kept geraniums in tomato cans outside on the windowsill, and assuming that I would do her a favor, I picked up one of the flowers, brought it home to my mother at noon and said: "Here, Mother, is a geranium for you." Then began the inquisition: "Did you buy it?" "No, Mother." "Did you steal it?" "Yes, Mother." She then sent me to my piggy bank and made me shake out of it fifty cents. I objected that the plant cost only ten cents and one single flower was not worth fifty cents. But she insisted that I make that kind of restitution. My act of dishonesty thus punished by restitution taught me for life that honesty is the best policy. In any case, when I took the money to Mr. Madden, he gave me two pots of geraniums.

All the time that we were in school my mother and father, both of whom believed in hard work, sent us out to one of the two farms they owned by this time, east and west of the city of Peoria. The tenant farmer would accept the Sheen boys as hired hands on weekends and during the summer months. In the early days during a lull in some heavy farm work, my father and some of his friends were seated together, and a jolly, fat neighbor, by the name of Billy Ryan, said to my father: "Newt, that oldest boy of yours, Fulton, will never be worth a damn. He's always got his nose in a book." My brothers rather enjoyed farm work; I suffered it. When I see thousands of young men running around in dungarees today, I remember how ashamed I used to be at having to wear overalls, which were the dungarees of those days. From the point of view of fashion, it was about as low as you could get.

Those who know me now find it hard to realize that there was once a time in my life when I plowed corn, made hay while the sun shone, broke colts to harness, curried horses, cleaned their dirty stalls, milked cows morning and night and in cold, damp weather, shucked corn, fed the pigs, dug postholes, applied salve to horses cut by barbed wire, fought potato bugs on the day that a circus came to town, argued with my father every day that farming was not a good life and that you could make a fortune on it only if you struck oil.

Without ever expressing it in so many words, I was brought up on the ethic of work. In Scripture work is described as a penalty for sin—the "primal eldest curse." It was not the work I disliked; it was the farming. Both my father and mother were hard workers. I can remember whenever we visited relatives, I could hear them say in the kitchen, "Ask Aunt Dee to leave the work to us," Dee being a nickname for Delia. My father, whenever he would go out to visit the tenant farmers, would help them build barns, reap the harvest and do anything to keep himself busy. Not only because it was parental training but perhaps because it was already ingrained in me, the habit of work was one I never got over, and I thank God I never did.

One day when I was ten, I was playing baseball in an open lot near our home in Peoria. My mother called me to go to the grocery store to buy something she urgently needed for dinner. I complained: "Why can't I finish the game? There are only two more innings to play." Her answer was: "You are out there for exercise. What difference does it make whether you are running the bases or running to the grocery store?" Years later when I fell into the wisdom of Thomas Aquinas I received the answer to her question. This learned philosopher asks: "What is the difference between work and play?" and he answers: "Work has a purpose, play has none, but there must be time in life for purposeless things, even foolishness." But when I learned that distinction it was too late for a clever answer to my mother. By this time she would hardly ever call me from a book.

Returning to the subject of education, St. Viator's College was also a seminary for the training of priests. When I graduated, Bishop Edmund Dunne of Peoria sent me to St. Paul's Seminary in St. Paul, Minnesota, to finish my studies for the priesthood. These were the days of World War I; food was meager and I developed an ulcer which required an operation. The courses were extremely good, especially in Sacred Scripture, history and moral theology. The music

Graduation from St. Viator's College in Bourbonnais, Illinois, c. 1917. (*Courtesy, Fulton J. Sheen Archives*)

teacher of Gregorian chant had to train all of us, whether we had singing voices or not. I was among those who could hardly carry a key on a ring. Grace Moore later on confirmed this. About twenty years later, however, when I returned to give a lecture in an auditorium in St. Paul, I was introduced by my music teacher, who praised me for my singing. I am sure the good man did not purposely lie; he just had a bad memory. They say singing is every man's birthright but it certainly never was mine. I didn't sound good even in a shower.

On Saturday, September 20, 1919, I was ordained a priest, by the grace of God, in the cathedral at Peoria. The stirrings which the Holy Spirit put in my soul in the early days were now fulfilled—or were they? I was now a priest. Yes. But is not that just half the story? I never asked myself that question the day I was ordained. In due time, and not in an easy way, I was to learn that a priest is also a victim. But more about that later.

Immediately after Ordination, I was sent to the Catholic University in Washington to work for a doctorate in philosophy, which required three years of residence and study. Some of the teachers were excellent—such as Dr. Edward Pace and the famous Dr. John A. Ryan, who was a leader in this country in the field of social ethics. On weekends I would make myself available for work in different parishes in Washington, a practice frowned upon by the university authorities. I was invited to give a Lenten course in St. Paul's Church by the venerable Monsignor Mackay. I was only twenty-four years old at the time and when I knocked at the front door of the rectory, the good Monsignor took a look at me and said: "Get back to the sacristy immediately with the rest of the altar boys." In the rain, and with a coat collar

As Fulton J. Sheen looked when he was
ordained in 1919. (*Courtesy, Fulton J. Sheen
Archives*)

over my own Roman collar, he did not recognize me to be a
priest.

The same year I was to offer Holy Week Eucharist in St.
Patrick's Church in Washington. The liturgy of that week is
slightly different from that of other days of the year and I
was a bit concerned as to whether I could do it properly. One
of the directions given in Latin during the course of the
Holy Saturday liturgy was to sing Alleluia three times. There
are about forty-nine notes in that Alleluia, which would test
even the skills of a Caruso. I did my best to give utterance to

all those black notes in the missal. I gave a sigh of relief at the end of the Alleluia, but old Monsignor Thomas, the pastor, who wore purple socks, shouted out from the sacristy in the hearing range of the entire congregation: "Sing it again!" I sang it again, simply because he ordered me to do it. When I finished the second effort, again in still louder tones, he cried: "Sing it again!" which I did in reluctant obedience and feeling very stupid for having to do so. But then I noticed at the end of the Latin directive about singing Alleluia the little word *ter*, which means three times. That incident always reminded me of the story of the man who had a choice of marrying either a beautiful servant girl who was unknown or an ugly opera singer who was quite famous. He opted for the opera singer. The morning after the honeymoon, he took a look at her and said: "For heaven's sake, sing."

After two years of graduate studies at the university, I felt that I did not have a sufficiently good education to merit the degree of Doctor of Philosophy. I confided my worries to one of the professors, who said: "What would you like to have in education?" I said: "I should like to know two things— first, what the modern world is thinking about; second, how to answer the errors of modern philosophy in the light of the philosophy of St. Thomas." He said: "You will never get it here, but you will get it at the University of Louvain in Belgium."

In September of 1921, I left for Louvain, Belgium, and entered the School of Philosophy. My brother Tom left with me to study medicine at the same university. Regardless of how long I live, I will never be able to express the depth of my gratitude to this great university for the brilliance of its teaching, the inspiration of its leadership and the development it gave to the human mind. There were no optional or elective courses—every course was required. So we had to learn metaphysics, experimental psychology, rational psychology, cosmology, Aristotle, modern space and time; these courses were part of the curriculum for all doctoral candidates. Everything contemporary was stressed in every area of knowledge. Even the professors of the Medical School gave us advanced courses in science. But along with being up-to-date, we were drenched in Aristotle, Plato and the ancients and immersed in the philosophy of Thomas Aquinas. The

Sheen at the University of Louvain in Belgium, early 1920s. *(Courtesy, Fulton J. Sheen Archives)*

way the professors handled Aquinas he did not belong to the Middle Ages; he was our contemporary. No assigned reading was ever given, but it was always assumed that any book which a professor suggested to be read could be brought up in the final oral examination.

The most brilliant professor I had was Dr. Leon Noel, whose last name was the same as his first, if spelled backward. One course he taught was on the philosophy of Bergson, who was then the dominant French thinker. Another course was on American pragmatism. On one occasion he called me into his office and said: "Have you read the Gifford Lectures of Dr. Alexander?" I told him that I had not. He said: "Well, they have already been published for at least thirty days. I advise you to read both of those volumes, and then go to the University of Manchester in England and consult with Dr. Alexander." Dr. Alexander had won a medal from King George for his philosophical treatise on *Space, Time and Deity*, his thesis being that Deity is evolving.

I asked Dr. Alexander if I might be permitted to follow one of his classes. I do not remember if he said: "It is on Kant" or "It is just cant," but in any case, he refused. He did invite me back to tea that afternoon. When I went to the building at the appointed time, I found a sign outside: "This afternoon at tea time, Dr. Alexander will debate Dr. Sheen of the University of Louvain." I did not yet have my doctorate from the University of Louvain, nor was I qualified to represent the university. But a tea table was prepared in the middle of the room for Dr. Alexander and myself. Hundreds of students sat around at various tea tables to listen to the discussion. Dr. Alexander began: "Well, what would you like to know?" I realized, for the first time, what it must be like to sit at the feet of Divine Omniscience. I said: "You do not believe that God is Infinitely Perfect, do you?" He said: "Have you read my books?" I said: "Yes, I have read them twice." "Well," he said, "if you ever read them with any degree of intelligence, you would know that I believe that God is perfect." I said: "May I explain to you your view as I understand it?" I then explained that Dr. Alexander's position seemed to me to be that God was an urge, or nisus, always one level above the present level of evolution. "When there was only Space-Time, God was a chemical; when chemicals came into being God was the ideal of plant; when plants came into the universe, God was the ideal state of an animal; when there were animals God was the ideal state of man; now that there is man, God is an angel. Someday we will reach that state. God will keep moving ahead as the Urge of the universe." And he said: "Yes, that is my theory; you understand it perfectly." I said: "Well, Dr. Alexander, your God is not yet perfect; He is on the way to perfection. A Perfect God would be One Who has at each and every moment of His Being the fullness of perfection." "I've never had that put to me that way before," he said. I asked him if he would be interested in reading the philosophy of Thomas Aquinas. "No, I would not be interested because you become known in this world not through Truth, but through novelty, and my doctrine is novel."

The examinations for the doctorate at the University of Louvain were oral. About twenty students or candidates at a time would be admitted into a large hall, where there were twenty professors seated at twenty desks. A student would choose any desk that he pleased, each student making for the desk of the professor he thought would be the easiest. The professor would ask questions until you could not answer; then he would tell you to go to another desk. The examination lasted the entire day, at the end of which each professor would give his own mark and then all the professors would unite and give a general mark.

When I visited the desk of Dr. Noel, he asked: "Tell me how an angel makes a syllogism." I said: "An angel does not have to go through the reasoning process, but rather has intuitive intelligence and, therefore, sees conclusions as clearly as we see that the part is never greater than the whole. Hence an angel cannot make a syllogism." Later on when I got to know him very well, I asked him if he recalled that question and why he asked it. He said: "You remember when I was lecturing on the philosophy of Bergson I said to the class 'I want you to read every single line St. Thomas has ever written on the subject of angels in order that you may understand angelic intelligence.' I just wanted to find out whether or not you had done the reading." A little later on while in Rome working at the Angelicum, I read through every single line that St. Thomas wrote at least once.

The university had a higher degree, which was called the agrégé. Agrégé meant one became aggregated to the faculty. There were several conditions to receiving the honor: one, the university must extend the invitation; second, a book must be written; and third, one had to pass a public examination before professors of other universities. I received an invitation to work for the agrégé. Since it was not necessary to stay at Louvain while one was working for the degree, I went to Rome for a year and entered the Angelicum, now referred to more properly as the University of St. Thomas Aquinas, as well as the Jesuit Gregorian University, studying theology. Then I was invited to give a course in theology in the Westminster Seminary of London.

The time came to take the agrégé examination before the invited professors of other universities. It began at nine o'clock in the morning and went on until five in the afternoon. A board was then selected from the visiting professors to decide on the grade with which one passed. They were always the same as they were for a doctorate: Satisfaction, Distinction, Great Distinction and Very Highest Distinction. That night the university would give a dinner to the successful candidate and induct him into the faculty. If you passed with Satisfaction only water could be served at the dinner; if with Distinction, beer; if with Great Distinction, wine; and the Very Highest Distinction, champagne. The champagne tasted so good that night!

I received two invitations to teach—one was from Cardinal Bourne of London, who suggested I go to Oxford with Father Ronald Knox and start some courses in Catholic philosophy and theology; the other came from Nicholas Murray Butler, who was then president of Columbia University in New York City, inviting me to teach a course in scholastic philosophy there.

I sent the two letters to my bishop: "Which offer should I accept?" His answer: "*Come home.*"

# Three

# THE GIFT OF THE TREASURE

Throughout all my graduate education I was already a priest. How did that desire begin and flourish in the clay? The treasure comes from God; the clay gives the response. As our Lord told His Apostles the night of the Last Supper: "You did not choose Me; I chose you." In the Epistle to the Hebrews: "Nobody arrogates the honor (of the priesthood) to himself; he is called by God." God does not put that sacred deposit in identical human natures, nor does He do it in the same way. He varies the giving from individual to individual. The vocation may come early, it may come late; it may come as it did to St. Francis, who was riding to a knightly contest in Apulia, or it may come after a life of sin, as it did to Augustine when he heard the voice of a child making reference to the Scriptures: "Take and read."

I can never remember a time in my life when I did not want to be a priest. In the early teens my father would send us to work on one of his farms. I recall doing spring plowing, watching the young corn come up under my eyes; as I saw the rich dark soil turned over, I would say the Rosary begging for a vocation. I never mentioned my vocation to others, not even to my parents, although others often told my parents they thought that I would become a priest. Being an altar boy at the cathedral fed the fires of vocation, as did the inspiration of the priests who visited our home almost every week. Not to be omitted was the Rosary, which was said every evening by the family before retiring.

My First Communion at the age of twelve was another special appeal to the Lord to grant me the grace of priesthood. But I always had one doubt—and that was my worthiness.

Never once did my mother or father say a word to me about becoming a priest, nor did I speak to them about it until the day I went to the seminary. Their only response then was: "We always prayed that you might become a priest; if it is your vocation, be a good one." I often would hear relatives and friends who visited my parents talk about me, saying that I would become a priest. And my younger brother Joe said that I liked to entertain visitors with little talks that I had prepared. For myself, I do not remember that.

A vocation is so very sacred that one does not like to

speak of it; I never mentioned it to anyone—my classmates, my parents, nor to the priests (except Father Kelly, a curate in the cathedral parish). Always associated with that sense of the gift of a treasure was the frailty of the earthenware pot which was to house it. I would often drive it out of my mind, only to have it come back again. For the most part, the religious vocation is rather a silent but insistent whisper, yet one that demands a response; no violent shaking of bedposts or loud noises in the night. Just "you are called to be a priest."

Neither is the vocation so imperative that it makes acceptance a necessity rather than a willing obedience. In the Old Testament story, when God spoke to young Samuel, there was no voice audible to anyone but the child. Nor was there anything to prove it was divine; that is why Samuel twice went to Eli after his name was called, believing that it was Eli who had summoned him. The experience of the aged priest, Eli, was necessary finally to convince the boy of the divinity of the speaker: "Eli perceived that the Lord had called the child." Samuel did not at first know it was the voice of the Lord. Neither do most of us, when first we are called, recognize it as such except by its persistence and the calmness and peace with which it possesses the soul.

The course of life is determined not by the trivial incidents of day to day, but by a few decisive moments. There may not be over three, four or five such moments in a human life. For many people, it would be the decision of marriage, the taking of a job or changing residence. Certainly a turning point in my life happened when I finished college. A national examination was given to college students. The prize was a three-year university scholarship. I took the examination and won one of the scholarships. I was informed sometime during the summer and immediately went up to St. Viator's College to see Father William J. Bergan, by now my dear friend. He was on the tennis court when I arrived. With great glee and delight I announced: "Father Bergan, I won the scholarship!"

He put his hands on my shoulders, looked me straight in the eyes and said: "Fulton, do you believe in God?" I replied: "You know that I do." He said: "I mean *practically*, not from a theoretical point of view." This time I was not so sure, and I said: "Well, I *hope* I do." "Then tear up the scholarship." "Father Bergan, this scholarship entitles me to three years of university training with all expenses paid. It is worth about nine or ten thousand dollars." He retorted: "You know you have a vocation; you should be going to the seminary." I countered with this proposal: "I can go to the seminary after I get my Ph.D., because there will be little chance of getting a Ph.D. after I am ordained, and I would like very much to have a good education." He repeated: "Tear up the scholarship; go to the seminary. That is what the Lord wants you to do. And if you do it, trusting in Him, you will receive a far better university education after you are ordained than before." I tore up the scholarship and went to the seminary. I have never regretted that visit and that decision.

Looking back through the years and studying vocations today, I find in my case and in many others there are three stages all illustrated in the call of the prophet Isaiah. It would seem today that many claim they have a vocation to the priesthood because they want to "work in the inner city," or "defend the political rights of prisoners," or "work for civil rights for the minorities," or "care for the handicapped," or "bring a religious mission to the political-minded in South America." No true vocation starts with "what I want" or with "a work I would like to do." If we are called by God, we may be sent to a work we do not like, and "obedience is better than sacrifice." If society calls, I can stop service; if Christ calls, I am a servant forever. If I feel my call is sociological dedication, there is no reason why I should enter a theological seminary. If I am convinced that a vocation is to be identified with the world, then I have completely forgotten Him Who warned: "I have taken you out of the world."

The first stage in vocation is a sense of the holiness of God. When Isaiah went into the temple he had a vision of the Lord seated upon His throne with angelic choirs singing:

*Holy, holy, holy is the Lord of Hosts;*
*The whole earth is full of His glory.*

Vocation begins not with "what *I* would like to do" but with God. One is confronted with a presence, not as dramatic as Paul when he was converted, but with a sense of the unworldly, the holy and the transcendent.

The second stage, which is a reaction to this, is a profound sense of unworthiness. The heart is shocked at the simultaneous vision of the clay and the treasure. God is holy, I am not. "Woe is me." God can do something with those who see what they really are and who know their need of cleansing but can do nothing with the man who feels himself worthy.

The Sheens of El Paso: Mr. and Mrs. Newton Sheen
and their four sons (standing l. to r.) Joseph, Fulton,
Aloysius, and Thomas, 1930s. *(Courtesy, Fulton J. Sheen
Archives)*

Isaiah was cleansed of his paltriness by the Seraphim who
took a burning coal from the altar and touched his mouth
and said: "Behold this has touched your lips, your guilt is
taken away and your sin is forgiven." This purgation begins
in the seminary and continues through life in the form of
physical suffering, mental anguish, betrayals, scandals, false
accusations—all of which summon the one called to become
more worthy of the treasure.

The third stage is response. After the purging, Isaiah

heard the voice of the Lord asking: "Whom shall I send?" And Isaiah answered: "Here I am, send me." That is what I said the day I was ordained.

The dialectic between the sublimity of the vocation on the one hand, and the frailty of the human clay on the other, is a kind of crucifixion. Each priest is crucified on the vertical beam of the God-given vocation and on the horizontal beam of the simple longing of the flesh and a world that so often beckons to conformity with it. The best vintage of wine is sometimes served in tin cups. To be a priest is to be called to be the happiest of men, and yet to be daily committed to the greatest of all wars——the one waged within.

But God is constantly remolding that clay, giving it a second and third, and even seventy times seven chances. The prophet Jeremiah was bidden to go to a potter's shop. Jeremiah said:

> So I went down to the potter's house and found him working at the wheel. Now and then a vessel he was making out of the clay would be spoiled in his hands, and then he would start again and mold it into another vessel to his liking.

The potter may have had the original intention to make a Ming vase, but even though the clay was marred, he did not give up; he fashioned it into another vessel.

The effort of restoring love succeeds even when God's original plan is frustrated by the material with which He has to work: "Where sin did abound, grace does more abound." At the close of life, one can well see the potter's intention to make a saint. But God has not given up, so that if the vessel is not fit to hold the rose, it can at least settle for being a tin can for a geranium. The Divine Potter can change the circumstances of the human clay, maybe adding a little suffering here and there. If we refuse to be molded into the original shape meant for us, namely, holiness and perfect imitation of Christ, He molds us into useful pitchers from which He can pour out His Divine Grace. God does not make anything with the purpose of destroying it. There is no waste in life. Childhood is not a waste. It has relationship to the rest of life.

That portion of us which is tried and tested, which is subjected to many trials, is not a waste. The tears, the agonies, the frustrations, the toils are not lost. All of these, which seem to militate against life, are worked into new forms. Life may be marred into a broken thing, but God can make it into a thing of beauty. So if I were asked if I had my life to live over again, would I live the priesthood as I have, the answer is: "No, I would try to love Christ more." The only sorrow in my life, or any life, is not to have loved Him enough. For I know now:

> That nothing walks with aimless feet;
> That not one life shall be destroyed,
> Or cast as rubbish to the void,
> When God has made the pile complete.

There are many more vocations to the priesthood than those which result in Ordination, as there are more seeds planted than those which bear fruit. St. Thomas Aquinas holds that God always gives the Church a sufficient number of vocations, "provided the unworthy ones are dismissed and the worthy ones are well trained." The best vocation leaders should be the priests themselves. We may not mount pulpits to urge parents to bear children, unless we priests bear spiritual children. On the last day, God will ask us priests: "Where are your children? How many vocations have you fostered?" Though it is not given to any of us to implant the vocation, it is nonetheless within our power to widen the capacity for receptivity. We fertilize the soil by good example and encouragement.

I believe that God gives some of us an intuitive sense of seeing vocations in others. I remember preaching Midnight Mass about the year 1960 at the Shrine of the Immaculate Conception in Washington. When the Mass ended about one-thirty in the morning, several hundred people gathered around me outside to exchange greetings. I saw a black boy with his father at the edge of the crowd and I called him to me. "Young man, do you ever think of becoming a priest?" He answered in the affirmative. I said: "I believe you have a vocation." I laid my hands on his head and prayed that if God called him, he might become responsive and immediately become aware of it. The father saw me talking to his son and inquired: "What are you saying to my son?" I told him that I believed that someday he would become a priest. The father said: "Ever since that boy was born, I have prayed morning and night that God would give him a vocation." I have never heard the final issue of that meeting. It is one of the things I will learn in Heaven.

Another circumstance was more certain. I was eating alone in the main dining room of the Statler Hotel in Boston. A shoeshine boy with a D-shirt—dirty—not a T-shirt, with a shoeshine box slung over his shoulder, began swinging on the large purple curtains that framed the entrance to the dining room. As soon as the headwaiter saw this, he shouted and chased the boy from the hotel. I left my dinner and went out of the hotel to the boy and asked him where he went to school. He told me he was going to a public school. I said: "With a name like that [his name was Irish], why don't you go to a Catholic school?" He said: "I got kicked out." "Who kicked you out?" I asked. "The pastor and the Mother Superior of the school." I promised: "I will get you back in." He asked who I was but I responded that I couldn't tell him. He then remarked: "No, they said nobody could ever get me back into Catholic school; I will never be allowed to return."

I went out to see the pastor and the Mother Superior of the school and I told them: "I know of three boys who were thrown out of religious schools: one because he was constantly drawing pictures during geography class; another because he was fond of fighting; and the third because he kept

Lake Champlain, summer of 1935; Alfred E. Smith, former governor of New York, is at far left. (Courtesy, Society for the Propagation of the Faith)

revolutionary books hidden under a mattress. No one knows the valedictorians of those classes, but the first boy was Hitler, the second Mussolini and the third Stalin. I am sure that if the superiors of those schools had given those boys another chance, they might have turned out differently in the world. Maybe this boy will prove himself worthy if you take him back." They allowed him to return to the school and today he is a missionary among the Eskimos.

When I was Bishop of Rochester, while walking down the middle aisle of a parish church, I passed a young boy in a pew who struck me as being rather unusual. I stopped and asked him if he ever thought of becoming a priest. He said: "I sometimes pray for it." And I said: "I am sure you have a vocation; continue to pray to our Blessed Mother that you may be strengthened in it." Recently I received a letter from the young man that he was joining the Jesuits.

Looking back on about sixty years of my priest-victimhood, how would I answer this question before God: "Do you think you have lived the life of a good priest?" When I compare myself with missionaries who have become dry martyrs by leaving their own country and family to teach other peoples, when I think of the sufferings of my brother-priests in Eastern Europe, when I look at the saintly faces of some of my brother-priests in monasteries and in the missions, and the beautiful resignation of priests in hospitals who suffer from cancer, and when I just even look at my many brothers in Christ whom I admire so much, I say: "No, I have not been the kind of priest I should have been or would have liked to have been."

But I know there is more to the answer of this question. When you put a painting in candlelight to examine it, the imperfections do not appear; when you put it under the full glare of the sun, then you see how badly chosen are the colors and ill defined the lines. So it is when we measure ourselves by God, we fall infinitely short; and when we compare ourselves with many who have given us inspiration, we feel a deep sense of unworthiness. But behind it all, and despite all of this, there is the tremendous consciousness of the mercy of God. He did not call angels to be priests; He called men. He did not make gold the vessel for his treasure; He made clay. The motley group of Apostles that He gathered about Him became more worthy through his mercy and compassion.

I know that I am not afraid to appear before Him. And this is not because I am worthy, nor because I have loved Him with deep intensity, but because *He has loved me.* That is the only reason that any one of us is really lovable. When the Lord puts His love into us, then we become lovable.

*Four*

# AFTER
# UNIVERSITY
# STUDIES

On my return from Europe, in response to
the "Come home" letter of my Bishop, I was
appointed to a parish where the streets were
unpaved, in that part of the city which was
called the "lower end" and from which the
well-to-do had left for other parts of the city.
The pastor, Father Patrick Culleton, was a
true man of God. I began preaching a Lenten
course; and this poor church which was
looked down on by the other parishes on the
hill soon became crowded. Some of the pastors later forbade their congregations to go

down to the "lower end" where "that young priest is preaching. Stay in your own parish."

As far as I could tell, this was to be my life. I was intellectually bent, loved teaching, but now I was an assistant in a parish. Editorials appeared in the newspapers against the Bishop. "Why does he waste talent of this kind? After spending money educating a man, why put him in 'a parish like that'?" I begged my parents never to take part in any conversation about the Bishop. I never complained, and I can say in my own heart of hearts that to me this was the will of God. I had to forget my desire to follow a more intellectual vocation, and was resigned to being a curate. This gave me a great peace of mind. It was my first test, as a young priest, in obedience. The will of God was expressed through the Bishop as a successor of the Apostles and that was sufficient for me. I began pleading in the confessional for daily attendance at Holy Mass and happily saw the number at the Communion rail increase from four to ninety. A renewal of the parish was undertaken and I was happy. After about a year the Bishop phoned: "Three years ago I promised you to Bishop Shahan of the Catholic University as a member of the faculty." I asked: "Why did you not let me go there when I returned from Europe?" "Because of the success you had on the other side, I just wanted to see if you would be obedient. So run along now; you have my blessing."

I was appointed to the School of Theology at the Catholic University of America in Washington, D.C., and assigned to the Chair of Apologetics. The appointment came from Bishop Shahan, the brilliant, gifted, saintly rector of the university. At the end of the second year, Bishop Shahan called a meeting of the Faculty of Theology. It is very much to the point of the story to know that Bishop Shahan was deaf and he used a little trumpet to pick up conversations of those who were near him. The subject of discussion was whether or not the Graduate School of Theology, which was then already established at the university, should open an undergraduate department and teach seminarians. The reason for the proposal was that the School of Theology had few graduate students. It was felt that the professors were not sufficiently occupied and challenged; they would be if they had more students to teach. One way to do that was to start

Returning from Europe aboard the SS *Normandie*, June 1936. *(Courtesy, Fulton J. Sheen Archives)*

an undergraduate School of Theology offering courses for seminarians. Before we went into the conference, almost every professor expressed opposition to such an idea. But that was before we went into the meeting. When the Bishop had made the proposal he extended his horn to each professor to ask his point of view. To my surprise all expressed agreement with the Bishop.

Inasmuch as I was the youngest professor, I was asked last. I took the horn from the Bishop and I said to him: "Your Excellency, it seems that instead of building the university up to high standards on the graduate level, we are tearing it down to meet a situation. Why not increase the level of teaching in our graduate school? Then the bishops of the country will send their priests here."

I was seated down at the far end of the table from the Bishop. He took off his little trumpet, rolled it up like a coiled serpent and pushed it down the whole length of the table toward me. Then he stood up and, flushed with emotion, said: "If I cannot get professors in this university to agree with me, I shall discharge them and get professors who will." And he left the room.

The other professors gathered around me and said: "Well, you certainly killed yourself. Here you are at this university only a year and now you are an outcast." I was troubled beyond the telling, went on teaching for the next week or two, but in the meantime received no word from Bishop Shahan. One day as I was walking up the lawn to teach my class, the Bishop passed in his car. He stopped and bade me sit alongside him. But he said nothing. He indicated for me to follow him into his office. We went up to the second floor of McMahon Hall, then into the bedroom, where he put on his cassock, zucchetto and pectoral Cross and cincture, came out and sat down in the chair.

He then said to me: "Kneel down, young man." I knelt down before him and he put his hands on my head and said: "Young man, this university has not received into its ranks in recent years anyone who is destined to shed more light and luster upon it than yourself. God bless you."

The Faculty of Theology continued to have other difficulties, and one of them involved the new rector, Bishop James H. Ryan, who was the successor to Bishop Shahan. The celebrated John A. Ryan, who had written so much about social justice, was then a professor of moral theology at the university. He wished to name as his successor in the department Dr. Haas, who later on became a bishop. Bishop Ryan presided at the meeting and said it was his duty to maintain the standards of the university. Dr. Haas had received his doctorate in philosophy from the university, but Bishop Ryan insisted that all the professors in the School of Theology must have a Doctor of Divinity in order to keep up academic standards. If, therefore, Dr. Haas would go to Rome, do graduate work and receive a doctorate in Sacred Theology, Bishop Ryan would consent to his appointment to the School of Theology.

Dr. John A. Ryan would not countenance the suggestion that Dr. Haas go to Rome for further schooling to get a D.D. before being named to the School of Theology. As a result, there developed a tension between the School of Theology and the rector. It was a question of Ryan vs. Ryan. Finally, the School of Theology drew up a document against Ryan, the rector. Copies of this letter were sent to several bishops and members of the board of trustees. Before the document

was sent, each professor of the School of Theology was asked
to sign it. I refused to sign. I thought it was unfair to send to
the bishops an accusation against the rector of the university
when the rector of the university had never been given a
hearing. I suggested: "Before sending out the letter why not
call in the rector, read to him the accusations you have made
and give him a chance to respond. If he cannot, then send
the letter, but I will not sign the document without giving
James H. Ryan the right to answer."

The next day there appeared on the bulletin board of the
School of Theology a notice to the effect that all of the classes
of Dr. Fulton J. Sheen had been suspended in the School of
Theology. James H. Ryan, the rector, knew the reason—
namely, because I defended him. He then transferred me to
the School of Philosophy, where I taught for more than
twenty years.

During the summer months following that incident, I
went to Rome, and one evening had dinner with Cardinal
Pacelli, the future Pope Pius XII, who was then the Secretary
of State. The next morning I visited him in his office and he
said to me: "Will you please tell me what you know about
the university and the opposition to the rector, James H.
Ryan." I answered: "Your Eminence, I beg to be excused
from any comment about the university and its rector." At
that point the Cardinal dropped the subject, and pulled out
a number of German newspapers from a file and began reading and translating them. For over an hour he spoke with
considerable vehemence against Hitler and Nazism.

At the end of the hour, as I left the room of the Secretary of State, there was waiting outside none other than the
rector, James H. Ryan. He asked one of the attendants the

name of the person in company with the Secretary of State for such a long period of time. He was told that it was Monsignor Fulton J. Sheen.

What thoughts do you believe must have been in the mind of James H. Ryan when sometime after that he was transferred from his beloved university to the Archdiocese of Omaha? Had someone spoken against him in Rome? Certainly it had to be that professor who was with the Secretary of State for over an hour. Before God, I never spoke of the university or Bishop Ryan to Cardinal Pacelli, but the story circulated that I had done so. This rumor became so widespread that when my name was proposed as rector of the university later on, Archbishop McNicholas of Cincinnati said: "I would not let Sheen be put in charge of a doghouse." He felt so bitter against what he thought was my injustice toward Bishop James H. Ryan that at the National Eucharistic Congress in Cleveland, when the speakers were Mr. Scott of Los Angeles, Governor Al Smith and myself, Archbishop McNicholas, who was seated with us on what was second base in the stadium, got up, walked across the diamond and out of the ballpark, rather than sit and listen to my address. I knew that he always felt I had done a great injustice to the rector by complaining about him to Cardinal Pacelli. But because my conscience was clear, I always made it a point to pay Archbishop McNicholas a visit every year when I lectured in Cincinnati. He always greeted me warmly and every conversation ended as it should end among priests. But that was only one interlude in the long years I passed teaching and lecturing.

*Five*

# TEACHING AND LECTURING

Being a teacher took up about a quarter century of my life. The career did not begin when I was appointed to the Graduate School of the Catholic University; rather it began in England when I was invited to teach theology at the seminary of the Westminster Archdiocese, St. Edmund's College, Ware. At the same time, I was working for my agrégé at the University of Louvain. I was assigned to teach dogmatic theology, though my specialty had been philosophy. Though I did audit many lectures in theology at the University of Louvain and later on at the Angelicum and the Gregorian in Rome, I was a beginner in every sense of the word.

One of my friends and distinguished colleagues there was Father Ronald Knox, a convert to Catholicism, whose father was the Anglican Archbishop of Birmingham. A graduate of Oxford, he was teaching Scripture and Greek at the seminary. Later on, he translated the entire Bible into English from the Hebrew and the Greek. Another colleague was Dr. Messenger, who was with me at Louvain and lived at a convent of nuns about two miles away from the seminary.

Each day Father Knox would write for his students a Latin poem describing the events of the previous day. One incident that gave him great scope was an explosion of the "starlight" equipment in the seminary. It was some kind of illuminating gas which was stored in the large toilets. The starlight used to leak into our butter and our bread so that we were constantly eating it. Of all the nights when the starlight plant should blow up in an English seminary, the one chosen by the starlight gods was the eve of St. Patrick's Day. We heard the explosion during the night. When we looked out on St. Patrick's Day, we found the lawn of the seminary strewn with toilet bowls. Knox wrote a brilliant Latin poem about it, but it was the last line which particularly annoyed Dr. Messenger: "Fragorem nuntius audivit" (Messenger heard the explosion).

I worked hard to prepare each lecture to the fourth-year students of the seminary. This particular day I was to lecture on the subject of "Theandric Actions." A theandric action is one in which both the divine and human nature of our Lord is involved. An example would be when He picked up dust, mingled it with spittle and applied it to the eyes of the blind

man and cured him. But no theological subject of this kind
is ever presented that clearly to students, for it is the business
of a professor to complicate the simple ordinary things of life!

I spent hours reading Bonaventure, Aquinas, Suarez, Bil-
lot and other theologians. When I went into the classroom,
if I met a theandric action coming out I would not have recognized it, so confused was I about the subject, but I lectured
for an hour. On the way out of the classroom, I heard one
deacon say to another: "Oh, Dr. Sheen is a most extraordinary lecturer, most extraordinary." I said to him: "What did
I say?" And in the best British accent he clipped: "I don't
quite know." and I answered: "Neither do I." That day I
learned that sometimes when you are confusing, you are mistaken for being learned.

Five years later I met a former student of St. Edmund's
who was by that time a priest in the Diocese of Manchester.
He inquired what I was doing. When I told him I was teaching at the Catholic University in Washington, he reflected: "I
hope you are a better teacher now than you were then." But
at least it must be said for me that I tried my pedagogy on
the English before I did it on my fellow Americans.

When I had completed the conditions for the agrégé of
Louvain, I paid a visit to Cardinal Mercier. "Your Eminence,
you were always a brilliant teacher; would you kindly give me
some suggestions about teaching?" "I will give you two: always keep current: know what the modern world is thinking
about; read its poetry, its history, its literature; observe its architecture and its art; hear its music and its theater; and then
plunge deeply into St. Thomas and the wisdom of the ancients and you will be able to refute its errors. The second
suggestion: tear up your notes at the end of each year. There

is nothing that so much destroys the intellectual growth of a teacher as the keeping of notes and the repetition of the same course the following year."

I tried to follow these wise counsels of the Cardinal. In addition to searching for knowledge of contemporary thought, I also resolved never to repeat a course. When I first went into the School of Philosophy I was teaching natural theology. I found that I was using some of the same notes that I had used before and, therefore, was not growing intellectually. I then decided to give a new course every year, but one that was related always to natural theology and to the existence and nature of God. So the courses throughout the years varied. There would be a course on the philosophy of history; another year the philosophy of Marxism, another the philosophy of religion, the philosophy of science, etc. All of these were presented in the light of the thought of St. Thomas.

In order to prepare for these new subjects, since I was not thoroughly versed in them, I would go to London every summer and spend the latter part of June, all of July and August and the first part of September reading up on the proposed course for the coming year. In the morning, evenings and on weekends I would serve as curate in St. Patrick's Church, Soho Square. In addition to that remote background preparation at the British Museum, I also spent a minimum of at least six hours more in preparation for every single hour of lecture in class. It is very easy for a professor to turn into a kind of dried-up intellectual without constant stimulation and study.

A perfect example of the philosopher who became dried up was Immanuel Kant. He never was outside the city of

Königsberg. He always told the same joke once a year, and on the same day. That joke was: "Why are there no women in Heaven?" Kant's answer was: "Scripture says there was silence in Heaven for half an hour." Kant always took exactly the same walk every day, so much so that the housewives of Königsberg could set their clocks by his promenade. The day he missed was the day of the publication of one of the works of Rousseau which very much changed his outlook and made him turn to the practical intellect. But that is another subject.

Going back to the early days of teaching, after the presidential campaign of 1928, when there was much bigotry against the Catholic Church, the bishops decided that there should be a School of Apologetics started at the Catholic University. I was asked by the rector, Bishop Corrigan, to draw up a plan for such courses. I drew it in the form of a pyramid, placing at the base of the pyramid such subjects as journalism, media, communications, psychology of religion, and then on the top the more theological subjects which were related to the defense of the Church. The rector accepted the proposal and asked me to find professors. I was granted permission to choose the professors from Europe. I further inquired: "Do I have the authority to tell them they are hired?" "Yes, if you find those that you believe are qualified." "What is to be their salary?" This was agreed upon. I went to Europe and I found about ten learned professors from England, France and Germany—all of whom spoke English—as the future staff of the School of Apologetics.

I wired the rector and told him of the ones whom I had chosen, and asked him to communicate with them and bid them to come as professors. By August they had not received any word from the rector, nor even in September. I was then deluged with telegrams from these professors: "What has happened to the proposal? Are we coming to the university?" Seeing that the rector had done nothing to engage them, I sent a wire to all of the professors saying that I had exceeded my authority and begged their pardon.

The next year the rector called me in again and said: "I want you to be head of a new School of Apologetics." I said: "I beg to be excused," knowing he had forgotten the incident the year before. The School of Apologetics never came into being.

For many years our dean in the School of Philosophy was Father Ignatius Smith, a Dominican, who was not only a most brilliant teacher, but also a most renowned preacher. My class every afternoon was at four o'clock. Before going into the classroom which immediately adjoined Dr. Smith's, I would go in and visit with him for ten minutes. He would walk out of the office with me and tell me a funny story as I was on my way to the classroom, so that I would enter the classroom laughing. My association with Dr. Smith, which lasted for years, was one of the happiest of my life.

On one occasion I was invited by the seminary authorities to sit on a board to examine seminarians for an S.T.B. degree. I did not recall immediately the dates of the early Councils and other such details required in seminary courses, so I had to use another approach. I asked the first student who came in: "Would you admit that, as a result of original sin, there was a disturbance in the universe: the beasts became wild and thistles grew, and man had to earn his bread by the sweat of his brow?" "Yes," came his reply. "If, then, you would admit that there was a general disturbance of nature as a result of original sin, why did God become man? Why did we not have pantheism instead of an Incarnation? Why did not God put Himself into all of nature which had rebelled against Him?" The other professors protested that the question was unfair, and I was asked to leave the board. My defense was: "I just wanted to find out if the student could think." The answer I would have hoped from the student was that since lower nature had fallen through man, it was fitting that all lower nature should be reconciled to God through man. That is why there was an Incarnation instead of pantheism.

I loved teaching. I loved it because it seemed so close to the prolongation of the Divine Word. The thought often came to me at the university: "Why is it that we teachers have tenure and football coaches do not?" There can be mediocrity in the classroom. A football coach who does not produce a winning team is forced to leave. Old generals may fade away—but poor teachers are just handed on. Teaching often becomes a communication from the notebook of the teacher to the notebook of the student without passing through the minds of either.

I felt a deep moral obligation to students; that is why I spent so many hours in preparation for each class. In an age of social justice one phase that seems neglected is the moral duty of professors to give their students a just return for their tuition. This applies not only to the method of teaching but to the content as well. A teacher who himself does not learn is no teacher. Teaching is one of the noblest vocations on earth, for, in the last analysis, the purpose of all education is the knowledge and love of truth.

Some practices I observed in teaching were the following:

my first rule was *never sit. Fires cannot be started seated.* If the students would have to "stand" for my lectures, I ought to stand for them.

I have given thousands of lectures but very few have ever been written out—either for the classroom or for general audiences. I always felt justified for not reading in the classroom or the pulpit by remembering a remark I once heard an old Irish woman make concerning a bishop who was reading a speech: "Glory be to God, if he can't remember it, how does he expect us to?"

If a survey were made of audiences who listen to speakers reading their speeches, it would be discovered that most of them are thinking about something else. G. K. Chesterton, after an American visit, observed: "My last American tour consisted of inflicting no less than ninety lectures on people who never did me any harm." I too found that even in giving lectures without notes, as soon as I would say "In conclusion," women would begin putting on their shoes. In any case, lecturing was a good preparation for radio and television.

In preparing lectures, I would first research the subject to be discussed; and then organize the research by arranging it, if possible, to a few clear points. The next step would be to make this material so much my own that I could readily communicate it to the students, or to an audience. This would be done by a learning process which might be described as follows: *I learned the lecture from the inside out, not from the outside in.* I did not learn the lecture by reading over the notes from my research. I would write out from memory my recollection of the points. Then I would check with the research to see how well I had absorbed the points. That paper on which I had first summarized the lecture would be torn up. One new plan after another would be drawn up and destroyed. I would repeat the process over and over again so that I was not allowing a piece of paper to dictate to my living mind.

As a mother cannot forget the child of her womb, so a speaker cannot forget the child of his brain. Why should a living mind bow down in subjection to research notes? What is so sacred about notes except their accuracy? But the mind can absorb that accuracy. The number of times that I would write out or even talk these points to myself would vary with the difficulty of the matter or with my memory. Finally, I would reach a point where the material was *mine*. It was like digested food, not food on the shelf. That was the reason I never used notes for a lecture or a sermon.

There would be less likelihood of my forgetting a subject if I used this method, though I remember once walking on the stage for a television show and completely forgetting my talk. I made a few "wisecracks" about forgetting and all the while I was trying to recall the subject of my lecture. Eventually, it came back.

A tragic failure of memory happened in Ireland at the Eucharistic Congress in Dublin. If there was ever any time in my life I wanted to do well, it was at the Eucharistic Congress, because it was in Dublin, because it was a Eucharistic Congress and because my grandparents on my mother's side did not come from Bessarabia. I was, as usual, talking without notes and so full of the subject I was using thoughts which would flash across my mind. One such flash that, for the moment, seemed brilliant to me was: "Ireland has never recognized any other king but Christ, and no other queen but Mary." The audience broke out in extended applause. At that moment I had intended to go into a poem of Joseph Mary Plunkett, a poem I knew as well as the Hail Mary:

*I saw His Blood upon the rose,*
*And in the stars the glory of His Eyes.*

While I was reciting the poem I was not thinking of the words; I was giving myself an intellectual spanking. Over and over I said to myself: no matter how brilliant you think a remark is, avoid anything that has a political reference. This is a Eucharistic Congress! I spanked myself so hard that when I came to the ninth line of the poem, I forgot it. I said to the audience: "I'm sorry, I forgot the poem." Thousands and thousands of Irish jaws dropped in disappointment, and when an Irish jaw drops, it collapses. There flashed across my mind then a line of Patrick Henry. Not the one most people know. Patrick Henry also said in the course of his life: "Whenever you are in difficulty in an oration, throw yourself into the middle of a sentence and trust to God Almighty to get you to the other end."

So I began a sentence: "I am glad I forgot; if I had ever wished to have forgotten anything . . ." Not knowing what to say, I started over again: "If I had ever prayed to have forgotten anything, I should have prayed to have forgotten these lines of Joseph Mary Plunkett. I believe there is beautiful symbolism in that forgetfulness, for standing on the anvil of Ireland's soil, one should be able to hammer and forge out the sparks of his own poetry and not be dependent even on a magnanimous soul like Joseph Mary Plunkett. When I finished the address, a number of bishops crowded around me saying: "That was a beautiful trick of oratory pretending that you forgot." It was not a trick. I had forgotten.

Experience has taught me that when there is a disturbance in a hall or a theater, it is good for the speaker never to raise his voice in order to make himself heard over it. The best trick is to lower the voice and to begin talking in a whisper. The audience reaction will be: "Oh, I'm missing something," and they will give back the attention which momentarily was taken away.

In lecturing, and here I refer to lectures outside of a classroom, namely, those given in auditoriums, theaters and to great concourses of people, I have found by experience that it is good never to plunge directly into the subject. The audience likes to have a chance to look you over. A touch of humor at the beginning is a good approach and the best humor is that which is directed against self.

An audience, I also learned, does not like to be made to feel inferior to the speaker. That is why a story in which the speaker is humbled gives them a feeling of equality. As I would use humor at the introduction of a lecture, so also was there humor at one or two points in the course of the lecture in order to change the mood, relieve the tension and give the audience an opportunity to relax. This would not be a humorous story for the sake of the humorous story, but would arise out of the lecture itself. I recall this example, when talking about a certain book related to the subject discussed: Two young women were discussing dates with young men. One young woman said she never could get a date, while the other was invited out every night. The second explained: "The trouble with you is you do no reading. Men are very intelligent; they like to talk about philosophy, literature, history and science. Start reading books. When you engage them in conversation, you will have material at hand to interest them." After weeks of study, the young woman finally got a date and as she sat down at table with a young man she said: "Wasn't that an awful thing that happened to Marie Antoinette?"

Often the target of humor is the length of time one has spent speaking. This incident really happened. On a crossing of the Atlantic before the days of airplanes, a deck steward came to me and said: "Are you the priest who preached the Mission Sunday sermon at St. Patrick's last year?" "Yes." "I enjoyed every minute of that hour and a half." "My good man, I never talked an hour and a half in my life." He said: "It seemed that long to me."

To me the conclusion of a talk must be strong, inspiring and elevating—and I would spend almost as much time on it as on many points in the lecture. As the comedians say: "It is very easy to get on the stage, but it is hard to get off." I guess the best lecturers are always those about whom the audience says: "I wish he had talked longer."

One area which occupied my time during latter years was talks in universities. I have been invited to secular universities several hundred times, many more than I have been invited to talk in Catholic universities. I have found that too often some in religion want to be secular; but on the other hand, I found the secular want to be religious. In talking in universities, I realized that the more divine the subject, the greater the response. At UCLA, on one occasion, I had dinner with about thirty or forty students. For the first half hour they

Street preaching in Alabama, 1930s. *(Courtesy, Fulton J. Sheen Archives)*

were abusive and insulting. I did not pay any attention to their abuse, but would pass their remarks off with a little light reflection. Then after a half hour they settled down and were perfectly normal. It seemed as if they just had to play a certain role—a role which they had assumed to be the correct role for that period of student life.

There is a tremendous potentiality for sacrifice among the young in this country. Certainly not the least of the difficulties is that the elders are not challenging them. The young people are rebelling against the bourgeois ethos of their parents, who believed in the American way of life, which judged prosperity by material achievements. But one thing that their parents never asked themselves was what they would do with themselves after they had bettered their condition. To some extent, religion fell in with this bourgeois ethics. It began to give not theological insights into the meaning of life, but rather psychological and sociological views to accommodate the bourgeois good life to religion.

One state university which I visited presented a problem. The president of the university met me at the airport and told me that the day before the students had burned down two buildings. He said: "I came to tell you that you need not give the lecture; I am afraid that something rash may happen. I have invited the board of trustees to sit on the stage with you, but they can offer no protection."

I told him that I would give the lecture. I forgot about the topic that I had chosen, but inasmuch as there was a difficulty in the university, I decided to talk on another subject. About ten thousand students showed up and I talked on chastity for about an hour in a way that the students could understand. At the end, they stood up and applauded and cheered and came to the platform to meet me.

The president of the university said: "I have been here twenty years, and this is the first time I have ever seen an incident of this kind." "What is so different?" I asked. "Well," he said, "other speakers come and take sides—black against white, yellow against green, blue against pink; or else they tell the students that their parents and the university governments are wrong." He said: "You challenged them; and challenged them with something they had never heard before and they are looking for a challenge."

As I said before, the more divine the talk and the more

the talk is related to the Crucifixion of Our Lord, the more
it involves the unknown element of self-sacrifice to our modern pagans, the more responsive they are. The Lord is never
wanting potential converts in any age. It is rather the actual-
ization of that potency that is the problem, and that depends
principally on us. How much longer the Good Lord will permit me to go on doing the work of giving retreats, I do not
know. But I do know that as long as He opens the doors, I
will try to walk in, and I will choose those doors which seem
to me to offer the maximum of spiritual opportunity. I beg
Him every day to keep me strong physically and alert mentally in order to preach His Gospel and proclaim His Cross
and Resurrection. I am so happy doing this that I sometimes
feel that when I come to the Good Lord in Heaven, I will
take a few days' rest and then ask Him to allow me to come
back again to this earth to do some more work.

# Six

# THE ELECTRONIC GOSPEL

I was born in the electronic age, when light waves are used to communicate the Word. Radio is like the Old Testament, for it is the hearing of the Word without the seeing. Television is like the New Testament, for the Word is seen as it becomes flesh and dwells among us. I delivered the first radio message from Radio City, New York, on the day of its opening. I also gave the first religious television show in New York when there were very few television sets in the entire city. The two dozen or more candles that were used at the studio altar under bright Klieg lights almost vanished in the heat.

I began broadcasting in the year 1928 when I was invited by the Paulist Fathers of New York to give a series of sermons in the church which were broadcast by the then very popular station WLWL. The vast church was filled upstairs and downstairs. Cushions were provided in the sanctuary for the overflow crowd and chairs were supplied at the side altars. I was invited by the pastor, Father Riley, who came out to hear me for the first few minutes, but then went back and said to some of his confreres: "I don't know why I ever invited that man." Father Lyons, who had been my confessor in Rome and whom I believe was instrumental in the invitation, begged him to go out and listen a little longer. As a result, I occupied that pulpit and broadcast over that station for many years.

Having been for a short time already a professor at the university and having given these broadcasts, the bishops of the United States chose me to be the first one to appear on national radio—an opportunity offered to them by the National Broadcasting Company. In those days there were so many preachers and priests appealing for radio time that CBS and NBC decided to control the requests by allowing only representative bodies of Catholics, Protestants and Jews to choose a speaker. Not only was there confusion because of the requests, but it often happened that those who appeared on radio took advantage of the opportunity to condemn their "enemies" or the opposition. Some control on the grounds of decency and charity was required.

I began my first national broadcast on Sunday evening in New York during prime time, at the same hour in which

"Amos 'n' Andy" appeared during the week. Scheduled shortly after the "Catholic Hour" program was the never-to-be-forgotten Fred Allen. The theme I chose was a popular presentation of Christian doctrine on the existence of God, the divinity of Christ, the Church and the spiritual life. The most vocal opposition came from the Catholic press in Milwaukee and Oklahoma City. Both of them pleaded that I be taken off the air and replaced by two men who could imitate Amos and Andy and who could discuss religion. Thus the tendency to imitate whatever was popular became a pervading spirit among some churchmen throughout the years.

After continuing on national radio for many years, my horizon expanded when in 1951 commercial television explored the idea of presenting a priest. By this time, after having lectured throughout the country, I was almost beyond the stage of yielding to experiment. The problem was: could a religious person be sponsored commercially on television? A survey was made of radio and television editors throughout the country. All agreed, except Boston. The Church and its bishops had nothing whatever to do with the invitation, nor were they ever involved in the sponsorship. One of the problems was remuneration. It was not so much a problem for me, for I was resolved never to take anything. Since by that time I had dedicated my life to the missions of the Church in Africa, Asia and other parts of the world, the mission office that I directed, the Society for the Propagation of the Faith, made the contract and merely used me as their spokesman. The fee given, I recall, was $26,000 a night. In the course of years, thanks to the gifts that were spontaneously sent, returns for the missions ran into millions of dollars, every cent of which found its way to some poor area

During early radio broadcasts of "The Catholic Hour," 1930s. *(Courtesy Fulton J. Sheen Archives)*

of this earth for the building of hospitals and schools and the further communication of the Word. We kept a record in our office of the mail received every day and for years it averaged between fifteen thousand and twenty-five thousand letters per day.

I did occasionally ask my listeners to send me a dime for the poor of the world. We were deluged from then on with coins taped to letters. Some even sent in their old gold jewelry. Students sacrificed their high school or college rings and sent the equivalent to the missions. In one telecast I said I liked chocolate cookies. The following week we could hardly get in the door of the office, which was blocked with boxes of chocolate cookies. We opened a yellow envelope and $10,000 in cash fell out. Scrawled in pencil was a note: "I don't need this any more. God told me to give it to the poor." Another letter asked me to give the $3,000 enclosed to an insurance company as conscience money, which was so delivered. Endless drawings were made of me, and countless photographs of young children dressed as I dressed on television came in daily. A blind couple in Minneapolis bought an Admiral television set to express gratitude for our sponsor, Admiral. A woman in New Jersey said that her cat always sat and looked at me during the show. (There'd be less objection to neighbors' cats if they all could be trained to look at television!) An elderly woman in Iowa would put on her best dress every Sunday evening to listen to me as if she were going to church. An actor, now famous, asked if he could use my name for life—Martin Sheen. In countless homes children were told to be silent while I was on television. I am surprised that the younger generation did not grow up with a hatred of my name; many persons whom I met as a result of television would be so surprised to see me that they would often say: "I've been an inspiration to you all my life" or "You have been a great admirer of mine for years."

The audience even included the White House. On the way to the Propagation office one afternoon, I saw President Eisenhower in a motorcade swiftly riding down Park Avenue in New York. A few days later, I received the following letter:

> *Dear Bishop Sheen:*
>
> *Last evening at the Alfred Smith dinner, I was told that as I was passing through the streets of New York you stopped at a street corner to greet me. I failed to see you, but I do assure you that I am more than complimented by your friendly thoughtfulness.*
>
> *I would have valued the opportunity to have stopped my car, however briefly, to chat for a moment.*
>
> 

*With personal regards,*
*Sincerely,*
*Dwight D. Eisenhower*
> 

I answered the letter as follows:

> *My dear President Eisenhower:*
>
> *In America, when the President passes a friend on street and fails, through no fault of his own, to salute him, he writes a personal letter of greeting. This is Democracy!*
>
> *In Russia, when the Dictator passes a friend without salutation, it means he is marked for liquidation. That is communism!*
>
> *Frankly, Mr. President, I am glad you missed me! The greeting would have lasted a second, your letter will last a lifetime.*
>
> *God Love You!*

Many requests also came to me. One, I recall, was from a Jewish boy in Pittsburgh who was told by his parents that he was not old enough to wear a yarmulke. He objected that: "Bishop Sheen wears one, why can't I?" In secret, he wrote to me asking for my zucchetto, which I sent him. Later on the Pittsburgh newspapers carried his picture with his episcopal yarmulke. A little girl in Minnesota wrote and told me her horse had died and she cried ever since. The family was too poor to give her another. She got the horse.

There was never any rehearsal for our television show, which meant a great saving for the producer. This was in part because I never use notes. *Time* magazine once sent a special writer to the theater to see what trick I was using week after week to give telecasts without the use of a teleprompter or idiot cards. The only prop that I used was a blackboard. It was on a swivel so that after writing on one side it could be turned over. I created the illusion that an "angel," who was one of the stagehands, would wash one side of the board as I moved away from one of the cameras' range. When the board was clean I would perhaps use the blackboard again but always attributing its cleanliness to the angel, who became nationally famous.

Because I was a teacher, I would sometimes write out words that I would explain or else draw crude pictures; I have no talent whatever in graphic arts. In fact, I was so poor that one of the art academies in New York offered me a free scholarship in order that I might learn to draw and not disgrace the human race. But it had one great advantage. It always allowed the audience to enjoy a superiority over the speaker, for they could draw and I could not.

I appeared on television just as a bishop in black cassock

and purple cloak called "ferriola." I was giving a lecture once in Longmeadow, Massachusetts. The auditorium was on the second floor. Some boys on the other side of the street on this warm night could see me on the stage and they shouted out: "Superman."

As a custom which started in kindergarten, I always wrote "JMJ" at the top of the blackboard, as I do on every piece of paper before I write—and which I hope someday will be put on my tombstone. In answer to many letters, the public finally recognized me and the words Jesus, Mary and Joseph.

Many televisions in bars were tuned to my program, which aired opposite Milton Berle. This was due in part to many taxi drivers who enjoyed my television show and who stopped working during that half hour. One taxi driver said to me one day: "Have you written a book?" I told him that I had. He said: "If I didn't already have a book, I'd buy yours."

The judgment of the viewing audience varied according to the way I appeared on their television screen. Assisting at an episcopal ordination in Brooklyn, I was marching into the cathedral with a number of other bishops when one woman on the sidewalk shouted: "You certainly look better on television!"

I would always have a large clock at the front of the stage when I spoke. This was in order that I might do my own timing. The television time which was without interruption lasted about twenty-seven minutes and twenty seconds. The trick to conclude on time without hurrying or without being cut off was to assign an exact time to the conclusion. If it were two minutes or three minutes long, I would break off from my regular theme and begin the conclusion so there was never any hurried cutoff.

I would spend about thirty hours preparing every telecast, which meant that enough material was gathered to talk for an hour or more. As in breathing, there is always more oxygen outside of the body than that which is taken in by the lungs, so the knowledge that one has on a certain subject must be far greater than that which is imparted. Though I would forget this or that point which I intended to deliver, I could draw on the store of accumulated information to take its place.

A day or two before the actual broadcast I would "try out" my comprehension of the subject by giving the talk in Italian to an Italian professor who was a friend of mine and also in French to a member of the staff who spoke French fluently. I did this not because of great expertise in either language but because I was forced to think out the ideas in another tongue and I knew that would help clarify the subject in my mind.

One day I directed a young lady who spoke French to a commercial organization which we hoped would circulate films we were doing on the missions. The head of the organization was a French Jew, so he was delighted to talk French to her. He asked her: "Do you see Bishop Sheen every day?" "Yes." "Do you talk to him?" "Yes." "Does he speak to you?" "Yes." "Did he tell you to come see me?" "Yes." Then he uttered a compliment the theology of which is shattering, but which nonetheless was meant to be a compliment: "For Christ's sake, he's another Jesus."

It may be interesting to recall how the mood of the country changed in the opinion of one who has had over fifty years' experience on electronic media. When I first began on radio nationally, the mood of the country was Christian.

Westover Air Force Base (Massachusetts), June 1950. *(Courtesy, United States Air Force)*

Hence, a "Catholic Hour" presentation of Christian doctrine was a popular approach. It did, however, provoke from a few bigots in the country a strong reaction—just because it was Catholic. One man in Pennsylvania wrote telling me that he had twelve books showing that the Pope was the Anti-Christ. He was prepared to send them to me, but I kept talking about "the Holy Father" and "the Vicar of Christ." "I was waiting for you to talk about the Pope but what you said about the Holy Father and the Vicar of Christ, I rather liked." In those days, there were not many letters that would be described as hate letters, or even neurotic ones.

When I began television nationally and on a commercial basis, the approach had to be different. I was no longer talking in the name of the Church and under the sponsorship of its bishops. The new method had to be more ecumenical and directed to Catholics, Protestants, Jews and all men of good will. It was no longer a direct presentation of Christian doctrine but rather a reasoned approach to it beginning with something that was common to the audience. Hence, during those television years, the subjects ranged from communism, to art, to science, to humor, aviation, war, etc. Starting with something that was common to the audience and to me, I would gradually proceed from the known to the unknown or to the moral and Christian philosophy. It was the same method Our Blessed Lord used when He met a prostitute at the well. What was there in common between Divine Purity and this woman who had five husbands and was living with a man who was not her husband? The only common denominator was a love of cold water. Starting with that He led to the subject of the waters of everlasting life.

This was the same method used by St. Paul at Athens

when the only common denominator he could find between himself and those who had lined the streets of the Acropolis with their gods was an inscription on one of them "to the Unknown God." From there he went to the concept of the true God. That was the way I tried to reach the vast television audience of America. And it worked.

I noticed during the television period a decline in bigoted letters. But there was an increase of correspondence that might be called neurotic. One wonders if Dr. Alexis Carrel was right when he said: "More people are suffering from nervous disorders than all other diseases put together." Apart from that detail, what was very noticeable in the country was a growth of good will. In proportion to the population, the greatest number of letters came to me from the Jews, the second largest amount from Protestants, and the third from Catholics. I felt repaid if I just brought one person a little closer to God. It would have been interesting to have kept the hundreds of thousands of letters of soul-searching and reaching out for Divinity which came to our office, but I felt I owed it to the writers to destroy their letters.

I personally answered as many as I could.

So many wrote to me expressing interest in the Church or searching for the gift of faith that I began instructions in large school halls, such as St. Patrick's in Washington, D.C., and St. Stephen's in the same city, as well as in Cathedral High School in New York City. Those who asked for literature on the Church were sent books and pamphlets.

In retrospect I had two approaches; one was the direct on radio, the other was the indirect on television. The direct was the presentation of Christian doctrine in plain, simple language. On television, I depended more on the grace of God and less on myself. If the subject of the telecast was flying, I might end it by talking about angels. Never once was there an attempt at what might be called proselytizing. It was for the audience to decide that I stood for something which they needed as a complement in their lives. The illumination that fell on any soul was more of the Spirit and less of Sheen.

An example of this was a telecast on the death of Stalin. About ten days before Stalin died I spoke about his death as if it were actually happening. I received telephone calls from newspapers in almost every state in the Union asking me what inside information I had. I told them I only knew that he was mortal and would have to pay the last penalty of sin which was death. And it was just pure luck that the telecast and his demise coincided. But as a further example of this second approach, after a lecture in a western city, I met a woman who told me that she became a convert after hearing one of my telecasts. I was very anxious to discover which one it was that so influenced her. To my surprise, it was the telecast on Stalin. There was absolutely nothing in that telecast that would draw a soul to the Church. God just used it as an instrument. "Paul plants, Apollo waters, but God gives the increase."

Very recently, a young priest told me in conversation: "I have already made seventy-two converts in six years of my priesthood." I said: "I would advise you to stop counting them, otherwise you might think you made them and not God."

There is a third approach to an electronic audience which will be in the future. It will not always be the direct, nor even the indirect which I used. It is what might be called the anthropological. I do not use this word in the sense of the science of man's beginning. I merely mean it as the roots of the word imply——a study of man. The presentation of religion had been principally from God to man, but now it will be from man to God. It will not start with the order in the universe alluding to the existence of a Creator of the cosmos; it will start with the disorder inside of man himself. It will take all the findings of our psychological age and use them as a springboard for the presentation of Divine Truths.

We bishops at one of our meetings recently decided to ask the people for $10 million for religious communications on radio and television. I was asked by the bishop-chairman to do a tape of about five or six minutes, which would be played in every Catholic parish in America, asking people to contribute. I finally agreed to announce the collection but not to ask the people for money, because we bishops had not yet decided how the money was to be spent. I could in conscience ask them for money to build hospitals and schools and clinics and churches in Africa and Asia, but to ask them for $10 million without a program of how it was to be spent seemed to me unwise.

Regardless of any harm that the electronic media may have done in other areas, they have been very good to religion. In any period of the Church's life in America there is always an audience at least as responsive or even more so than the one I enjoyed. I often wish that I were younger so that I might use this third approach which I have mentioned, namely, starting with the unhappiness inside of the human heart. The audience is always there, the opportunities are ever present. There is need to take hold of tortured souls like Peter, agnostics like Thomas and mystics like John and lead them to tears, to their knees or to resting on His Sacred Heart.

I have often been asked how to prepare sermons, and I can only speak of my own experiences after a long life of preaching.

All my sermons are prepared in the presence of the Blessed Sacrament. As recreation is most pleasant and profitable in the sun, so homiletic creativity is best nourished before the Eucharist. The most brilliant ideas come from meeting God face to face. The Holy Spirit which presided at the Incarnation is the best atmosphere for illumination. Pope John Paul II keeps a small desk or writing pad near him whenever he is in the presence of the Blessed Sacrament; and I have done this all my life—I am sure for the same reason he does, because a lover always works better when the Beloved is with him.

When the general plan of the sermon has been formulated. I will then talk my thoughts to Our Lord, or at least meditate on it, almost whispering the ideas. It is amazing how quickly one discovers the value of the proposed sermon. That is why the French speak of *l'esprit de l'escalier*—"the spirit of the stairway," or the recollection of what one *should* have said in the conversation that evening. Generally there are three different formats to any lecture or sermon: what is written; what is delivered; and what you wished you had said. That is why "giving the sermon before Our Blessed Lord" is the best way for me to discover not only its weaknesses, but also its possibilities.

After the material is gathered and the points formulated, I follow with either a meditation or a quiet vocalization without ever referring to notes. The material of the sermon is not wholly that which comes from the paper to the brain, but which proceeds from a creative mind to the lips. I have asked many a comedian what he thought was his best joke, and the answer I received was "the one I have most often told."

I am convinced that preaching and lecturing are impossible without much studying and reading. This perhaps is one of the weaknesses of the modern pulpit and lecture platform—the neglect of a continuing education. Books are great friends; they always have something worthwhile to say to you when you pick them up. They never complain about being too busy and they are always at leisure to feed the mind. One can almost tell the decade or the year when some priests were ordained by looking at their bookshelves; some have Tanquerey and Wapelhorst; younger ones have books on the revolutionary sixties, but some have not bought a serious book in decades. When the intellectual larder is empty, it is difficult to prepare a homiletic meal. The higher the building, the more materials have to go into it. One need never fear of exhausting material if there is serious study.

After I had been a professor for about six years at the Catholic University, and had been on national radio and given many lectures throughout the country, a fellow professor who was a very good friend of mine, and afterward became an archbishop of another country as a representative of the Vatican, asked me to discontinue radio and lecturing. The argument he used was: At the speed you are traveling, there is only a limited amount of material that you can use and you soon will have exhausted it and there will be no more

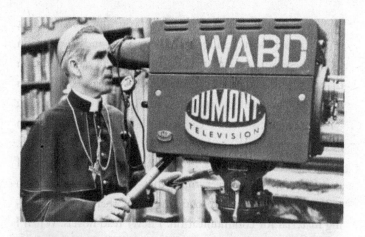

Sheen enjoying "behind the scenes" at DuMont television studios, May 1952.

opportunities of influence. I advise you, therefore, to just limit yourself to teaching in the university and to abandon all of these outside activities. I asked him the same question that the Lord had asked the scribes and Pharisees: "Do you say this of yourself or has someone else told you?" He said: "You are right; someone else told me to tell you." We both knew who it was. We continued to be friends until his death.

My reading embraces literature, science, philosophy of politics—in a word everything that would be useful for a priest in instructing or discoursing with others, or in supplying material for communication. I never read novels. When I was in college, I had great difficulty reading all of the novels assigned in class, but I do read book reviews of novels and also studies of contemporary literature which summarize their trends. When I was instructing Jo Mielziner, the famous theatrical artist, this particular afternoon as I rang his doorbell, he told me that Humphrey Bogart had just dropped in. Jo told Bogart that I was coming for instructions and that he could listen if he wanted to do so. Otherwise he could go into another room. Bogart said: "Why should I listen to any priest; I know more about the Catholic Church than any priest." I pretended to know nothing about the conversation, but when I went into the room with a few others, the subject being discussed was "novels." I admitted that I had not read any of the novels they were discussing; "Whether or not this was inherited from my father, I do not know," I said, "for he could never read novels." Humphrey Bogart, who had just boasted of his great knowledge of the Catholic Church, asked: "Was your father a priest too?"

The first subject of all to be studied is Scripture, and this demands not only the reading of it, but the study of commentaries. For practical purposes and for the busy priest, I have found no commentary to equal the *Daily Study Bible* of William Barclay, which appeared in about fifteen small volumes. Protestant commentaries, I discovered, were also particularly interesting because Protestants have spent more time on Scripture than most of us. In general, I found Arthur W. Pinks's three-volume *Exposition of the Gospel of St. John* to be one of the best from a spiritual point of view.

Since my life has covered such a long span, it has undergone several influences in style. The greatest influence in writing was G. K. Chesterton, who never used a useless word, who saw the value of a paradox and avoided what was trite. At a later date came the writings of C. S. Lewis, who, with Chesterton and Belloc, became one of the leading apologists of Christianity in the contemporary world. Lewis' style was concrete, pedestrian, full of examples, analogies, parables and always interesting. Malcolm Muggeridge, too, has become another inspiration to me. He is always sparkling, brilliant, explosive, humorous. And I must not forget poetry, particularly *The Oxford Book of Mystical Verse*—especially the poems of Studdert Kennedy and, above all, Francis Thompson. Through the years I have kept a file of favorite poems, many of which I have learned by heart.

# Seven

# COMMUNISM

Shortly after I was appointed professor at the Catholic University of America and particularly after Russia became an ally of the United States in World War II, communism began to have an appeal to many Americans. This prompted in me a deep interest in communism. As a philosopher, I was trained in the philosophy of St. Thomas Aquinas, which is complete and total in the sense that it embraces God, man and society. Communism also has a complete philosophy. Cajetan, in commenting on a text of Aquinas, observed that if one starts with a wrong assumption and is logical from that point on, he never will get back on the road to truth.

As a preparation for communism, I have read through the writings of Marx, Lenin and Stalin. Their philosophy can be summarized rather simply: man has been "alienated" from his true nature in two ways—by religion and by private property. Man was alienated from himself by religion, because it made him subservient to God; man was alienated from himself by private property because it made him subject to an employer. If, therefore, man was ever to be restored to his true nature, religion and private property must be destroyed. Atheism and the economics of communism are inseparable.

Communism had its origin in the brain of Karl Marx, who, on both his father's and mother's side, was descended from a long line of rabbis. However, he became Christian with his family, for political not religious reasons. Later on, he received a degree by correspondence from the University of Jena.

The subject of communism became very intense during the Spanish Civil War in 1936. One incident of that period is worth recalling. The foreign policy of the United States was considering lifting the embargo against sending arms to the Communists in Spain. In order to combat this movement, a meeting was held in Constitution Hall, Washington. The speakers were three: a former Spanish ambassador, a young woman who had been in Spain and had fought against the Communists, and myself. Thousands were turned away from Constitution Hall. It is very likely that that meeting had something to do with the breaking down of the movement to send arms to the Communists.

The day after that meeting in Constitution Hall, I had a

meeting with President Roosevelt. Its purpose really was to ask for an assignment to the Housing Committee for a friend of mine who was defeated for a second term in Congress. I was always opposed to asking any favor from a politician, but because this man had been a good friend of mine for years, I broke my resolution.

When I went in to see President Roosevelt he was angry. I thought he was angry with the Secretary of War, who had just left the office. I soon learned that he was angry with me. He had the Washington *Post* laid upright before him on the desk. When I came in, he began: "There is one thing that I will not tolerate in this country, and that is giving speeches such as you gave last night in Constitution Hall." I asked: "What was said, Mr. President, that offended you?" He read a line from the paper. I *knew* no such statement was made. I then asked: "Mr. President, let me see the paper." Recognizing that he was not quoting from the speeches at Constitution Hall, but from another meeting in Washington, he quickly rumpled up the paper and threw it into the wastebasket: "You must take my word when I say anything." "I can take your word," I assured him, "unless it is not true." He said: "You think you know a great deal about the Church's attitude toward communism, don't you? I want to tell you that I am in touch with a great authority, and he tells me that the Church wants the Communists to win in Spain." I said: "Mr. President, I am not the least bit impressed with your authority." He said: "I did not tell you who it was." I said: "You are referring to Cardinal Mundelein, and I know that Cardinal Mundelein never made the statement that you have attributed to him."

He then changed the subject, and began attacking the Archbishop of Baltimore. He said: "Imagine, that man who is seated on the chair that was once occupied by a cousin of mine called the Ambassador from Spain to the United States a 'liar.' I will have no dealings with any man who cannot contain himself and uses words of this kind to destroy public servants." And he went on: "Another thing, one of my bodyguards went over to St. Augustine's Church last Sunday. He said that the priest asked parishioners to join a protest against Roosevelt, who is in favor of sending arms to the Communists in Spain." The President then shouted: "That man is a liar." Recognizing that he was using the word that he had condemned in the mouth of Archbishop Curley, he laughingly said: "You know how it is, we men in public life become a little excited now and then."

Seeing that we were getting nowhere, I said: "Mr. President, I came to see you about a position in Housing." He said: "Oh, Eddie voted for everything I wanted in Congress. He wants to be in Housing, does he not?" "Yes." So he wrote on a pad his name and said: "The moment you leave this office I will call Mrs. So-and-So [he mentioned the name of a woman who was in charge of Housing] and you call Eddie and tell him he has the job."

When I left the White House I called Eddie and said: "Eddie, I saw the President. I am sorry, you do not get the job." He said: "Is that what the President said after all I did for him?" I said: "No, he said you would have it." My friend never received the job.

My courses at the university not only had the regular registered students, but there were always auditors—in fact so many that chairs had to be brought in for almost every afternoon lecture. One afternoon just before I went into class, a distinguished, slightly graying gentleman came to me and said: "I want to talk with you; it is very important." I said: "I am about to begin my class; if you wish, you may come in, and after class I will see you." I was talking on the Soviet Constitution that particular afternoon. After the lecture, he said: "I am an escaped Soviet. My father owned a circus; my brother was sent to Siberia; my sister was shot. I resolved to leave Russia, so I joined a shipping unit and one night jumped into the sea to escape. I was in danger of drowning,

Photograph of an oil painting done by Gerald Brockhurst of Rt. Rev. Msgr. Fulton J. Sheen, 1940s. Lourdes in background. *(Courtesy, Society for the Propagation of the Faith)*

so I prayed to Christ and was saved." He then handed me a small booklet with his name, entitled *The Story of My Escape from Communism*. He said: "I want you to read this carefully and then call me." He gave me his telephone number. "I know you travel around the country talking about communism. I want to travel with you. At the end of your lectures, I would like to have ten or fifteen minutes to tell the audience my firsthand experience with communism. It would be a very effective way of destroying the system which I hate."

Afterward I went to the telephone and called the head of the Communist Division of the FBI, to whom I gave the man's name. He reacted quickly: "Oh, he is a very well-known spy; we didn't know that he was in the United States. The last we heard, he was in the Philippines. He's very dangerous; your life is in danger. We'll take over from this point." I never heard again from the man, and never learned what happened to him.

Because of my lectures at the university and my public appearances, my anti-Communist position was well known. I suppose it was natural, then, for someone who defected from the party to come to see me. I met this man through a telephone call at an appointed place. He told me that he was one of the members of the presidium who sat on the stage in Madison Square Garden in New York with Earl Browder and the other top Communists. He had just attended one of the top Communist meetings in New York where they not only worked together during the day, but also slept together at night.

I asked him how I could be sure that he was honest because he wished to give me material from the inside of the party. I said: "Give me your Communist card." He said: "You know you could have me killed with this card. All you would have to do is call up the Communist headquarters and read off my code number. Within a few short weeks it would be noised about that I had died in an accident." I was still unconvinced. Whenever he came to visit me, he would change taxis two or three times, and always asked to be admitted into the cellar, where he could change his clothes before coming up, because he had been at one of these night meetings of the Communists.

To make absolutely certain, I made an appointment with him at the Plaza Hotel in New York. I engaged two rooms, one adjoining the other. I called the FBI, told them I was meeting this particular man who was a top member of the Communist Party and who promised to give me information. I asked them to make a thorough investigation of his integrity. Their answer: "You hold a conversation with him; we will enter the room adjoining his, and when you leave with him, flush the toilet. That will be a signal for us to leave. We will follow him and in a month we will report to you."

In a month I received the FBI report indicating that I could trust him absolutely. He then gave me considerable information about the inside of the party, told me of false photographs that were made of me, and said that at one meeting I was called "Public Enemy No. 1." We kept in correspondence for several years until his source of information dried up, since he eventually stopped attending Communist meetings.

I angered a White Russian who accompanied me as a bodyguard throughout the country as I lectured on communism. On one occasion I was speaking in Westchester. It was the custom of the bodyguard to sit on the stage with me af-

ter being introduced as a friend; he would hand me a program on which he would mark the well-known Communists
seated in the audience. In this particular hall, he handed me
the program with one big "X" on it, which meant that everyone in the hall was a Communist, and I must be prepared.

So I changed the nature of my lecture, and said that I had
often been accused of being unfair to the Communists because I would quote statements of theirs which might not be
verifiable. I continued: "In order to correct that impression,
I will read only Communist documents, but in order that I
might not be accused of misinterpreting them, I am going to
ask various members of the audience to come to the stage
and read the Communist documents." Not a single person
came forward, and the rest of the lecture went on uninter-
rupted.

At the close of World War II, I was giving a lecture on
communism in Akron, Ohio. Several lawyers sent in word to
the sponsors of the lecture that they would not attend because I was unfavorable to Russia. In those days, many were
well disposed toward Russia. It was a very unpopular approach to dare say anything against our so-called ally. I was
staying in a rectory in Akron where a well-known prelate was
also visiting. He asked: "What are you talking about tonight?" I said: "About Russia and Eastern Europe and how
Russia will take over all of Eastern Europe, Poland, Lithua-
nia, Albania, Czechoslovakia, etc." The prelate said: "You're
crazy; Russia is a democracy; it is no longer Communist." I
said: "I have spent my life studying communism and I am
convinced that they intend to take over Eastern Europe." I
started down the stairs. It was an old rectory and there must
have been twenty-five steps. As I put my foot on each step,

my friend, who stood at the top of the stairs, pointed his finger at me and at each step repeated: "Sheen, you're wrong! You're wrong! You're wrong! You're wrong!" until I reached the bottom step. I looked up at him and said: "Someday you will discover that Eastern Europe will belong to the Communists."

The editor of a newspaper chain was in the audience that night. The next day he published a cartoon about me attacking Russia. The idea behind the cartoon was that I was destroying the unity of America and Russia.

Because of the position I took concerning Russia, my radio talks were carefully monitored. Someone stationed in the booth would shut me off the air in case I veered from the then-popular position of Russia being a democracy. I sent in a manuscript for one broadcast that contained the line, "Poland was crucified between two thieves—the Nazis and the Soviets." I received a telegram from the Bishops' Conference asking me not to say that, because I was implying that one of the thieves was Russia. I answered the telegram by suggesting: "How would it be to call Russia the 'good' thief?"

Just before World War II when Russia and Germany were still enemies, I made the prophecy on radio that as "Pilate and Herod were enemies and became friends over the bleeding Body of Christ, so one day communism and Nazism, which are now enemies, will become friends over the bleeding body of Poland." The prophecy became true as the Nazis and Soviets were united.

Despite my opposition to the evils of communism, I have always loved Russia. The chalice I use every day in Holy Mass was used in St. Petersburg in its days of faith. It may very well be that the basic reason why communism appealed to

With ex-Postmaster General James A. Farley, late 1940s. *(Courtesy, Society for the Propagation of the Faith)*

Russia was religious. Deeply embedded in the Russian soul were passionate religious convictions: the universal vocation of Russia to call all men to brotherhood; the need of sacrifice and pain to accomplish this mission; and the supreme need of resigning oneself to God's Will. Communism in the face of a declining Church promised the people the realization of these three ideals, but without clearly telling them that they would be emptied of God. Brotherhood became a revolutionary proletariat; sacrifice became violence, and the Will of God became the will of the dictator. Communism is a religion, a surrender to an absolute. That is why it appeals to those who are without faith, and why Soviet Russia is today regarded as the last hope of the Western man who lives without God.

The little tabernacle in my private chapel is a replica of a Russian church. Thus do I express my hopes for the ultimate conversion of Russia. Not in war, but in prayer must we trust that the land which once was known as Holy Russia may become again the wellspring whence a pure stream of Christianity may flow. Then shall we see fulfilled the words of the Russian poet Khomyakov, who was conscious first of Russia's great sins:

> But now, alas, what sins lie heavy,
> Many and awful on thy soul!
> Thou art black with black injustice,
> And slavery's yoke has branded thee,
> And godless flattery and baneful lying
> And sloth that's shameful, life-denying,
> And every hateful thing in thee I see.

But then he saw in his land a vessel of election summoning souls to penance:

> For all that cries for consolation,
> For every law that we have spurned,
> For sins that stain our generation
> For evil deeds our Fathers learned,
> For all our country's bitter passion,
> Pay ye with tears the while we live.
> O God of Might, of Thy compassion
> May'st Thou forgive! May'st Thou forgive![*]

---

[*] A. S. Khomyakov et le Mouvement d Slavophile: Les Hommes, Tome I, trans. A. Gartieux. Copyright © 1939 Editions du Cerf, Paris, France.

## Eight

# DESIRING THE EPISCOPACY

How many priests wish to become bishops?
There is no way of knowing, for only God
knows what goes on inside of the human
heart. St. Paul wrote: "It is an honorable ambition to aspire to be a bishop." Perhaps this
was because, in the early days, many of the
bishops became martyrs. It was a much more
uncomfortable post of leadership than it is
today. I must confess I started praying when
I was a young priest to become a bishop.
What was clearly the motive was the desire to
be a successor of the Apostles. I do not re-

member exactly when, but I believe it was during my first- or second-year graduate work at the University of Louvain. I remember the form the petition took. On the way to class, I passed the Church of St. Michael, on the walls of which were paintings of the Seven Dolors of the Blessed Mother. A Hail Mary at each of the Seven Dolors was offered for that intention, and I have continued that prayer though I have been a bishop for many years.

Along with that prayer to God went a resolution never to do anything by myself, or to cultivate any friendship, or to use any human means to achieve that "honorable ambition." I had occasion to put that resolution into practice.

As a young professor at the Catholic University, I was asked by Bishop Kelly of Oklahoma City for permission to submit my name to Rome as a bishop. I asked for a few days to think it over; then I wrote: "There are two ways in which one advances in the Church. One is by a push from below, the other is by a gift from above." By a "push from below" I meant influence or intercession by another. By a "gift from above" I meant an appointment by the Holy See under the inspiration of the Holy Spirit and without the influence of men. I concluded the letter by saying that since his invitation was a "push from below," and not a "gift from above," I would have to refuse. Archbishop Quinn of San Francisco, who was formerly the Bishop of Oklahoma, told me that he saw that letter in the files of the diocese.

Shortly after being named National Director of the Society for the Propagation of the Faith, I was ordained Bishop in the Church of Sts. John and Paul in Rome on the eleventh of June 1951. I afterward learned that this was done through the good graces of Cardinal Spellman.

A very crucial moment in my life began when a considerable amount of money came into my hands as a result of television. Along with gifts and wills, the sum ran into millions of dollars. Since I was director of the Society for the Propagation of the Faith, my life was committed to the spreading of the Gospel, the building of hospitals, leprosaria, schools etc., in Africa, Asia, Oceania and other parts of the world. But since I was appointed by the Holy See to this position, and since I dearly loved the missions of the Church, I insisted on giving not only every cent that came in through the ordinary channels—that is, through the diocesan offices—but through my own personal efforts, to Rome and its Sacred Congregation to be distributed for the planting of the Church throughout the world. What does it mean to be a bishop? When Our Blessed Lord first called Peter and the other Apostles to Himself, He said that from now on they would catch souls instead of fish. Whether or not a promotion in the Church increases the ability to fill nets is another matter. Statistics do not prove that one can catch more fish seated on the bank dressed in purple than when dressed in black. Rather, it would seem that the responsibility increases because a fisherman uses only a hook, but a bishop uses a crosier, or a crook. That means that he is to increase Christ's fold whether they be fish or lambs, both "by hook and by crook."

The Christian law is that the higher we go, the lower we are to become. Our Blessed Lord said, "Let the greatest among you be as the least." There is a danger of the pomp and circumstance of the treasure making one forget the clay. A sense of elation comes with the pectoral cross around one's neck, and some of us who start fumbling with it when

Solemn moments during consecration of Msgr. Fulton J. Sheen as Auxiliary Bishop of New York. Adeodato Giovanni Cardinal Piazza presided in Rome's Church of Sts. John and Paul, June 1951. *(G. Felici)*

it is first put over our shoulders never stop until the end of our days. It is called a pectoral cross, not a crucifix. The ring on the finger, the zucchetto on the head and the title "Bishop"—all these things have a ring about them and all contribute to a sense of false euphoria, which I confess having had.

In England and in Ireland, a bishop is addressed as "Lord" or "My Lord." There is the story of a newly ordained bishop in England who was asked: "How shall I address you?" He answered: "You may address me as 'My Lord,' but do not address me as 'My God.' " I also confess to the joy at the privileges that are given to a bishop—his place at table, the extra-soft prie-dieu and the reverence born of faith. In a very short time I discovered that I was no different than before, that the clay was just as weak as ever, that the esteem people paid me was not necessarily the way the Lord looked on me. It took me some time to discover that the jewel in the ring does not necessarily become a jewel in a crown of Heaven.

Working as I was for the missions, and seeing the poverty of good men and women who were spending themselves and being spent for Christ, along with the growing sense of my own weakness and sinfulness, made me realize how far I was from where Christ wanted me to be. I then began wearing a very small silver ring with a mother-of-pearl image of the Blessed Mother in it, which I continued to wear until the Second Vatican Council when Pope Paul VI gave every bishop a simple gold band. I then began using a crucifix rather than a cross at the end of the chain worn about the neck. The crucifix, which I grew more fond of, was one which a community of nuns sold to a jeweler for the price of silver—the story of which is told on another page of this book.

The supreme joy of being a successor of the Apostles is the power to ordain or to beget other priests. Physical generation is denied us by virtue of celibacy, but to lay hands on young men and to anoint their own hands with the power to forgive sins and to offer the Body and Blood of Christ is a spiritual begetting of the celestial order. This brings burdens, for the Lord holds us responsible for ordaining those who are unworthy. As Bishop of Rochester, I rejected a few deacons who were presented to me for ordination. I had felt in examining them, and also from observing them in the seminary when I made visits, that their intentions were not worthy. When the news finally got about concerning the rejection of certain members of the class, a mother of one of the young men came to me and said: "Thank God you are not ordaining my son. He is not worthy to be a priest." Several other members of the class came to me and asked: "How did you know? Your judgment was right."

The worth of a bishop is determined by his *donation to life, not its duration.* Because I am in a position of eminence, it could be very easy to judge my life by the monies I collected for the poor of the world and set them down in terms of dollars and cents. Or, if one is in a diocese, to list the schools and churches that have been built, forgetful that all this has been done through the gratuities of others. God will judge me rather by how much I reflected Him, not only in work but in word and life.

When finally the sands of life run out, the test of worth is not how long we served, or how much we did, but whether or not the people in our charge remember the Bishop as one who is Christ among them. This is a difficult and frightening assessment, and I shudder at the responsibilities that are mine after over sixty years in the priesthood and almost thirty in the episcopacy. No one can count the times that my soul shuddered, reading from St. John Chrysostom that the life of a bishop should be more perfect than the life of a hermit. The reason he gave was that the holiness which the monk preserves in the desert must be preserved by the bishop into the midst of the evil of the world. St. Thomas Aquinas taught that the spiritual life of the bishop makes greater demands for perfection than the religious life: "Perfection is a prerequisite for the episcopal state; that is why Our Lord, before committing the pastoral charge to Peter, asked him if he loved Him more than the others." The Lord has blessed me with duration both in the priesthood and in the hierarchy. But what of the donation? It certainly has not been a total donation of self; nor has every human coin of opportunity that has been dropped in my path—whether copper, silver or gold—been stamped with the image of Christ.

Looking back over my office of bishop, three observations have struck me:

1. Bishops are a *gift* of the Father to the Son.

2. Bishops continue the Mission of Christ.

3. The Lord is not always pleased with us.

1. The prayer of Our Blessed Lord the night of the Last Supper was for His bishops, namely, the Apostles. And

how did He describe us? As "gifts" of the Heavenly Father to Himself: "Whom You have *given* to Me." Notice the closeness between the bishops and Himself. Our Blessed Lord in that prayer said: "I have come from the Father," and now He tells the bishops: "You have come from the Father; that is why I have you; you are His Gift."

2. The first gift of the Spirit after Good Friday and Easter was to the bishops and it was for their mission. Pentecost was not the initial breathing of the Spirit. On Easter Sunday night, doors of the upper room were barred, Thomas was absent and the Lord suddenly appeared to ten bishops, three of whom slept in the Garden, one of whom denied, and only one of whom was present at the Cross. What Our Blessed Lord might have said to all of them was: "Shame on you, shame, shame." But what did He say? "Peace." And He showed them His hands and His feet and His side. Our Lord was not a superstar; He was a *Superscar.* He said the word "Peace" twice. The first time he meant reconciliation; that was why He showed His scars to prove that we were united again to the Father. The second "Peace" was not a mission of reconciliation, but a mission of service: "As My Father sent Me, so also I send you." And He breathed upon His bishops.

In the Greek or the Septuagint version of the Bible, there is only one other time when that word "breathed" is used, and that is in Genesis; when He created the first man, He breathed into his nostrils the breath of life. This is the second breathing and it was on the Apostles or the bishops. The first breathing made Adam; the sec-

ond breathing made the new creation—the Church and
its mission to the world.

3. The Lord was not too pleased with His bishops as they
appear in the Book of Revelation. John the Evangelist
was on the Isle of Patmos, exiled because of his faith.
There he writes about the first bishops of the early
Church, whom he calls "angels" of the respective churches.
There is no doubt that he is talking of the local authority and how it is being exercised in the community.
Through these churches with the bishops at their head,
Christ exercises His power and renders His judgment
about each one. The truer the Church is to Christ, the
greater will be her tribulation. But it is in the midst of
this Church with all her faults and failings that the Lamb
bears away sin. The Church is not made up of saints, but

Sheen "on the set." (*William Kahn*)

of sinners who are trying to be saints. This is true of the bishops.

St. John may be recording either the historical condition of each bishop at the time, or he may be unfolding the simultaneous state of the bishops at any period of history—or even both together.

St. John writes of the seven bishops in seven different churches or dioceses of Asia. Of these seven dioceses, the first mentioned was Ephesus: the bishop was zealous, orthodox and a great organizer, but there was not love. Smyrna: the bishop was humble, dedicated to his flock, persecuted and approved. Pergamum: the bishop was timid in the face of evil, and compromising. Thyatira: the bishop was good, but he failed to do anything about teachers of false religion. (How modern this sounds!) Sardis: the bishop was a pretender; he deceived himself; he called himself living, but he was dead. The Church of Philadelphia: the bishop was a good shepherd and kept his word. Laodicea: rich on the outside; poverty-stricken on the inside.

The church is always judged by the bishops; that is the lesson of the Book of Revelation. And in many instances in which St. John writes about these churches, he said: "I know your works," that is your administration, finances, social service and schools. I know all of these—then there comes a "but" ... What was forgotten was love of Christ, or orthodoxy, or self-denial. I once heard of a preacher who was developing the theme about the three young men who were called by Our Lord. Each of them said: "I will go, but ..." and then each gave an excuse. The preacher ended up by saying: "It seems to me that many people are going to Hell on their 'buts.' " Well, here there is a "but," such as lost love, a cold church or allowing false prophets to teach. The only two churches that were approved without any criticism were the churches that suffered.

Today bishops are often criticized for a wrong reason. In the Book of Revelation, we are condemned for want of spirituality. The danger today may be the primacy of administration over love. Few who criticize the bishops know what goes on in our hearts—our worries and our heartaches. I remember once landing in the Los Angeles airport. The porter

Sheen at his famous blackboard on national television, November 1952. *(The New York News)*

who took my bag said to me: "Everybody knows you; it must be wonderful to be a bishop." And I said to him: "Suppose you had four hundred children and ten were very sick and five were dying. Would you not worry and stay awake at night? Well, that is my family. It is not as wonderful as you think."

I believe bishops are strong on two conditions. First of all is reliance on Peter and his successors. Our Blessed Lord told His Apostles: "The devil had asked to sift you as wheat." There is no indication that Our Blessed Lord denied that there would be a demonic trial or testing; there is even a suggestion that He permitted it. Though the other Apostles were there, He spoke only to Peter: "Peter, I have prayed for you." Our Lord did not say: "I will pray for *all* of you." He prayed for *Peter* that his faith fail not, and after he recovered from his fall that he confirm his brethren. I think bishops are strong *only* when they are united with the Holy Father. As we begin to separate from him, we are no longer under the prayer of Christ. And if we are not under the prayer of Christ, we are no longer protected, nor are we strong guardians or angels of the churches.

As I see it, the second source of strength lies in the communication and interflow of life and wisdom between the members of the episcopal fraternity—a deep fraternal spirit of love. This was made clear the night Our Blessed Lord washed the feet of the bishops, bidding them to wash one another's feet. There was to be a community of service between us. The Vatican Council affirmed this in the sense that it asked for the Collegiality of Bishops. In each country there was to be an Episcopal Conference, allowing the bishops to express their common problems and solutions.

I think, though, the Episcopal Conference is weak when it depends on human resources and power instead of on the divine. The Sunday after Easter there were seven bishops in a boat; they went out on their own; they were not sent. They labored all the night and took nothing. The Risen Lord appeared on the shore in the early morn but they did not recognize Him at once. He told them to cast their nets on the other side of the boat. Now they were under divine direction; new Power was let loose.

They dragged in a net containing 153 fish. They counted them that day. It was a reminder by Christ of the original mission He gave them to be "fishers of men." Implicit, too, was the truth: "Without Me you can do *nothing*" . . . nothing. Before He gives strength, He makes us feel our emptiness.

*Nine*

# MISSIONS AND MISSIONARIES

Evangelization is inseparable from professional teaching ever since the Word became flesh. Not even Eternal Wisdom could remain within the theological center of the Trinity, but He became a roaming Teacher, an itinerant Instructor. Nature decreed that certain things kept to themselves spoil. Almost everything in the universe was made to be spent. Wealth hoarded makes its keeper a miser. Learning for the sake of learning makes the student proud. University professors desiccate by never making their knowledge available to those who do not sit at desks. The Logos or Word of God taking a child on His lap will forever remain the mission of education—to share it as wealth must be shared.

All during my teaching career, I would travel to New York, Boston and other cities almost every weekend to instruct converts and preach. Evangelization took on other forms. I also built several churches in Alabama. One summer I traveled in a trailer with a priest who later on became a bishop—Bishop Durick—through the state of Alabama, talking on road corners and in cornfields to anyone who would listen. A considerable legacy I received was used to build the first maternity hospital in the United States for blacks in Mobile, Alabama. On one occasion I received a letter from a black woman inviting me to the village where I gave a mission on the steps of the public school; afterward a church was built on the main street. It was in the diocese of Bishop McGinnis, which was the entire state of Oklahoma.

In 1950, the bishops of the United States invited me to become National Director of the Society for the Propagation of the Faith. This meant opening the narrow door of a classroom to the world. It would be my duty to represent in the United States the Sacred Congregation for the Propagation of the Faith in Rome, charged with the evangelization of a great part of the world. That meant directing local offices in each diocese in the gathering of funds to support the Church for the spread of the Gospel in Africa, Asia and many other places. From now on, I would have to drop the *Contra gentes* of Thomas Aquinas which was directed to the conversion of the Moslem, and take up the globe of the earth and direct my efforts to all people.

It was very consoling to have a universal mission and to

consider the world as my parish. I can very well imagine how Our Blessed Lord must have felt restrained when His Heavenly Father restricted Him to Israel. He had come to be a "ransom of sin" for all men in the world, but He left that universality of evangelization to His Apostles. It was when He was stripped of His garments on the Cross that He became the "Universal Man." Up until then, He wore the garments that identified Him as one coming from a territory that was as small as from New York to Wilmington. But when He hung naked on the Cross, He became the Man of the world.

The world, to me, was suffering from two kinds of hunger. Our Western world, with its affluence, was suffering from hunger of the spirit; the rest of the world from hunger of bread. The affluent part of the world was Christian. Take

Departure ceremony for missionary priests going to Pakistan, St. Vincent Ferrer Church, New York City, August 31, 1956. (*Frank Bauer Photo; Courtesy, St. Vincent Ferrer Church*)

a circular map of the world, and run a finger around the 30th parallel, raising it slightly above China, and it will be discovered that most of the wealth, health, education, scientific advancement is above the 30th parallel and much of the poverty and ignorance is below it. Christianity is above the 30th parallel; that is why it bears the burden of aiding the world's poor.

Furthermore, Our Blessed Lord said: "Go into the world and make disciples." Here was not only a cosmic mission, but also a personal one, namely, to bring souls under the discipline of Christ. I came into this office of the Society for the Propagation of the Faith at just the moment when the Church was beginning to sense a conflict between divine salvation and human liberation, between working for personal salvation of those in a parish or in a community and having a concern about their social welfare. God never intended that individual and social justice should be separated, though they very often were divorced. In the sixties, in particular, youth developed a passionate interest for social justice in restricted areas, but they showed very little concern for individual justice, that is to say, their own relationship to their parents and to God.

What the appointment as National Director brought to my life was the opportunity to see that Christian salvation has both an earthly and a historical dimension; that the conversion of a single soul may not be alienated from the promotion of human rights as required by the Gospel, and which is central to our ministry; that soul-winning and society-saving are the concave and convex sides of the love of God and love of neighbor; that in addition to begetting children of God through evangelization, we have to give the witness of fraternal love in a sensitiveness toward humanity's desire for freedom and justice; that as Christ is both divine and human, so the mission of every Christian is to be transcendent in lifting eyes to Heaven but also imminent in the care of the way he lives on earth; that earthly liberation is an integral part of evangelization and that they are united as Creation and Redemption; that when we separate the two there is the danger to politicize faith and relate it to Marxism as is done in one part of the world, or else to create a dichotomy between the two by remaining in the Church but doing little for its spiritual life, while identifying the mission of Christ only with the social Gospel.

When I would sit with the other national directors of the world at the annual meeting in Rome, and with the distinguished members of the Sacred Congregation, I would see how we distributed our money not only for the building of churches and for evangelical centers, but for hospitals, housing, leprosaria, credit unions, aid to legal groups to prevent injustices to the poor, even down to answering this telegram I once received from Rome: "Send $200,000 immediately for the starving children who are eating sand in Pakistan." There it was that I saw the balance between the personal and the societal, between the vertical and the horizontal, between the human and the divine. I published a report at the end of every year for the diocesan directors showing how every cent was spent, and with practically no overhead because our missionaries were giving their lives for the Gospel and for the poor. My successor, Bishop Edward T. O'Meara, has continued that publication and expanded it in a way to be a compelling appeal to all men to unite love of God and love of neighbor.

I should write here how I first met my successor. The Society for the Propagation of the Faith was holding a national meeting of its directors in St. Louis. After a meeting one evening, a number of the diocesan directors and myself decided to make a visit to the Blessed Sacrament in the St. Louis Cathedral, but we found it closed. I met a young priest outside who said: "I will open the cathedral for you." He turned on all the lights, was extremely gracious and kind. Afterward I wrote to his archbishop asking if he would permit the then Monsignor Father O'Meara to become Assistant National Director of the Society. And thus, Providence prepared the way for the well-being of the Propagation of the Faith by a seeming chance meeting with a priest before the closed door of the St. Louis Cathedral.

Divine Providence indeed opened a way for a vast increase of aid to the missions of the world. As I mentioned earlier in this book, I was invited not by the bishops of the United States, but by a television network, to appear on a weekly show for which I was paid $26,000 a night. This, along with the gifts that came to the office as a result of television, made it possible to give millions of dollars to the poor of the world over the course of one year. In addition to that, a column in the Catholic newspapers of the United States entitled "God Love You" made an appeal to the Catholic laity for "sacrifice" for the spread of the faith. The response of the faithful was beyond our wildest expectations. Many, giving up their vacations or sacrificing in the way of food and clothing, added contributions to the General Fund of the Propagation of the Faith. I had no right to dispose of any of the monies thus received, though sometimes there was much pressure from outside to do so, but it was my assignment from the

Holy Father to gather alms and send them to the Central Office of the Sacred Congregation in Rome, where the distribution would be made according to needs.

Another factor which should be mentioned as most important in the growth of the spirit of sacrifice was the practice of daily prayer in the National Office. Every day at two forty-five our whole office staff would recite the Rosary together. Later on we used the fifteen minutes to give a spiritual commentary on certain passages from the Bible, and during my fifteen years there we went through practically the whole of Scripture in our office meditations.

Not to be forgotten was the devotion of the office staff, who had to work extra hard because of the tremendous volume of mail that came to our office as a result of television. Reports in our office showed the daily mail was between 18,000 and 25,000 letters. Everyone in our office was a missionary—those who opened the mail and typed, kept books, did the secretarial work, answered the mail. It will be remembered that King David went out to battle and found that several hundred men were too ill to go after the victory at Ziklag. The victors in the army sat down to divide the spoils. David intervened: "No, those who stayed behind to watch the luggage will share equally with those who fought." The good and faithful friends in our office are, therefore, considered sharers in the heavenly triumphs as much as those who left home for foreign missions and those who made sacrifices for the missions every week.

As the Holy Father has bishops from all over the world visiting him, so the National Director is privileged to have missionaries come daily to dine at his table. Hardly a day passed without our hearing the story of these "heralds of

At the desk of his Manhattan office as National Director of the Society for the Propagation of the Faith, 1950s. *(Nat Fein; Courtesy, Queens Borough Public Library)*

the Gospel" as they brought inspiration to my life and to my office and to my pen, for I used many of their stories in my "God Love You" column. Instead of narrating anything that I may have done for the Society for the Propagation of the Faith, I prefer to recall some of their stories or else my own experiences as I visited mission lands.

# NEW GUINEA

I remember Father Zegwaard, a Dutch missionary, who worked with the cannibals in New Guinea. I was curious as to how he ever gained entrance to a camp of cannibals. "Providence," he said, "took care of that. I wandered through the forests and the day I first spied them I fell ill with diphtheria. Ready to die, I stretched out on a log where they discovered me. I was too sick to eat, so for weeks they just stood around me in curiosity. When I got well, we were friends. The cannibals lived near the sea; the women did the fishing and the men fought. Anyone who came from a neighboring tribe was considered as coming from another world. That is why they had a right to kill him and even, in some instances, to drink his blood in order to absorb his strength."

He came into my office and asked that I give him three hundred axes which he felt would help civilize these people. The reason he wanted axes was that they had to build their houses in trees because of the high tides; they had no steel with which to cut limbs, but only big fish bones. Returning to them, he promised he would give each of them an ax provided they would never kill anyone. Each cannibal would take the ax, seat himself on the log with the ax between his teeth to impress ownership of that ax and also to indicate thanksgiving. After some period of time, Father Zegwaard's own ax was stolen. Stealing was very rare among these people. The day his ax was stolen, a missionary airplane flew over his camp to see if he were still alive. By coincidence, the day the airplane appeared in the sky, smallpox broke out among the cannibals. Since they have a deep sense of retribution, they said: "These spots on our faces have come from that spirit up above because we stole Father Zegwaard's ax." It was a crude way of acknowledging Divine Justice.

They returned the ax and, in reparation, they gave him one of their own boys, whom Father Zegwaard later sent to Australia to study for the priesthood. That boy has since become one of the first "cannibal" priests of the modern world.

## BORNEO

Bishop Antony Galvin visited me from Borneo. His people lived in almost a single apartment house, one floor with no walls or dividing lines between families. This crude structure would be strung through the trees, sometimes a block long. As there was no boundary wall between families to denote territorial imperative, so there were no marks on the river where each family could fish; but no one ever violated the fishing territory allocated to each group. Bishop Galvin on one occasion was instructing his people on the commandments. When he came to the commandment "Thou shalt not steal," they asked him: "What is stealing?" He said: "If I should take this gourd and bring it back to my hut, that would be stealing." These primitive, uneducated and uncultured people asked: "Does anyone in the world steal?" We call these people "primitive"!

## PACIFIC ISLANDS

I asked a missionary from the Pacific Islands what was the greatest virtue of his people. "I will tell you their greatest virtue in terms of their greatest vice. It is the sin of 'kai po,' the sin of *eating alone*. They would go without food for several days until they could find someone with whom they could share their blessings."

This same missionary told me that he visited a tiny Pacific island in his motorboat. He asked the chief if he might come to visit again to evangelize, to instruct and to convert. The chief said that he would grant him permission if the missionary would give him a motorboat, since the chief had never seen a boat that moved without man-power. Some

Sheen with Maryknoll Sisters he had commissioned for overseas missionary service, May 1957. (*Courtesy, Society for the Propagation of the Faith*)

months later Father returned with a motorboat as a gift. The chief arranged a banquet at the seashore, where roast pig and Pacific fruits were strewn on mats.

On leaving, the chief had made no reference about allowing the priest to teach his people. "Aren't you going to give me any souls?" Turning to a sixteen-year-old girl, the chief replied: "Yes, there's one; you can have her." Her name was Kaza.

He took her back to the island, put her in the charge of the Sisters and after several years she became a Catholic and expressed a desire to become a nun. The missionary said: "No, you will have to return again to your island, and remain for some time with the people in order to test your vocation." When she returned to the island there was considerable opposition to her because of her Christianity. However, she did convert her mother and father as they were dying; but an aunt in whose care she was placed raised opposition to her because of her faith. Poor Kaza was almost on the verge of surrendering her faith, when one day at the seaside, the son of this aunt was bitten by a shark. The waters were tinted with blood and the people on the shore shouted out: "Yaweh, Yaweh." No one knows where they ever got the Hebrew name for God. "Yaweh, Yaweh, why have You done this?" Then someone said: "Maybe because of the way we treated Kaza." Here again was the sense of Divine Retribution.

Kaza was then allowed to return again to the other island and she did become a nun. Later on, as Sister Gabriel, she returned and evangelized her whole island. I corresponded with her for several years afterward.

# CHINA

I flew into Peking, China, in 1948 with Bishop James A. Walsh of Maryknoll. Seated alongside him, I was reading Confucius, which prompted this remark: "I believe you and I are the only two missionaries in China who have read Confucius. We have to know the Chinese way of thinking. Before you can lead people to where you want them to be, you have to know where they are." As we landed he said: "I will never leave China unless I am put out." Everyone knows the story of Bishop James Walsh and how, after many long years of imprisonment, he was finally sent out of China—a beautiful example of what a missionary was meant to be.

Because of the many sufferings of our missionaries under Communist rule, there should be in the catalog of sanctity a new type of saint. "Wet" martyrs are those who shed their blood for the faith. But since the Communists did not always kill, though they tortured, a new kind of martyr arose: the "dry" martyr. What they agonized through a period of years far exceeds in pain what other martyrs suffered in a brief interval. Each day, hour and minute was a profession of Faith. Including the persecution in Eastern Europe, the Church has had more martyrs, wet and dry, in the last seventy years than in the first three hundred years of her history. Not to be forgotten either are the victims of Auschwitz, Dachau and other furnaces, for these Jewish people were guilty of no other crime than believing they were the chosen people of God. Bishop Walsh was not a "wet" martyr, but he is certainly recorded in the scrolls of Heaven as one of the glorious "dry" martyrs of the Church of the United States.

There was one missionary bishop, Francis Ford, whom I did not know directly. However, his secretary—a nun who served with him in China—told me many interesting stories about the good Bishop.

When he was twelve years of age in Brooklyn, he heard an Italian missionary lecture on his work among the lepers; he gave a nickel to help the missionary and in those days a nickel represented a large portion of his spending money. And what stuck in his heart were the last words of that lecture by the missionary: "My one ambeesh is to die a martyr." And that is how he later came to die!

When the Communists came into power, Bishop Ford was arrested. The Bishop told Sister: "I am afraid the Communists are going to take over my property. Here is the key to my chapel; I want you to take out the Blessed Sacrament before It is desecrated." She took a loaf of bread and the key to the Bishop's chapel on the second floor of his home, removed the Blessed Sacrament and hid It in the loaf of bread. As she closed the chapel door, a Communist colonel who was known all over that part of China for his cruelty said: "I am taking over possession of this chapel; I have a key." He tried to open the door, but it would not open. "Here, you open the door." She said: "I cannot; my hands are filled with bread." He said: "Give me the bread." She passed the bread to him and he looked down at it, "as if it were an infant," she recalled, but he had his gun cocked all the while, as she opened the door. She removed the Blessed Sacrament to safety and later on was imprisoned.

When the Communist police closed in on his mission,

some Sisters who were teaching catechetics were arrested along with him. On the way to the prison my informant told me that he addressed them, saying: "Remember, the Church is not only a triumphant Church, but also a suffering Church; with Christ you may expect not only joy but sorrow, but He is always with you." As he was led from his mission at Kaying, many who were sympathetic to the Communists spat at him and threw stones and offal. One carried a sarcastic banner reading: "The People's Government welcomes the spy—Bishop Ford." While all this ridicule was being heaped on him, he made the sign of the Cross as best as he could, though he was handcuffed.

The good Sister who was in prison with him for a time said that he was too weak to stand, so he leaned against a prison wall. His hair was long and white and his beard matted, his face emaciated and pale from torture. He was the only one, for reasons that only Providence could explain, who was given bread and wine in prison. This was not done out of respect for Bishop Ford, but was God's way of giving him consolation. The Sister told me that no Mass in a Gothic cathedral could ever equal in splendor the beauty of Bishop Ford moving his fingers along the cement tray, his burnt-out eyes as candles, his vestment the black padded Chinese gown, his miter a stocking cap, his music the groans of the suffering, his missal the memory of Calvary, the sanctuary bell the death knell about to strike—and saying "Qui pridie . . ."—the day before He suffered.

The Bishop's Chinese cook, who had served him for many years, and whom he regarded as a good friend and a good Christian, was the man who delivered him over to the Communist authorities and falsely accused him. Despite the fact that he knew how the Bishop had solaced the sick and buried the dead, he nevertheless delivered him over to suffering. The reward the houseman received was to be made chief of police of that village.

The women with whom the Sister had been incarcerated were not permitted to eat unless everyone confessed to being a Communist. She refused. The result was that they turned on her. "The only kind person in the cell," she said, "was a prostitute."

A Communist guard came into the cell one day with a lead pipe and told Sister to hit every woman over the head. She laid the lead pipe gently on the shoulder of each woman. The Communist guard shouted: "You're not a Communist!" "Why not?" she asked. "Because you don't hate." After much torture, she promised that she would write out a confession. The guard went to get the paper but immediately she was seized with the worst toothache she ever had in her life. And when he came back, she refused to sign. She has borne in her mind and body ever since the memory of those torturous days for her fidelity to the Church.

Whenever Bishop Ford was given a walk outside the prison, being unable to support himself, he leaned on two Chinese fellow prisoners. Then came the day of the death march. He was put out in line between the two other prisoners. The Chinese Communist colonel who had seized the chapel tied a sack around his neck weighing over twenty pounds. He tied it in such a way that the rope would tighten as he walked. The Communists would not kill anyone; they would just let him die. The good Sister, seeing what was done to the Bishop, broke the line of march, for she was behind with the women. She came up and shouted at the

Informal gathering of students and a Sister of St. Joseph, discussing young people's role in helping the missions, at national office in New York, August 21, 1957. *(Photo by H. Earl Eakin)*

colonel: "Look at the man." It was a kind of "Ecce homo." For the first time he seemed to see pain etched in the face of the Bishop. Later he came to his Communist consciousness and called her a "dog" and ordered her to get back in line. She watched the weaving of the prisoners in the death march, her eyes forever on the Bishop. After two miles he was still standing, supported by the two Chinese aides, *but the sack was not on his back.* I said to her: "Why do you think the sack was taken off his back?" She said: "It was taken off his back by the Communist colonel. The reason, because he once carried the Blessed Sacrament." For that aid to the Bishop, the Communist colonel was put in prison and that was the last time that the Sister heard of him.

After Bishop Ford died a dry martyr in February of

1952, the former cook went back to the chapel, threw a rope over a rafter and committed suicide.

Elsewhere in China, a priest had just begun Mass when Communists entered and arrested him and made him a prisoner in a house adjoining the little church. From a window in that house he could see the tabernacle. Shortly after his imprisonment, the Communists opened the tabernacle, threw the Hosts on the floor and stole the Sacred Vessels. The priest then decided to make adoration to Our Lord in the Blessed Sacrament as much as he could day and night. About three o'clock one morning, he saw a child who had been at the morning Mass open a window, climb in, come to the sanctuary floor, get down on both knees, press her tongue to

At mission on a location in Sasolburg, South Africa, November 27, 1960. (*Courtesy, Society for the Propagation of the Faith*)

the Host to give herself Holy Communion. The priest told me there were about thirty Hosts in the ciborium. Every single night she came at the same time until there was only one Host left. As she pressed her tongue to receive the Body of Christ, a shot rang out. A Communist soldier had seen her. It proved to be her Viaticum.

## AFRICA

On one of my visits to the missions, I went to a leper colony in Buluba, Africa, where there were 500 lepers. I brought with me 500 silver crucifixes, intending to give one to each of the lepers—this symbol of the Lord's Redemption. The first one who came to meet me had his left arm eaten off at the elbow by the disease. He put out his right hand and it was the most foul, noisome mass of corruption I ever saw. I held the silver crucifix above it, and *dropped it*. It was swallowed up in that volcano of leprosy.

All of a sudden there were 501 lepers in that camp; I was the 501st because I had taken that symbol of God's identification with man and refused to identify myself with someone who was a thousand times better on the inside than I. Then it came over me the awful thing I had done. I dug my fingers into his leprosy, took out the crucifix and pressed it into his hand. And so on, for all the other 499 lepers. From that moment on I learned to love them.

## AUSTRALIAN DESERT

Another friend of mine, who worked among the primitive people in Australia, was Father Vincent Shiel. This missionary, slightly beyond middle age, came to my office with this story. "I am a missionary in the desert district of 125,000 square miles in Australia. Only two classes live there: sheepherders and opal miners. The opal miners are naked and live underground, cutting holes in the walls for places to sleep. I have no rectory, other than my Volkswagen. The heat in the desert averages about 125 degrees. Almost the only kind of food I can carry are cans of peaches. It seems that any other kind explodes in the desert. I asked my bishop if I might become a Trappist; he refused. I then sought his permission to visit you in America, to tell you why I wanted to become a Trappist, namely, because I felt I had failed some of my people in the desert." The Bishop agreed that if I saw in him a vocation to the Trappists, he might join the community to do penance for any remissness in pastoral duties.

When I asked him to describe his life to me further, it developed that, in crossing the desert, he would sometimes be 350 miles or more from a single human being. In one crossing, a stone flew up and cracked his battery, making further journey impossible. The limit of life, he told me, walking in such heat without food and drink, would be less than a day. There was nothing to do but pray for help or resign oneself to death. As he leaned his head over the steering wheel, making his act of resignation to God, he heard the rumble of a truck in the distance. The truck was carrying a spare battery and thus his life was saved.

After hearing the unimaginable sacrifices he was making for his people, and learning that he would often go down into the opal mines to read Mass for his people and instruct them, I said: "My dear Father, I think that you are looking for a plastic cross instead of a wooden one." By that I meant that there was no sacrifice he could make in an ascetic community which could equal the sacrifices he was making in the desert. Just a few moments before, I had given him a personal check to buy a new Volkswagen, since he had told me that the one he owned when he left was swept away in a flood. But he tore up the check and left, showing considerable resentment against my reference to the "plastic cross."

A few weeks later he came back and apologized, saying: "You were right; I am fleeing from a difficult mission. I shall return and give my life." This he has done, and to such a noble extent that it is difficult to find anyone who will take his place in that desert mission.

# PAKISTAN

One of the first visitors whom I received in my role of National Director was a bishop in Pakistan. He told me that at the outbreak of the war he, being an Italian missionary bishop, was arrested, put into jail and told that he would not be released until the war was over. A few days later he received a visit from a thirteen-year-old girl named Clara Mark, a Hindu whom he had converted to the Faith. She said: "Bishop, you will not be here in this prison very long; you will be released at the end of six months and will continue to serve as a bishop for years to come."

The Bishop inquired how she knew he would be released from prison. She said: "I have offered my life for you, and for the success of your work." Six months later the authorities unlocked the prison door and told the Bishop that he was free to continue to live as a bishop in Pakistan. His first visit immediately after leaving prison was to Clara Mark, and he learned from her parents that she had died that morning.

## KENYA

I went to Kenya in East Africa to consecrate Father Joseph Houlihan, a St. Patrick missionary from Ireland, who had just been named Bishop of the newly established Diocese of Eldoret. The morning after the Ordination, the Bishop asked me to drive out into the bush with him to survey his missionary territory and to meet his people. As we drew near one place, he said: "We are now coming to an area where all the people are naked, but I have never been able to get through to them or to gain a hearing. We will see if it makes any difference now that I am a bishop." As our car drove among these people, the chief, wearing nothing but an abundance of feathers on his head, came running to meet the Bishop. They both spoke warmly in the native tongue of the chief, who explained to the Bishop that he was at his Ordination and he would be very happy to have him come among his people. The Bishop said: "If I had six hundred dollars I would start a clinic tomorrow." He was assured of the $600 and those people now are being evangelized for the Faith.

In Eldoret, Kenya, Archbishop Sheen stands next to a young African bishop, Kenya's first, who is now Maurice Cardinal Ottunga, Archbishop of Nairobi. *(Yves Tourigny, W. F.)*

## UGANDA

One night I stopped at a small missionary center where priests would come for a week or two of rest after having been in the mission field for a long period of time. It was a single-story house with about four rooms. That particular night there were so many missionaries coming and going that I slept on the cement floor near the front door. About four o'clock I was awakened by one of the priests leaving. He car-

ried a large sack on his back. "Father, where are you going?"
I inquired. "I don't know," he said. "When will you be back?"
"In about six months." He was on his way to establish a new
missionary station.

## NEW GUINEA

Visiting a very primitive mission, I asked the missionary how
he ever found these people and what was the manner of his
contact. He said that he heard about them being in the wilds
and finally discovered them one day as they were doing a war
dance. They noticed his movement among the bushes at the
edge of their camp and they started throwing spears at him.
He took a mirror out of his bag and caught the reflection of
the sun and began shooting the sun in the direction of the
warriors. They became so entranced by the reflection of the
sun in their eyes, which seemed to them like a light gun, that
they stopped in their tracks, had him come forward, and he
finally became their friend.

*Ten*

# IN
# JOURNEYINGS
# OFTEN

Al Smith, on the occasion of our trip to Europe together, remarked: "The two best days of any trip are the day you leave and the day you get back." St. Augustine saw it in another light: "The world is a book and those who do not travel read only a page." Travel depends on what you bring to the places you visit. It is very much like attending an opera; if one's knowledge of music is nil, one is constantly waiting for the orchestra to play a tune that one can whistle. What would the scene of the Battle of Waterloo mean to one who knew nothing about Napoleon?

I have traveled much in the world, except to Russia and behind the Iron Curtain, though I once was behind the wall in East Germany. Though I visited Europe much during and after World War II, I am here concerned with those trips overseas which affected me spiritually and intellectually.

In 1922 a distinguished French novelist, Emile Baumann, came to the University of Louvain to give a lecture. He had just won the Prix de Balzac for eminence in French literature. I was invited to dine with him and the rector of the School of Philosophy. At dinner Monsieur Baumann asked the rector if he would recommend a graduate student of the university to accompany him on a trip tracing the travels of St. Paul, about which he would later write a book. (That book was subsequently printed in French and went through over one hundred editions.) The rector suggested that he take me along as his companion. I was embarrassed at the thought, for he was a distinguished man of letters while I had all the imperfections of one unskilled in the French language. But it turned out to be a happy trip together. Inasmuch as the footsteps and the sea journeys of St. Paul which we followed are already in M. Baumann's book, I will limit myself only to three places which influenced my life. Little did I know in those days that it would be given me through radio and television to address a greater audience in half an hour than Paul in all the years of his missionary life.

The psychology and the theology of conversion have always been one of the major interests of my life, hence my deep interest in a visit to Damascus, where Saul was given the gift of faith. Paul, or Saul as he was known before he became an apostle of Christ, was completely turned around at Damascus. Before entering the city he intended to persecute those who were Christians. On the way out he loved both Christ and Christians. I do not believe there is anything in Scripture which so much reveals the nature of the Church as this conversion of Paul. One moment he is the major bigot in Christian history and a persecutor "breathing out threats against the Church"; the next he is the greatest of all apostles "born out of due time." The date is certainly before A.D. 50. Christ has already risen and was glorified in Heaven. Yet the heavens open and the voice speaks: "Saul, Saul, why do you persecute *Me*?" Saul asked: "Who art Thou, Lord?" The answer came back: "I am Jesus Whom you are persecuting."

How could Saul be persecuting Christ, Who was already glorified in Heaven? If someone steps on the foot, does not the head complain? Saul was touching the Body of Christ which is the Church and the Head protested, for the Head and the Body are one.

Desirous of finding some way to express my thanks for having been near the spot where Paul was called to be the greatest of apostles, I sought out a little chapel on the roadway which had been dedicated to him and which traditionally marked the spot of his conversion. On the right side of the altar there had been a heroic painting of the saint. Someone had gone into the chapel the night before and slashed the painting to ribbons. Before the ruined image of Paul I recalled the words of Christ to Saul during his conversion: "It is hard for you to kick against the goad." In other words, "It's no use trying to resist My grace. For a long time I have had great things in store for you. Try no longer to be My enemy. I have marked you to be a great apostle. It is hard. I have struck thee down as a persecutor, but I will raise you up as a chosen vessel unto Me."

As the Damascus scene impressed on my early priesthood the continuity of Christ through history in His Body which is the Church, so the Athens scene taught me that the central theme of all our preaching must be Christ and Him crucified.

Paul first preached in the marketplace, where the philosophers, particularly the Stoics and Epicureans, disputed. Many of them were students of the University of Athens, but since they were searching more for novelty than depth they compared St. Paul to a small bird which picks up different seed for its food. He was not unprepared to meet the diverse philosophers, one of whom was devoted to pleasure and the other to a puritan way of life, for he had acquired a familiarity with their doctrine in his own city of Tarsus. In any case, St. Paul defended his position so well that the crowd proposed that he should go to the top of the Areopagus, or Mars Hill—the most famous spot in Athens. It was a place of sacred judgment and the center of arbitration on religious matters. Pericles had stood there.

On the way up the hill, Paul passed through streets that were lined with the statues of gods. In fact, I observed many images of the ancient gods still remaining as I made my way to the hill. What struck me was not just idolatry, but that these stone images were yearnings in the hearts of men for God to appear among them. If their gods would not come down from their Olympian heights, they would force them to come down by incarnating them in rock and gold and silver. These were unconscious cravings for Emmanuel or "God among us."

Every night I went to Mars Hill and reread that famous speech of St. Paul in chapter 17 of Acts. From the point of view of rhetoric and pedagogy it was a perfect speech. First, he began with a tribute that was to win their souls. Paul spoke of how God made the universe, was the Lord of Heaven and earth, did not dwell in temples made with hands (such as the beautiful one he was looking on); that He made of one blood every nation of men that dwelled upon the face of the earth, fixing the limits and extent of their habitation, and inspiring them to seek God even though they might be groping in the darkness. God, Paul said, was not far from any one of them. As the poet put it, "We are all His offspring." Paul then jumped to the subject of Judgment and the Resurrection.

He made only two converts—Dionysius, and a woman named Damaris. The talk was not a success. It was rather one of Paul's great failures. He left the city immediately after the talk and walked to Corinth. He never went back to Athens, never wrote a letter to the Athenians, and there is no record that he established a church in Athens. As I sat evening after evening reading that speech, it finally dawned on me why St. Paul had failed in that talk. He had failed to mention the Name of Christ and His Crucifixion. I am sure that as he walked that dusty road between Athens and Corinth he must have said over and over again what he later wrote to the Corinthians: "I am resolved among you to know nothing but Christ and Him Crucified."

One other moment in the voyage among countless ones that affected me was the visit to the city of Ephesus. When I saw it, it was a wilderness; when St. Paul saw it, it was called the "Treasure House of Asia." He looked out on the great glory of the Temple of Diana as she was called in Latin, or Artemis as she was known in Greek—one of the Seven Wonders of the World. It was 425 feet long, 220 feet wide and 60 feet high. The altar itself had been carved by Praxiteles, the greatest of all the Greek sculptors. Each of the 127 columns was of Parian marble weighing 150 tons, measuring 60 feet high and decorated in gold and precious stones. Eight of these columns I saw later in the Church of Santa Sophia in former Constantinople. All that remains now is the open amphitheater facing the sea, which seated thirty thousand people, and a few ruins of the library, which contained many volumes of magic and superstition. Large stones of the street somewhat resembling those of the Appian Way still could be seen. But of its glory, its temple is a mass of shapeless ruin, its harbor a reedy pool whose silence is insulted by the noisy flights of crows. "All the air a solemn stillness holds." The government insisted that we take guards with us because of the robbers who hid in the ruins. On one occasion they did dash out from the long subterranean passage but were quickly repulsed by the soldiers.

Paul began preaching in the synagogue and then later on after it rejected him, he taught in the school of Tyrannus, the heathen Sophist who specialized in rhetoric and philosophy. During the month of May, which was the sacred month of Diana, Paul noticed that the drunkenness, debauchery and worship of Diana was beginning to decline, since he preached that there were no gods made with hands. Consequently, there arose in Ephesus muttered curses against him; finally, the ill-concealed exasperations came to an end when the chief victim of the decline of idol worship began to protest against Paul. His name was Demetrius; he had built a considerable business in the manufacture of little silver shrines and images of Diana which he sold to pilgrims on their visits to the temple. Also affected were the sacred slaves and musicians of the temple, as well as skilled artisans and ordinary workmen.

A mob was quickly organized which ran over those large stones heading for the amphitheater. Nothing hinders men more from going to or from an opinion than the interest they have in holding it; they see they cannot have the honey unless they burn the bees; they cannot have their profits, their orgies and their gain unless they dispatch Paul.

Paul had never said anything against Diana. On the contrary, when the mob went into the amphitheater, shouting for the death of Paul, the town clerk told the people that he had not mentioned Diana by name. For two hours the crowd in the arena shouted praises to Diana of the Ephesians until it reverberated on every side. Then a recorder, an important civic official, calmed the angry crowd.

Two of Paul's companions in travel, Gaius and Aristarchus, had been carried into the theater with the crowd. Paul himself was on the point of going there but his disciples bade him to hide. St. Paul, looking back on those moments, said: "We were weighed down exceedingly, beyond our power, inasmuch as we despaired even of life itself." Paul was obliged to leave the city later on.

Ephesus taught me that preaching of the Word will always provoke antagonisms. Whether it be against communism or against greed, whether it be directed against divorce or abortion, there will be not only individual harassment but organized revolt. Sometimes a seeming zeal for religion can be nothing more than a disguised love of profit, as was the case with Demetrius. Despite all that, Paul established the Church in Ephesus—to which he later addressed one of his epistles—while its bishop was the first of the seven to whom the Book of Revelation is addressed. Interesting still is the fact that in the Church of St. Mary the Virgin in 431, the Council of Ephesus was held. As the gods of Athens were yearnings for a god among men, so it happened that Diana, the Moon Goddess, found her fulfillment in Mary, who is described as having the moon under her feet.

Many travels in Africa, Asia and Australia were a combination of my duties as National Director of the Society for the Propagation of the Faith and also the bounty of being asked by Cardinal Spellman to make a trip with him and Archbishop Bergan of Omaha, Bishop Boardman of Brooklyn, Bishop Walsh and a number of priests from April until the middle of June 1948.

Everywhere on that trip then was a tremendous outpouring of people for Cardinal Spellman. The very first night of our arrival in Sydney, I addressed 25,000 people inside the cathedral and another 15,000 heard the sermon through loudspeakers outside. The next morning I gave four broadcasts. At the lord mayor's welcome to the Cardinal, the latter told a story of visiting an Arab sheik. Toasts were offered at a dinner at which lamb was served. The sheik took the eye out of the lamb in the center of the table and gave it to the Cardinal as a tribute. Later on the sheik asked him how he liked it. The Cardinal, of course, responded that he loved it. The sheik then gave him the other eye, which he could hardly swallow.

Almost every talk I gave there was recorded and then played the next day on radio. Fifty thousand people attended the reception at the show grounds. Cardinal Spellman spoke for a few minutes and then, without any warning—as was his custom—called on me to finish the talk. That evening at eleven there was a broadcast, the next morning another broadcast, then a public Holy Hour at the cathedral.

One of the very unusual customs occurred when the Cardinal of Australia and the bishops attended the Grand Centenary Ball at the Town Hall in Melbourne. Cardinal Gilroy presided, Cardinal Spellman was the guest of honor and there were thirty bishops and twenty-five monsignori. We sat on the stage from eight-thirty until nine-thirty when the dancing began. The bishops' attendance at balls was to lift the moral tone of dancing and then it became a stamp of approval. The Cardinal spoke about twenty-two minutes and then called on me to give a talk. He introduced me with the words: "This will be his ninety-ninth talk today." The two prize remarks at the ball were those of Archbishop Mannix, who with a twinkle in his eye said to the bishops: "Dancing is optional"; and of Archbishop Bergan, who remembered that John the Baptist lost his head at a dance.

As I left that Town Hall, I felt sorry for more than a thousand people who were unable to pay a pound to attend the ball, but manifested devotion by greeting the prelates and the dancers as they went in. One of the joys of that visit in Melbourne was the return of a lost sheep to the fold. A woman wrote me that her husband had been away from the Church for about forty years. I phoned her and asked him to call at Cardinal Gilroy's house. After a brief greeting with the husband I said: "Please kneel down." He said: "What for?" I

said: "You're going to Confession." And without further ado
he made a very good confession. He was almost dancing
when he went out. Long corridors are not always necessary
as entrances to a palace room. When the Holy Spirit stirs a
soul there is very often a greater desire to return than we realize.

A letter to one of the newspapers in Melbourne by a
reader who called himself reverend, declared that I was "the
greatest menace that has yet visited Australia." Afterward, I
addressed hundreds of priests at meetings sponsored by the

Bishop Sheen and Bishop Thomas Gorman at the airport in Dallas,
Texas, October 1952. (*Dallas Morning News*)

Eucharistic League and that evening, which was called "men's night" at the exhibition hall, gave another address to 20,000 while 15,000 more stood outside listening to loudspeakers. I spoke at the racetrack to 100,000 people.

In Sydney, I shared a room with a monsignor who had an extraordinary snore. It was a bubble snore combined with a dying gasp: it mediated between the gurgling of a baby and the death rattle of an octogenarian. If it had been a consistent snore I could have slept; but just when I was sure it was over, it would start again. Thank God he's not married!

Cardinal Spellman, responding to a welcome in Sydney, wanted "to say a word about Monsignor Sheen, who in America is doing more than any archbishop or any bishop to make the Faith known and loved. He is one of the most truly apostolic souls of our times. He has the ear of Catholics; he has the ear of non-Catholics, and I rejoice to know that the Australians love him as much as we do. I brought him on this trip to give him some recognition and to pay a debt. But I find that I have only increased the debt—if there be such a thing."

On our voyage across Australia to Darwin I planted a tree at four o'clock in the morning. En route we came down in Commonweal, an emergency airport, because we were running short of fuel; we struck a small toolshed as we went down and had to wire for another plane. Flies were everywhere and they immediately attacked the face. We had to brush them off with our hands. I asked one of the radio engineers if they troubled him. He said: "No, after a time you get used to them." Bishop Walsh and I walked to a little town of sixty souls where we bought some soft drinks to take back to the rest of the party. When a new plane arrived the pilot

insisted that he could not carry all the bags. The Cardinal
then said that he would leave some of his bags. He would always get on the plane last and take any seat that was left. He
turned to Monsignor Quinn and asked which bag he should
leave. Monsignor answered: "The bag with your speeches in
it!"

Arriving in Batavia, Java, I could not help but recall that this
was where *Pithecanthropus erectus* was discovered in 1891. I also
noticed that there were 683 zillion mosquitoes in Batavia
alone and that half of them bivouacked in my bedroom the
first night. They are generally not as quick in flight as our
mosquitoes but their mufflers are better and they carry plenty
of bombs. When you hang your clothes up at night they
hold their maneuvers in your sleeves, drills in your trousers,
and they attack in formation when disturbed. We were tired
and one good Jesuit asked to take us to the Botanical Gar-
dens. He told us how interesting the fauna and the flora
were. But no one seemed to be interested in the fauna nor
was anyone interested in the flora. So we stayed in the hotel
and enjoyed the best coffee in the world, remembering that
this, of course, was Java.

In Singapore I read Mass for sixty Sisters and two hundred
orphans who had been left behind by the Japanese; I later
was given a national hookup to the nine states of Malay and
Southeast Asia on the subject of impressions of Singapore.
After the broadcast I made four records of fifteen minutes
each on the subject of communism which were to be broad-

cast on the stations later in the week. In Bangkok it was interesting to observe Siamese architecture, in which the roofs had horns on the ends that pointed upward. This was in order that the evil spirits would slide off the roofs. Surpassing anything in splendor was the temple of the Emerald Buddha, which stood about thirty feet in the air on top of a gold tabernacle. The Buddha himself was about three feet high and was carved from one piece of emerald. I wrote in my notes: "Someday Buddha and Confucius may be to the Eastern Catholic theology what Plato and Aristotle were to St. Thomas and Augustine." I did not see a single Siamese cat in Siam. In the cathedral in Saigon, I preached a sermon in French. There were 100,000 Catholics in Saigon itself in 1948.

In Hong Kong I was assigned to stay with the British governor. During the war, the Japanese shelled Hong Kong and destroyed the beautiful residence of the governor. They then restored it brick for brick, exactly as it had been—with one exception. They put up the magnificent fireplaces, but they left out the chimneys. After broadcasts and several talks during the day, we were invited to a dinner by General Wang. No knives or forks, only chopsticks of ivory. Each course was put in the center of the table. Course 1 was "bird's nest," a gelatin made of the saliva of mountain swallows. (Next came washrags; each guest would wipe his face and hands.) 2. Shrimp with meat sauce. Nothing is served on the plate; everything is in the bowl and eaten with chopsticks. 3. Chicken cut in rectangles. 4. Partridge with mushrooms, kidney beans, cashew nuts. 5. Sliced squab. 6. Duck sauce surrounded by lobster rings. 7. Fish cutlets. (Every course was served in the same bowl and we were supposed to eat everything.) 8. Noodles and mushrooms. 9. Fried rice. 10. Little cakes and lotus seed. 11. Nuts served in what looked like miniature grapefruit. Finally, wet towels to finish the washing which started round two.

Arriving in Shanghai, we stopped at the Cathay Hotel, where Cardinal Spellman signed a check for dinner which cost him, in those days, 33 million in Chinese money. The Cardinal then announced that I was to accept no more talking engagements or broadcasts without his permission. He considered me too exhausted from speaking. The mayor of Shanghai, Mayor Wu, invited us to dinner. Thirty-two of us sat down to table. By this time we learned that toasts were given to practically every guest. And when you drank a toast you were to take the glass in your right hand, touch the lower half of the glass with the left hand and say something that sounded to me like "Gamboy" which means "bottoms up." I asked the mayor if there was any way of avoiding drinking incessant toasts. He said yes, it was to say something that sounded like "suhbeen," which in American became "soybean," and which we were told meant "as you please." I asked the distinguished gentleman who sat next to me if the rice wine caused intoxication. He said: "You can drink a dozen glasses without any effect, but then all of a sudden it catches up with you." At that moment, he fell off the chair intoxicated.

On the afternoon previous to the dinner, I gave a lecture at Aurora University and the next day gave a broadcast to China. I said that God had kept China behind a veil all these

A First Holy communion ceremony in Taormina, Italy, April 1953.
*(Courtesy Society for the Propagation of the Faith)*

centuries and allowed it to keep a five-thousand-year-old culture to become one day a great Christian nation. After the
broadcast, Bishop Walsh told me that Pius XI had told him
that very idea some years before.

The next day Bishop Walsh and I had tea with Mme.
Chiang Kai-shek, in one of the most lavishly decorated
homes I had seen on the trip. She told of how through the
years she became closer to God through suffering and that
she and the Generalissimo prayed together every night. She
was discouraged that America had done so little for China,
adding, "There will never be any peace in China until China
becomes Christian." It seemed to me during the conversation
that she thought of Our Blessed Lord *becoming wiser* as He
lived. I took the occasion to speak to her of the Eternal
Word and His sacrifice and how it was prolonged in the

Mass and invited her to Mass the next morning, but she
pleaded another engagement.

The following day I gave a lecture at the National University and had dinner with Generalissimo Chiang Kai-shek.
He told us of his deep affection and gratitude for American
aid during the war, how much he trusted in God's will. The
Minister of Education, who sat next to me, said that he had
a Chinese copy of the *Summa* of St. Thomas Aquinas which
was done by the missionaries in the sixteenth century.
Whether he read it or not I do not know, for he said that he
had accepted the economic interpretation of history and not
Providence. The next morning called for another sermon at
the cathedral and a national broadcast to all of China. That
evening at dinner the Apostolic Delegate, Archbishop Riberi,
and Archbishop Yu-Pin of Nanking asked the Cardinal if I
could remain in China to make a tour of all the Chinese universities and give a series of broadcasts. The Cardinal refused, feeling that I had worked too hard on this trip and was
needed at home.

After Hankow, where Communist soldiers were landing
in the airport, we flew to Peking. Cardinal Tien and twelve
Chinese bishops, Mayor Fu and a large cheering crowd met
Cardinal Spellman and his party as they became convinced
that the Catholic Church is not all French or bearded. After
a broadcast in the afternoon, a very unusual courtesy was
shown to the Cardinal and his party: a formal dinner in the
Forbidden City, where we had some "one-thousand-year-old
eggs" and the usual starvation that accompanied my use of
chopsticks.

On June 7 we flew to a port city where we were met by
Admiral Badger, who was the chief logistic officer to Admi-

ral Ernest King in the war and was now Supreme Commander of the Port. Admiral Badger invited the Cardinal and
myself to dinner in his private study. During the meal he
spoke off the record about the Chinese and the Russian situation, using a pointer to indicate the spots on the map
which he felt were vital. I distinctly remember him saying: "I
asked the State Department for a thousand Marines to be
sent to northern China to stop the Communist advance. The
State Department refused."

In Tokyo, a dinner was given to the Cardinal and his party by
General Douglas MacArthur. He always looked you straight
in the eye when he talked and gave the impression of authority and power. I personally believe that he was one of the
greatest characters that America has ever produced. Among
the reflections he offered at dinner were these: he wished he
had eight hundred Catholic missionaries for every one now
working in Japan to bring that country to Christianity. The
world struggle, he said, is not economic or political but religious and theological; it is either God or atheism.

The next afternoon at three I gave a lecture at Sofia University and later on a broadcast to Japan and another lecture
to the leaders of the Diet, at which the mayor, the Cabinet,
the ministers of the state and professors of the Japanese university were present. The next day I met my good friend General Charles Willoughby, who accepted in MacArthur's name
the surrender of the Japanese during the war and whom I got
to know very well in America when he dined at my table in
Washington. He had come to my home to challenge me
about something that was quite untrue. He towered over me

like a great giant as we stood together and he made the accusation. I then reached up and grabbed his starred shoulders, pushed him down on the couch and told him the truth. He said: "You have done me a great favor and for this I shall help the Catholic Church in Japan." I cannot give the details of what was done, but I can say that he did help the Church in Japan and I shall always be grateful to the great General Willoughby.

At another dinner which was given in honor of the Cardinal, I sat between General MacArthur and Admiral Griffith. The latter told me that the Japanese at the beginning of the war could have annihilated our fleet if they had sent theirs out in its entirety, but never more than 25 per cent of their strength was ever mustered. The result was that at the beginning of the war the battles were stalemates. Finally, the Coral Sea battle destroyed their air power. After dinner, the general arranged a showing in a private theater of a dancer wearing sixteen kimonos. I could not help but remark that if Salome had danced that way neither Herod nor John would ever have lost his head. The little dance we saw was a kind of play written in the sixteenth century and reveals that while Shakespeare was doing his tragedies so full of emotion and action, the Orient was passive in its drama almost to the extent of immobility.

The next morning we called on the Emperor of Japan, before whose door two thousand Japanese soldiers committed suicide the day of the Japanese defeat. The building was rather unpretentious; the Emperor did not sit on the throne but on a chair. He said that he tried to prevent the war but could not and was glad that it was over. He rejoiced in the work of the missionaries and that of the United States Government in rehabilitation.

The next day I gave a talk at Habiya Hall, the largest hall in Tokyo, from which thousands were turned away. I took as my text "The Unknown God," which St. Paul used when he talked to the Athenians, suggesting that Japan had an "unknown god," expressing the hope that Japan—which was the Land of the Rising Sun—would soon understand that the sun is the Son of God who is the light of the World. Two broadcasts followed and then another lecture at the Habiya Hall to students. These talks were also broadcast. The next day we drove to Yokohama and gave a lecture in the stadium and later on in the church. That evening I had dinner with General Eichelberger, former head of West Point. The general believed that the American occupation of Japan was the most successful in history.

On the way back to America, we stopped at Wake Island, where we had our first experience of the gooney birds. Here were one thousand people living in an area of eight square miles, mostly Navy personnel. When the naval officers met us at the airport, they drove us to the Gooneyville Hotel a half mile away. It takes its name from the thousands of gooney birds which inhabit the island. It was dark but the searchlights revealed many birds on the roadway. The Navy drivers would drive over the lawns in order not to disturb the gooney birds. As they explained it: "The gooney birds were here first." They resemble large ducks, though few are white; they feed their young on regurgitation.

The reason they were named "gooney" by the Americans was because though they have wings they have to learn how to fly. They use the runways for their practice and properly start off against the wind. They rise about ten feet above the ground and after a clumsy start most of them fall flat on their tummies. Some get up, discouraged, and in July and August when the goonies migrate, the non-fliers generally die for want of food since there is no known way to feed them artificially. When they do learn to fly they shriek with great delight. Sailors once found some of them standing on a sand dune; and when they shouted to them, the gooney birds turned around but without adjusting their feet—so they fell backward. Almost everything they do seems to be gooney. As we were flying to Honolulu on the way home, Archbishop Bergan accused the Cardinal of hiding a gooney bird under his coat.

In China, what interested me particularly was their philosophy of *yang* and *yin*. Yang is hot, active, light, dry, masculine; yin is cold, moist, passive, dark, feminine. Yang is movement and yin is rest. The interplay of these two principles in Chinese philosophy produces everything that is. Looking at a mountain at the beginning of the day, one may see sunshine on one side and shade on the other, but in the evening this arrangement is reversed. Both sides have yang and yin. Yang is more closely related to heaven and yin is more closely related to earth. All these terms were unfamiliar to me. I could see that they were actually no different from *matter* and *form* in the philosophy of Aristotle and later on in the philosophy of the Scholastics. Everything that is is made up of a determinable element which is the *materia* and a determining element which is the *forma*. I could see that this dualism in

Western language was the conflict of good and evil, right
and wrong, true and false.

The more I familiarized myself with the Far East, the
more I saw that the Western mind knows the world better
than it knows man, but the Eastern world knows man better
than it knows the world. Our Western world can tame nature, the Eastern world learned to tame itself. The former is
an extrovert and produces a technological civilization; the
latter is an introvert and seeks to develop wisdom through
contemplation. The Western world regards the head the lo-
calization of wisdom, but the Eastern world often makes it

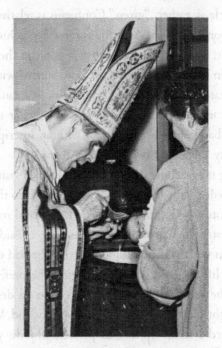

Baptizing an infant, early 1950s. (*Courtesy,
Society for the Propagation of the Faith*)

the navel. It looked for the center of personality there, as the
Hebrews found it in the bowels. In many statues of Buddha,
I noticed that the center of gravity was in the navel. Japanese
wrestlers, before they enter into a match, stare at the navel of
one another to develop a full concentration over the oppo-
nent. In fact, this concentration went on so long that a law
was passed to limit their staring to fifteen minutes. It struck
me during the trip that it might be shortsightedness on our
part to impose the Aristotelian philosophy on the Eastern
mind; that it would have been better to have gathered up the
good religious aspiration of the Eastern people in the natural religions to bring them to Revelation. God is not proven
to them; He is, rather, "given." Confucius is relatively just as
good for some minds as Aristotle is for others. Our missionaries, I felt, should start with what is good in the religions
they find in their countries as Our Lord started with a drink
of cold water in converting a Samaritan, as Claudia began
with a dream in understanding Christ far better than a rational husband, and as Paul began with an inscription to a
pagan deity to convert two souls in Athens.

During my teaching days at the university, I visited Mme.
Koo, the wife of the last ambassador of China to the United
States before the Communist takeover. She told me she was
not interested in Christianity because she considered that
original sin was the most stupid doctrine she had ever heard
of in her life. I asked her what religion she preferred. She
told me she was Buddhist. I then asked her to describe for
me the eightfold path of Buddha, which she did. When she
had finished I said: "If man is perfect, why do you think
Buddha offered these ways of purification? Was it not because he saw that in human nature there were certain en-

demic evils as well as emotions and instincts which had to be controlled?" Mme. Koo saw the light and later on brought her Buddhism to perfection in Christianity.

Traveling in Moslem countries as well as Moslem parts of Africa again brought me face to face with the role of Christianity. The Moslems are firm believers in God. Indeed, they have rejected Christ, Whom they consider a prophet announcing Mohammed. But this may be partly due to the scandal in those countries of warring theologians as they disputed the Trinity and the Hypostatic Union. Mohammed led the people out of those conflicts and out of polytheism into a recognition of the absolute sovereignty of God. It is to the credit of these people that they are prayerful; it may be there is more prayer to God in the Moslem world than there is in the post-Christian civilization of the Western world. Here we are not speaking of the judgment or quality of prayer but merely the number of people who, at least five times a day, bow down to God. I recall taking a bus trip in Cairo to the pyramids. At one of the appointed hours of prayer the bus driver stopped his bus, took his prayer rug out to the sand, knelt down upon it and made his obeisance to the Almighty.

A deep spiritual bond exists between Christians, Moslems and Jews, for as Pope Pius XII said, all Christians are "spiritual Semites" because we are descended spiritually from Abraham. The Moslems trace their genealogy, however, through Ishmael and not Isaac. In addition to having Abraham as a father, they also have a devotion to the Blessed Mother. The nineteenth chapter of the Koran, I discovered, has forty-one verses on the Blessed Mother. They believe in original sin, and have a vague concept of the Immaculate Conception. I often wonder if there is any connection between the revelation of Our Lady at Fatima and the ultimate conversion of the Moslems. Why did the Blessed Mother choose a tiny, insignificant village like Fatima so that she might be called Our Lady of Fatima? The daughter of Mohammed bore the name of Fatima. Writing after her death, Mohammed noted: "Fatima is the most holy of all women in paradise next to Mary." The Moslems occupied Portugal for centuries. When they were finally driven out, the Moslem chief in that locality had a beautiful daughter by the name of Fatima. A Catholic boy fell in love with her. She not only stayed behind when the Moslems left but even embraced the Faith and became a Catholic. Her young husband changed the name of the town where he lived to Fatima. Thus, the place where Our Lady appeared in 1917 has a historical connection with Fatima, the daughter of Mohammed.

Trips to India, as well as many years of dealing with East Indians as director of the Society for the Propagation of the Faith—along with constant study of other religions—have brought me to somewhat the same conclusion I had come to concerning Oriental religions and the paganism of the Athenians. St. Paul quotes Isaiah: "I was found by them that did not seek me. I appeared openly to them that asked not after me." Christ is hidden in all world religions, though as yet His face is veiled as it was to Moses, who asked to see it.

I have always contended in talking to missionaries that we are not so much to bring Christ *to* peoples as we are to bring Christ out of them. When Christ assumed a human nature He had no human person. (There is a difference between *na-*

*ture* and *person.* Nature answers the question "What?" "What is it?" Person answers the question "Who?" "Who is responsible?") Christ has two natures or principles of operation: divine and human; but only one person, which is the Word or Son of God. Because His person was divine, every single human nature in the world was potentially in that human nature of Christ. Our missionaries are lawyers bringing to other peoples a will and a testament, reminding them of the wealth that has been bequeathed to them by the Cross and Resurrection of Christ. The good Hindu, the good Buddhist, the good Confucianist, the good Moslem are all saved by Christ and not by Buddhism or Islam or Confucianism but through their sacraments, their prayers, their asceticism, their morality, their good life.

The combination of travel, the study of world religions and personal encounter with different nationalities and peoples made me see that the fullness of truth is like a complete circle of 360 degrees. Every religion in the world has a segment of that truth.

Serving the missions makes one sick at heart if anyone is left out of the ark of salvation. A blind boy at Lourdes was cured during the Way of the Cross as his father asked God to restore his son's sight. The first words of the boy as he saw his father and others were: "Everybody's here!" That will be the missionary's cry at Judgment when he sees his flock and is overwhelmed by the goodness of God. Everybody is here who wanted to be here.

Travels in the older civilizations provoked theological musings, but other parts of the world shifted my emphasis from ideology to economics, politics and the social order. Here I am referring to countries called the Third World, without excluding those countries in Asia which were ravished by Communist infiltration and tyranny. I saw in one Latin American country women and children with festering sores rummaging among exposed garbage, fighting the birds for rotting crumbs. As one man told me who had moved from the mountains to the city slums: "I was once just a man. Now I am many men." Rio de Janeiro has the finest beach in the world. But about a mile back of that beach is a small mountain in which thousands are existing in cardboard boxes, as hundreds crowd around a water spout to slake their thirst but not to satisfy their hunger. How happy I was that the Good Lord had made me a beggar for his mission cause, to give at least a trickle of aid, for hunger is not just an economic problem. It is a moral and spiritual problem. As W. H. Auden wrote: "We must love one another or die." I gave a series of broadcasts in Rio in the presence of that apostle of the poor, Archbishop Helder Camara. As I look back on them now, I wish I had said nothing about communism, for such statements seemed to comfort the landowners, who were already oppressing the poor. I did not have the same feeling in Buenos Aires, Argentina, where I lectured in the law school and later gave broadcasts for a week on spiritual subjects. Time has proved that it is not only the backs and stomachs of the poor that have been affected by indigence. It is also the thinking of those teachers, even at times Christian thinkers, which perverted the very Christian truth which could help in liberation of the needy. By reducing theology to politics, by stressing social needs to the neglect of personal sin in the oppressor, by identifying Mark with Marx, they take all the air out of Christian trumpets which could call international attention to the plight of the people. The bishops have kept the true balance of fearlessly telling the rich, as did Cardinal Landazuri Ricketts of Lima, that luxury spending helps spread sentiments of desperation among the poor. Another bishop commenting on the rapid sale of bonds to fight communism declared: "They buy bonds not to end social injustice but as an immediate form of self-defense for their possessions."

What made the apostolate difficult in some parts of Latin America was that mothers discouraged their boys from studying for the priesthood on the grounds that they would be poor and impoverished like themselves. I gave a broadcast in Colombia in which I addressed myself to the boys and young men within my hearing. "I know that many of you have in your hearts a vocation to serve Christ and the poor in your own land, but parents have dissuaded you lest the burden of poverty which He endured would be too heavy for you." I asked those who felt they had a vocation but had never spoken to their parents or a priest about it to write to me. I received over two hundred letters, which I turned over to Church officials hoping they would make contact with these youths and bring the call of God to fruition.

Poverty has many inconveniences besides want of food, drink and housing. I was preaching one Sunday in a small church in the bush in Kenya. During the sermon and the Holy Eucharist, my eyes watered constantly. I mentioned it to the pastor afterward and he said: "Oh, I forgot to tell you that we did not have money enough to make a floor for this church, so we used cow manure with clay. It was probably that odor that disturbed you."

While making my Holy Hour later in that church, I found a woman about fifty years of age rapt in almost ecstatic prayer. I asked her about her condition and she told me she had ten children and her husband had deserted her and she knew not his whereabouts. Her only consolation was in the Lord.

Sometimes, the only way one can understand the poor is not by writing a check but by direct contact. I was reminded of the meaning of the Incarnation. God did not remain aloof to the agonies, pains and injustices of this world, but took a human nature like ours, in all things save sin, to prove that true love is identification—not just in the flesh, as in marriage, but in hunger and need.

On another visit to South Africa, I came face to face with the horrors of apartheid. I shall not mention the injustices against the blacks in the hope that all these will gradually be remedied. But to indicate how much needed to be done, I recall a visit I made to one of the towns outside Johannesburg where the blacks were restricted. The director of the Society for the Propagation of the Faith told me of one of the catechists in that area who had brought thousands to the faith. I asked him if I might visit her. It was quite unusual for white people to visit the blacks in such restricted areas, but more unusual still for a white person to take tea with a black woman in her own little hovel. The next day I left South Africa. I was told later that it was quite fortunate that I left when I did, for the government was about to ask me to leave for having made that visit.

One cannot spend fifteen or more years serving the underdeveloped nations and the poor of the world by begging for them without developing an entirely new point of view with regard to the world. I began to think less of the problem of poverty and more of the poor; less of the problem of crime and more of the criminal; less about age and more about service to a Stranger Who lives with all the slum dwellers who have no place to lay their heads. All the little children separated from parents are as one child to that Stranger; all the delinquents, all those who are crying, weeping and complaining against God are really looking for that Stranger. Even all their bitterness against affluence, aggrandizement and unshared wealth in the face of the world's poverty seems to me as the wrath of One who drove buyers and sellers out of the temple. This Stranger will rise out of the slums, the dumps, the hovels, the emptiness of stomachs, the parched tongues, the burning fevers and the white sores of leprosy. He will stand before all who helped, saying: "I was hungry and you gave me to eat." Travel merely confirms the teaching of theology that humanity is one. The accidental differences of color and race and what jingles in the pocket are of little concern. The longer I live the more I become convinced that in the face of injustices we must begin to say I love. Kind deeds are not enough. We must learn to say I forgive.

In light of that concept I have always had great sympathy for the poem on the Black Virgin by Father Albert Abble:

*I'm looking for an African painter*
*Who will make me a Black Virgin*
*A Virgin with a fine "Keowa"*
*Like our mothers wear.*
*Look, Mother,*
*The yellow races have lent you*

*Their yellow tint.*
*The Redskins have made you*
*Like their own wives.*
*The Whites have pictured you*
*As a Western girl.*
*And would you refuse*
*To take our color?*
*Anyway, since your Assumption,*
*Since the glorious day*
*When you were triumphantly*
*Carried away into Heaven*
*You no longer have any color.*
*Or rather, you are all colors;*
*You are yellow with the yellows*
*Like a mother who might have several children*
*of different shades*
*But who could be found in them all.*
*Isn't it true, Mother, that you*
*Are the Mother of the Blacks, too.*
*A Black Mother carrying the Infant Jesus*
*on her back.*\*

# THE LAND CALLED HOLY

Of all the places on earth, to me the three most precious are
Rome, where the successor of St. Peter, the Vicar of Christ,
continues to feed the lambs and sheep of Christ; the Holy

*\*Les Prêtres Noirs S'interrogent.* Copyright © 1957 Editions du Cerf, Paris,
France. Used by permission of the publisher.

Land, on which once trod the feet of the Word of God made man; and Lourdes, the shrine of Our Lady at the base of the Pyrenees. And along with these must be mentioned Fatima in Portugal. The difference between Fatima and Lourdes is that Lourdes is the place of faith and Fatima is the scene of penance.

He who brings only a knowledge of topography to the Holy Land cannot take away as much as he who sees it

At the wedding of two close friends, Havana, Cuba, May 1957.
*(Karren Photo; Courtesy, Society for the Propagation of the Faith)*

through the eyes of faith. I made two pilgrimages to the Holy Land, the last in 1959, when five of us joined, as pilgrims—the famous photographer Yousuf Karsh, the well-known South African journalist and author H. V. Morton, myself and my two grandnephews—to set out to find the "missing link" between being just humans and being adopted sons of God. What we found was not the beast under the earth, but Heaven on earth; not the man *in* the tree, but the Man on the Tree—the Son of the Most High. Not until we looked at the land in which the Lord exercised His apostolate, a land no more than two hundred miles long, did we realize the truth of the words of St. Paul: "He emptied Himself."

He made Himself a zero. He was not like a prince becoming a peasant to win the people; He was rather like a man anxious to save dogs who were mistreated, throwing off his human body and taking on himself the body of a dog, but keeping his human mind. All the while he knows that he is superior to all the other animals who surround him and to whom he tries to teach obedience. Yet he limits himself not to speech but to barking. But that humiliation of a man becoming a dog is nothing compared to God becoming a man. The similarity, however, heightens when one thinks of the dogs turning on the man, killing him, for indeed man turned on his Lord and crucified Him.

The "emptying" of God becoming man was found even in the land He chose, for politically it was enslaved and economically it was poor. The very ground itself almost seemed as though it were stoned from Heaven. The rabbis used to say, "When God made the world He had two bags of stones—one He scattered over the world, the other He dropped on Palestine."

Because I do not wish to make this chapter a travelogue, I limit myself to those areas which made a deep and profound impression on me. Very little of what one sees now is as it was when Eternity became time, when Omnipotence was found in bonds, and the Bird that built the nest was hatched therein. The Sea of Galilee is unchanged. Most of the other scenes are like the ancient palimpsests—those old manuscripts on which a later generation wrote over the script of a previous generation. One has to strip off layer after layer of history, invasion, pillage and war to get back to a primitive scene.

Though a large church is built over the site where Christ was born, I was very much struck by the fact that to enter the basilica one has to stoop under a very narrow and low door. One can still see the remains of a larger and more fitting entrance that was walled up centuries ago to deter armed Moslems from dashing into the church on horseback. Since Christ was born in a cave, it was also necessary for both shepherds and Wise Men to stoop to discover the Babe from Whose fingertips tumbled planets and worlds. Humility is always the condition of discovering divinity; divinity seems always to be where one least expects it. As one kneels before that spot on the floor, which is marked with the inscription *Hic de Virgine Maria, Jesus Christus Natus Est*, one calls to mind the visit of the shepherds and the Wise Men: those who know nothing and those who know they do not know everything. They seem to be the only two who ever fathom a mystery. The scribes, or the learned theologians of Jerusalem, told Herod where the Babe was to be born, but they did not go. Greater respect was shown by the Persians who burned the Church of the Holy Sepulcher and other churches in 1614, but refused to burn the Church of the Nativity because they saw a mosaic of the Magi in Persian dress.

In Nazareth I visited every carpenter shop just to bring back to me the flavor of the Architect of the universe working as a carpenter. Thirty years of His life He spent obeying, three years teaching and three hours redeeming. "Is this not the carpenter's son?" was not intended to be a question seeking information, but a slur on the lowliness of his profession. I recalled a painting by Holman Hunt. It shows Our Blessed Lord, tired at the end of a day's work, stretching out His arms wearily; as He does so and the sun shines in the door, the Mother can see on the opposite wall the shadow of the Cross.

I had memorized this poem by Father Leonard Feeney which I quoted to my fellow travelers in one of the carpenter's shops:

*Whenever the bright blue nails would drop*
*Down on the floor of his carpenter's shop,*
*St. Joseph, prince of carpenter men,*
*Would stoop to gather them up again;*
*For he feared for two little sandals sweet*
*And very easy to pierce they were*
*As they pattered over the lumber there*
*And rode on two little Sacred Feet.*

*But alas on a hill between earth and heaven*
*One day——two nails into a cross were driven*

*And fastened it firm to the Sacred Feet*
*Where once rode two little sandals sweet.*
*And Christ and His Mother looked off in death*
*Afar——to the valley of Nazareth*
*Where the carpenter shop was spread with dust*
*And the little blue nails all packed in rust*
*Slept in a box on the window sill;*
*And Joseph lay sleeping under the hill.*

A particularly touching sight was a visit to the synagogue. The building itself was not the important thing, but it recalled for me the scene when Our Blessed Lord as a young Man began to read one of the lessons on the Sabbath Day. It was the prophecy about the Messiah Who was to come. He then told the story of two Gentiles who were healed, and on whom were worked miracles in the Old Testament, indicating that the Gospel and the Kingdom of God would be opened to the Gentiles. When He told the audience that Scripture was fulfilled in Him that day, they reacted: familiarity does indeed breed contempt. The speaker's suggestion was that other peoples of the earth would be important in God's eyes. This was a little too much for the Nazarenes, so they rushed Him out of the synagogue, brought Him to the bow of a steep hill and threatened to throw Him over to His death.

The interruption of His discourse and breaking off of devotions proved they were not worthy to have His presence. Later on, as the Gospel of John tells us, they would attempt to stone Him, but because His Hour was not yet come, He either blinded their eyes as God did to the Sodomites and Syrians, or filled them with confusion so they could not do what they had intended to do—to throw Him over the precipice. His work was just begun. He left Nazareth and never went back. It became a place, as one of His Apostles claimed: "no good could ever come from." But it was also a place where the world learned "a man is without honor in his own country."

The Jordan River was disappointing when one considers its historical importance, its bearing the ark when the Jews returned from exile, and being the site where Christ was baptized. Down the road from it was Jericho, where Moses had once sent his spies and where lived Rahab the prostitute who later on became one of the ancestors of King David and therefore the bar sinister in the human genealogy of Christ. The river could not have been forty feet wide; my grand-nephews threw coins across the river, recalling the story of George Washington throwing the silver dollar across the Potomac. I bottled some water from the Jordan, brought it back with me and later on used it for the baptism of some of my relatives. The Jordan is probably the one holy site in the Holy Land which appeals only to the heart and not to the mind.

Despite the commonness of the scene, but the richness of the memory, I allowed the rest of the party to go down the road to Jericho while I sat and meditated on the words that John the Baptist said about the One Whom he baptized: "As He grows greater, I must grow less." Therein was the secret of the Christian message. As the ego deflates, divinity takes up the abode. Nothing can be occupied by two objects at one and the same time. To decrease is to be less and less occupied with self. That was the day perhaps more than any other that I learned that humility is not something that is directly cultivated; otherwise one becomes proud of his humil-

In Brussels, at First Communion of
princess from the Belgian royal family,
1964. *(C. Niestadt)*

ity. It is a *by-product*; the more Christ is in the soul, the less
the "I" weighs it down.

The Dead Sea is something special in a visit to the Holy
Land. Everywhere else there are recollections of compassion,
mercy, sympathy and love; here is the sordid history of divine justice, retribution, even wrath. Here it was that Abraham, who had been accompanied by Lot in all of his
wanderings, separated from him as their flocks grew in size
and the shepherds quarreled. Abraham gave Lot a choice of
land that stretched before them and Lot "lifting up his eyes

saw" the rich valley and the Lake of Sodom. For Abraham there was nothing left but the comparatively barren hills of Judea before him. But Lot was to learn that happiness does not consist in the abundance of things a man possesses. Five cities later grew up about that lake and all of them became conspicuous for the most vile forms of lust and homosexuality. That day on which the sun was described as having come up brightly, God started a train of natural causes turning the destruction of cities into a judgment described as "a rain of brimstone and fire from God out of heaven." The whole neighborhood of the Dead Sea abounded in sulphur and bitumen, furnishing the materials which burned; lightning from heaven struck it, accompanied by an earthquake that threw up fresh masses of combustible material. The cities seemed like a vast furnace from which a cloud of smoke rose to the heavens.

All that remains of that Divine Judgment is what is called the Dead Sea, into which fish flow from the Jordan River and within a few moments die, giving them the phosphorescence of life but the smell of death. The sea is so salty that one can float on the waters. I dipped my finger into it and the taste was nauseous, and if one leaves the water on his finger, it becomes encrusted with chemicals.

While I was there I noticed a resort hotel had been built upon the shore; multicolored umbrellas on the beach gave it a kind of carnival flavor. I noticed a macabre advertisement at the entrance to the hotel: "The lowest spot on earth."

History can be studied in many places on the earth, whether they be caves where there is scribbling by a primitive mind, or the plundered tomb of a Cyrus, or the vestigial remains of a Troy; but I believe that the greatest of all places to understand history is on the banks of the Dead Sea. Our Blessed Lord Himself used those cities of the plain as examples of rehearsals for the Last Judgment and of those who would not receive His Message: "I tell you this: on the day of Judgment it will be more bearable for the land of Sodom and Gomorrah than for that town." Shakespeare himself spoke of Heaven using wars as a punishment for perversities, lusts and passive barbarianism:

> *If that the heavens do not their visible spirits*
> *Send quickly down to calm these vile offenses,*
> *It will come*
> *Humanity must perforce prey on itself,*
> *Like monsters of the deep.*

A kind of a holy fear came over me as I looked out on that Dead Sea—a fear inspired by two reflections: one from Scripture and the other from Greek drama. From Scripture: "Wherever the body is there shall the vultures be gathered together." The vultures come when the corpse of civilization decays. Balthasar gave a great feast with the vessels stolen from the sanctuary of Jerusalem and that very night the vultures in the form of the army of Cyrus were already outside the gates. Those winged scavengers of cliff and peak that encircle and whirl dizzily overhead, waiting for the scent of a body that taints the air, are the condensed image of the judgments of God on peoples and nations throughout history which have lost the life which resisted death.

The other subject of contemplation came from the Greek tragedies, which were often divided into three sections. The first was *hubris* or pride, in which man began to exalt and de-clare himself even superior to God. The second section was *nemesis* or a moment of success when eternal truths begin to be hidden from the mind because of the overemphasis on the erotic and the monetary and the supremacy of the self. Finally *ate* or a time of judgment when the evil that men do produces heinous effects.

I am sure that those who were sipping tea that afternoon when I sat on the banks of the Dead Sea never once thought of the meaning of crisis in history. The word "crisis" is from the Greek word *krisis*, which means judgment. It was a frightening experience for me to watch the salty and murky waters and those lazy bodies that never even had to swim to keep afloat.

One of the lighter moments of the pilgrimage was a photograph which Mr. Karsh wished to take of me leading a flock of sheep, symbolizing my role as a shepherd. We found a flock of several hundred sheep and a shepherd who, in the tradition of the country, accompanied the sheep. The photograph which Mr. Karsh projected was for me to be at the head of the sheep as if I were leading and shepherding. He ran ahead several hundred feet with a stepladder and his camera, climbed up the ladder, adjusted the film, and by the time I got to the ladder, the sheep were all ahead of me and I was behind. He tried it two or three times and in each instance the sheep were unable to be photographed because they went beyond the camera's range. Finally dashing ahead more than the usual distance in the hope that he could capture me at the head of the flock, he saw the sheep advancing rather rapidly and shouted: "Tell the sheep to wait!" (which proved that Mr. Karsh knew absolutely nothing about sheep). I remember one of the trick problems that was given in school when I was a boy: "If there are twenty sheep in one field and one of them goes into an adjoining field, how many are left in the first field?" The answer is "none," because all sheep follow one another.

I would love to linger over other recollections, particularly of the Garden of Gethsemane and the Lithostrotos or pavement in the basement of Pilate's palace on which the Feet of Christ trod. But all this has been written in the book that resulted from my pilgrimage, *This Is the Holy Land.*

I conclude with what was one of the most touching

At the Sea of Galilee, where Christ said: "Simon, feed my lambs," c. 1958. *(Photo by Yousuf Karsh)*

scenes of the trip: an early morning visit to the Sea of Tiberias. I went down to the site where Our Lord met some of His disciples the week after the Resurrection—the site being easy to identify because of the great rocks mentioned in the Gospel story. I began reading the twenty-first chapter of the Gospel of John, which, to me, is a kind of an epilogue to the first chapter of John, which is the prologue. John always has a mystical meaning hidden behind every event, but here the correlation is rather evident. The opening chapter of his Gospel begins: "In the beginning was the Word." That Word became flesh through the power of the Holy Spirit in the Virgin Mary and Christ appeared before man as the Son of the Father. That opening line of John is intended to exhibit the Eternal Life of Christ before He comes into the world. Chapter 21 is the epilogue or what is to happen to His Church when He returned to Heaven; a symbolic exhibition of the Church after He founded it on Peter. Christ standing on the shore represented Himself in eternity, the sea being the world. The disciples are directed from the shore to cast nets on the other side, Christ manifesting His power by working with them in their seemingly lonesome toil, and exhibiting His love in providing food for them.

It was four o'clock in the morning when I went to that shore and sat by those two large rocks, with a fire between them. About a hundred yards out on the sea from where I was sitting there were seven men in a boat. This was one of the many coincidences with the Gospel that struck me during my visit. The description of the scene is as follows:

*Jesus appeared to His disciples again afterwards, at the Sea of Tiberias, and this is how He appeared to them. Simon Peter was there, and with him was Thomas, who was also called Didymus, and Nathaniel from Cana of Galilee, and the sons of Zebedee and two more of His disciples. Simon Peter told them, I am going out fishing, and they said, we, too, will go with you. So they went out and embarked on the boat, and all that night they caught nothing. But when morning came, there was Jesus standing on the shore, only the disciples did not know that it was Jesus. Have you caught anything, friends, Jesus asked them, to season your bread with? And when they answered no, He said to them, cast to the right of the boat, and you will have a catch. So they cast the net, and found before long they had no strength to haul it in, such a school of fish was in it, whereupon the disciple whom Jesus loved said to Peter, it is the Lord. And Simon Peter, hearing him, said, you say it was the Lord, and girded up the fisherman's coat, which was all he wore, and sprang into the sea. The other disciples followed in the boat (they were not far from the land—only some hundred yards away), dragging their catch in the net behind them. So they went ashore and found a charcoal fire made there, with fish and bread cooking on it. Bring some of the fish you have caught, Jesus said to them. And Simon Peter going on board, hauled the net to land. It was loaded with great fish, 153 of them, and with all of that number the net had not been broken. When Jesus said to them, Come and break your fast, none of the disciples ventured to ask Him, who are You? Knowing full well it was the Lord. So Jesus came up and took bread, which He gave to them, and fish as well. Thus Jesus appeared to His disciples a third time after His rising from the dead.*

As I meditated on those words of John, I wondered why Peter went back to the fishing business since the Lord had called him away from it to make him a fisher of men. He must have been a natural leader, for when he suggested that he go fishing, six others willingly jumped into the boat with him to return to their former trade.

When Peter first came to His Lord on shore, he jumped back in the sea again. That was because he saw the fire, which reminded him of his denial ten nights earlier. For a long time I asked myself, why, at that scene, did Our Lord speak of lambs and sheep? Generally, almost all of the Lord's illustrations were taken from the immediate scenes about Him like "when the sower went out to sow his seed," or "a fisherman threw his net into the sea," but a seashore seemed so alien to the conversation with the disciples which followed.

Because Peter had denied Our Lord three times, Our Blessed Lord asked him three times if he loved Him. We have only one word in English for "love," which is the source of the confusion and often the identification of sex and love. The Greeks had at least three words for love—two of them are used in the Gospel. One Greek word for love is *philia*, which means a natural human love and affection. The other is *agape*, which means a sacrificial love. Peter had already been made the "rock of the Church"; now Our Lord commissions him further—to feed His lambs and feed His sheep. Before doing that, He asked if he loved: "Simon, son of John, do you love Me?" In challenging Peter, the Lord gave him the opportunity of three times confessing and proclaiming His divinity after three times denying it. In the first question, the Lord challenged the *superiority* of Peter's love (*agape*); in the second, He challenged if Peter had any love at all (*agape*); in the third question, the Lord challenged even his affection (*philia*). This was the most searching question of all and it pierced the heart of Peter and made him sad. The Lord wounds only that He may heal. After each of the triple confessions of Peter came the commission to "feed My lambs and feed My sheep"; that is to say, to minister spiritual nourishment to His people and to the young.

I could find no answer to the queries that went through my mind about the Lord speaking of the future members of His Church as "sheep and lambs." As I gave up mentally trying to find a solution, someone tapped me on the shoulder. It was a shepherd. He had in his arms a three-day-old lamb which he placed in my hands. I said: "Where did you find this lamb?" He said: "I am a shepherd and I graze my flock on this field adjoining the Sea of Tiberias." That was the answer! The Lord changed the metaphor from "fish" to "sheep and lambs" because the sheep and lambs were probably there that very day.

Now I can see why the Lord called His bishops first to be lords and then to be shepherds, because He wants us to prosper spiritually, by hook or by crook!

As I cradled the lamb as a symbol of the firstlings of the flock in the Church, Mr. Karsh and Mr. Morton arrived and on that very shore where the Lord stood, Mr. Karsh took the favorite picture of my life—an unworthy shepherd holding a precious lamb in his arms.

*Eleven*

# THE BISHOP IN A DIOCESE

My appointment by Paul VI to the Diocese of Rochester in 1966 brought a new joy, namely, close association with people and with priests particularly. The priesthood is the greatest fraternity in the world. No introduction is necessary to another priest; there is nothing to live up to; nothing to live down. The mere fact that he is a priest means that he is a brother. Being made a bishop of a diocese binds one with the cords of grace and the cords of Adam to every priest and religious, and to each of the laity. Nothing better symbolizes this than the fact that the name of the diocesan bishop is mentioned every single day at Mass.

Before recalling events *within* the diocese, it would be well to recount events *outside* the diocese, that is, the spirit of the world. The sixties had a peculiar philosophy, which affected every person regardless of his faith or lack of faith. It might be described in two ways: first, what was generally good in the spirit of the sixties was the shift from the individual to the social. In the sixties, a social consciousness arose in which love of neighbor was too often purchased at the cost of neglect of God; at times, individual justice was ignored so long as one was fighting for social justice.

The second characteristic of the sixties, which seems to be in contradiction but is not, was the emphasis on the *me*. The "I" of each person is accepted as the valid criterion. In the beginning is not the Word, but in the beginning is the I and it was good. Anything that stands opposite the self is a negation of self. This became identified with authority. In the extreme form, as Sartre put it, "My neighbor is hell"; and by "neighbor" Sartre included even God, for God opposes the self as the absolute. As a consequence of these two assumptions, a sense of personal guilt and sin began to vanish. The only sins were social sins. This made it difficult for religion and morality in the sixties. Ordinary Christians often succumbed to the position that evil lies only in society. It took someone who has passed through the fallacy of that view to remind us of the truth: "Gradually it was disclosed to me that the lines separating good and evil passed not through states nor between classes, nor between political parties either—but right through every human heart . . . I have come to understand the truth of the religions of the world:

the struggle with the evil *inside the human being* (inside *every* human being). It is impossible to expel evil from the world in its entirety but it is possible to constrict it within each person."* I mention this philosophy of the world in the sixties because it was also the time of the Second Vatican Council. But it is quite wrong to think the Vatican Council brought on changes in the Church. The Church does not live in a vacuum but in the real world.

As brother priests constitute the heart on which every bishop leans, so the people are the breast from which he derives consolation. Every man or woman who looks at him is really asking the question whether he is a minister of redeeming love. As did the woman at the well, each soul repeats: "Come and see a man who has told me everything I ever did. Could this not be the Christ?" To me the people—Catholic and non-Catholic— were a joy and a consolation. How often in the midst of the daily solicitudes of the Church would I be thankful for an old woman saying "God bless you" while reaching out of a pew with a smile, or for that three-legged dog that met me at the entrance of the church on Confirmation day. Because the people are not homogeneous, the Bishop has to use a paradoxical approach, for the Lord told him to be not only "the salt" of the diocese, but also "the light."

Salt is used to prevent decay and deterioration. Light is that which illumines and reveals the dark cavernous parts of the soul. On the one hand, the bishop should stop the spread

*Alexander I. Solzhenitsyn, *The Gulag Archipelago* III-IV (Harper & Row, New York, 1975), pp. 615–16.

of evil; on the other hand, he is to promote goodness and truth. It was very clear under the guidance of Scripture that I was not to be exclusively either an episcopal saltcellar or a switch that turned on light. I learned to see that to work in the inner city was not worldliness but love, and on the other hand, to wash my hands of the city of God was not love but worldliness. That strict balance between the salt and light had to be kept for the good of all.

I recall a visit to Dansville, New York, to celebrate afternoon Mass on the feast of the Assumption of Our Lady. Four or five priests made the trip with me. On the way, a few miles outside the city to which we were traveling, we saw a vacant shrine on a front lawn—but no statue. As we arrived at the parish, people gathered about the car and I was obliged to remain there a little while to talk with them while the other priests went into the house. Finally, I left the car and went up to the second floor to wash and prepare myself for the afternoon Mass. On the way down, I saw a man on the back porch and I said to him: "Thank you for taking care of the rectory while the priests are in the church." Lo and behold! I was not in the rectory; I was in a neighbor's house. Father Michael Hogan, my secretary, quipped that they were going to put up a brass plaque in the bathroom, the latest version of "Kilroy was here."

During the sermon I mentioned the fact that I had seen an empty shrine in front of one of the homes. I promised that if the family who lived in that house would visit me after Mass, I would give them a statue of Our Lady. It developed the family had been to an earlier Mass, but the grandmother came to me afterward, and asked me to visit the family on the way back to Rochester. We promised to give them a statue of Our Lady, which I saw in the niche on later visits. The young wife inquired of Father Hogan his father's first name. It developed that her mother had once been courted by Father Hogan's father—that is how close I came to missing a good secretary!

Father Hogan was good in announcing beforehand to any pastors whom I visited that I did not care for chicken. Generally bishops are overfed with chicken on Confirmation tours. I was spared that diet because of the warning. My prejudice dated back to when I was a young boy visiting one of my father's farms during the summer. The tenant farmer, anxious to win the favor of the Sheen children, used to give us chicken every day except Friday. In the course of my young life, I wrung the necks of about 22,413 chickens. At night, I do not have nightmares; I have "night-hens." That childhood experience ruined me for what many consider a delicacy and I was spared it on my episcopal trips.

I finished a triduum in one parish. The church was crowded and we invited the young children to sit in the sanctuary. There were probably fifty or sixty of them under the age of ten. I went into the church about an hour before the sermon and knelt down on a prie-dieu to meditate. Afterward the sheriff of the town told me that his little daughter was among those who were in the sanctuary that night. She asked her father: "Why did the bishop kneel there looking straight at the altar so long?" "He was probably talking to God." The little girl said: "I thought he was God."

Providence guided us as we journeyed to the southern part of the Rochester diocese. On the way back we visited several parishes and pastors. We needed gas in one city and while at the filling station, I met some children and I asked

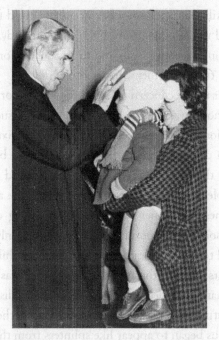

Blessing a young child in Buenos Aires, late 1950s. (*Courtesy, Society for the Propagation of the Faith*)

them where I could buy them some ice cream. They told me that ice cream was sold at the filling station. About twenty or thirty children appeared immediately; they seemed to come out of the gas tanks. We bought them ice cream cones and Father Hogan and I took a walk with the children. One little girl asked: "Will you come and visit my sister?" "Yes, where is she?" "She's dead; she is in the undertaker's parlor." We went to the undertaker's parlor and there was a little girl aged seven. She looked alive and appeared like an angel. Alongside the corpse were the weeping parents. The little girl had been killed in an automobile accident. I told them how much good would come from this seeming tragedy. Actually, it resulted in two conversions and the reconciliation with the Church of two other members of the family.

Another major concern of a bishop is the poor, and very specially those in the inner city, where there is such a large concentration of unemployed. Any bishop in the sixties would have had a deep interest in this group not only because he was under the inspiration of Christ and wished to follow His example, but also because it happened to be a "mood" of the times. The inner city because a rallying cry of an awakened social consciousness. Some nuns suddenly felt they were called to this work rather than to teaching children, and some priests also felt that working in a parish was less their mission than their dedication to the socially disinherited. Some beautiful examples of self-sacrifice among these priests and religious began to appear like splinters from the Cross. I remember traveling in the southern tier of the diocese with a young priest and asking him who lived beyond those hills. He told me the area was outside his parish and that therefore he did not know, but that he was willing to find out. Left free for that work, he found a small army of migrant workers whom he organized into parishes and he taught the children their catechism. Sisters rented vacated houses and began taking care of children of fatherless families whose mothers eked out a bare existence by working themselves at menial jobs.

One of the most cherished possessions of any bishop in a diocese is a seminary. Rochester had a seminary which educated not only its own priests, but those of about a dozen other dioceses. In the late sixties, many seminaries began to put less emphasis on the doctrinal and spiritual, and more on the sociological and even the political. Not only in this country but throughout the world there began to be a fission between the priesthood and the victimhood of Christ. Sometimes there was an acknowledgment of the priesthood without the victimhood or co-redemption with Christ; on the other hand, victimhood was sometimes interpreted solely in terms of service to the world rather than also bearing the guilt and sin and poverty of the world in the Name of Christ.

To give the seminarians the best possible education, I invited some priest-professors from Europe to teach. In addition to that I felt it was necessary to let our seminarians know how much Christians in Eastern Europe were suffering for their Faith. One specialist in this area was Reverend Michael Bordeaux—a graduate of Oxford who had studied in Moscow. His specialty was "Religion Behind the Iron Curtain." He has since become a world-renowned expert on this subject and circulates the most authentic records the extent of the persecution of Christianity behind the Iron Curtain. Anxious also to arouse an evangelical spirit among the seminarians, I invited the famous ex-Communist editor of the London *Daily Worker*, Dr. Douglas Hyde, to teach techniques in dealing with converts. It was his business to translate the many methods he used in his early life to make converts for Communism into techniques for making converts for Christ after his own conversion to Him.

Another domain of the bishop, and the most important of all, is his relationship to brother priests and religious. In order to soften the administrative and juridical associations of a "Chancery Office" we changed its name to a "Pastoral Office." Five mornings of the week, all the officials of the Pastoral Office would meet to review common problems, personnel, requests and petitions. This was done in order to avoid individual and arbitrary action on the part of the bishop, and to receive benefit of the corporate judgment of those who were closely associated. Among them were two auxiliary bishops—Bishop Denis Hickey and Bishop John McCafferty—both of whom had remarkable good sense and were of inestimable help to me.

Immediately upon entering the diocese, I knew there was need of episcopal assistance, so I asked the priests of the diocese to recommend a priest among them who was known to be "spiritual, of sound moral character, interested in the problems of the diocese and worthy of being called to the episcopacy." After this consultation, the results of it were forwarded to the Holy Father who later named those mentioned above as auxiliaries.

My secretary, Father Hogan, was a joy and an inspiration to me. An automobile agency in Rochester, typical of the kindness of the people there, offered to loan me a new car every year. At the end of the year they would take back the car we had driven, and give us a new one. I said to Father Hogan on the occasion of the second car: "When the Good Lord was on earth, He had to go around Jerusalem on an ass; but it is my privilege, thanks to you, to be driving a Plymouth around the diocese." Father Hogan answered: "Yes, but you still have an ass to drive you."

It is customary in reviewing a bishop's life in a diocese to do so in terms of the churches built and schools erected. But these are built by the money of the people and their sacrifices. All the spiritual good done is through the grace of God. *The Wall Street Journal* and *Time* magazine, without my knowledge, sent reporters to Rochester to write a review which later appeared in both publications. The diocese itself and the people also have their own record of accomplishments. I would like to dwell on the clay that was found in the treasure, or rather, things that I would like to have done but failed to do.

One concerned the Catholic press, which in our country has undergone many changes. It began because the secular press printed no Catholic news. The Church needed its own organ to communicate information concerning the church, the diocese and the world. The Catholic press, in any case, reached only a small number of the faithful in any diocese. The idea struck me to buy a page in the secular press, once a week. Thus the entire diocese would be covered, since one newspaper chain circulated throughout it. After two or three months negotiating in secret with the secular press, it was finally decided that we would buy a page once a week. This page would be free of any editorial restrictions on the part of the secular press. Our aim was to print Catholic news in brief, somewhat in the fashion of national weeklies like *Time* and *Newsweek*. Also, it was sought to divide the Catholic news into categories, like "Pontifical," "National," "Diocesan," "Liturgy," "Catechetics," and "Morals." Everyone reached by the secular press would be a potential reader of Catholic news and of the Church's position on many subjects of the day. In addition to saving money, such a plan would mean wider circulation, and also enable us to bring Christ's message to everyone. But when the plan was finally proposed, it was discovered that the Catholic press had a contract with a printing company with two or three years yet to run. So the proposed new format for the Catholic press had to be abandoned.

Another idea which proved to be more clay than gold was prompted by the insufficient medical help given to the poor, particularly in the inner city. I proposed to buy an ambulance and to equip it for medical service to care for pregnant mothers, sick children, the aged and the otherwise disabled in the poor quarters of the city. Approaching a hospital, to which I offered the ambulance, I asked them to supply two nurses and an intern for a few days a week. Nothing ever happened.

Traveling throughout the diocese I noted that there were almost as many cars in front of large supermarkets as there were outside of a church on Sunday. Inasmuch as the laity gathered in such large quantities almost every day of the week, why not rent a small store in the supermarket area in order that our Catholic people might visit Our Blessed Lord in the Blessed Sacrament, assist at Mass and go to Confession? It was also hoped that non-Catholics might come for prayer and for instruction. This, too, failed because the report given to me was that it was impossible to find a place to rent in a supermarket area.

I failed in the area of housing. I discovered that only forty or fifty units for the poor people in the inner city had been built in the course of four or five years. The federal government was slow to institute any kind of housing. I decided—why not give up a church with all of its property to the federal government, on condition that they use that block—if it be a block—as a beachhead for housing? Let it build, say, a hundred or two hundred units in that area given by the Church, and then begin to fan out through the inner city in order that the poor might have better quarters.

The Secretary of Housing at that particular time was the Honorable Robert C. Weaver, to whom I wrote:

*Dear Mr. Secretary:*

*Gibson Winter, as you know, has written about the suburban captivity of the Churches. I write out of a conscience that there might also be an inner city captivity of the Church. By that I mean that sometimes the right to property is preserved in the midst of the property-less. New means of service are sought when we ought to be saying about some of our property "take it down; why encumbereth the ground?"*

*The Church must do something now like St. Laurence did centuries ago. He gave away precious vessels of the Church to help the poor. We now want to give away a Church. We do this not because we do not need it, nor because we are not finding new expressions of apostolate in a tightly circumstanced environment, nor because it is a burden to our budget, but because the poor are a greater burden on our conscience.*

*We are under the Gospel-imperative not to be just a receiving Church, but a giving Church. We are under the necessity to be not just a ministering Church, but a surrendering Church. We are moved by the Spirit to do this in order to crash the giving barrier, just as technology crashed the sound barrier.*

*Would you, therefore, be willing to accept from the people and the clergy of the Diocese of Rochester the free, total and unqualified gift of one of our parishes in the inner city? We will pass the Church and all the property attached to it, to you or to any person whom you may designate, so long as on that property is built within the shortest possible time, housing for the poor. We are giving not just what we have, but we are giving what we are in recognition of our servanthood in the self-forgetfulness of Him Who had compassion on the multitude.*

*Faithfully in Christ,*
*†Fulton J. Sheen*

I then went to Washington to see Mr. Weaver. He told me that for a long time the federal government had been hoping that the Catholic Church or other Churches of the country would give some of their property in order that the government might start federal housing. He said that this offer was so very encouraging that he would present it to President Johnson. President Johnson was so much in favor of it that he asked that some publicity be given to it at a proper time.

In order that the property might be given, I had to receive permission to alienate Church property. This permission was given by the Board of Consultors, by the Apostolic Delegate and eventually by Rome itself. The question, then, was—which church? I asked the federal government to come and investigate the area; they chose the Church of St. Brigid, which occupied a square block in the inner city, and had a zealous pastor, but only about one hundred parishioners. Once that parish was selected, we then made the announcement.

To our great surprise, there was opposition, though artificially stimulated. Telephone calls were made throughout the diocese to oppose the Bishop for "giving away a church." Girls in a community college were loaded into automobiles with placards, and marched in front of the Pastoral Office, condemning the Bishop for ruining a parish. That evening when I visited a school, I was surrounded by several hundred people who had been organized to protest against "the destruction of our parish." Many threw pebbles at the car as I passed by. That night I withdrew the offer. That empty church, rectory and school stand abandoned today in the inner city—a monument to my failure to do anything about housing.

On another occasion, I invited union leaders in the field of housing, electricity, construction, bricklaying, carpentry and allied arts to my home for dinner. I outlined for them the need of house repairs among the poor of the inner city, and asked if they would be willing to send some of their men on Saturdays to work with black youths to help them

At a press interview with the new Bishop of Rochester, 1966. *(Courtesy, Society for the Propagation of the Faith)*

repair their own houses. The idea was for the craftsmen to train apprentices so that they might later do work among their own people. This idea was rejected because the training of apprentices "would hurt union labor."

A wrong impression would be created by dwelling on failures which were generally outside the general practice of episcopal administration. They were clay vessels that broke in my hands as they did in the hands of the potter whom Jeremiah visited. But clay has another quality than failure on the wheel; it also has the opposite property of "stick-to-it-iveness." It consolidates and commixes into a mass. Though the bishop and priests are only earthenware pots of clay to hold the treasure of the ambassadorship of Christ, they nevertheless form a fraternity the like of which exists nowhere on earth. No ironmonger of France feels an inner unity of soul with an ironmonger from Pittsburgh. No voter in the 15th Congressional District ever greets another voter from that same area with warm bonds of affection. Even alumni of the same college have little to exchange at their meeting except reminiscences. But when a bishop meets a bishop, and when a bishop meets a priest, and when a priest meets a priest, there is no introduction required; Christ has already introduced them one to another. We know what each other is in his heart. They may call on one another at any time and for any need; regardless of any attitude that a priest may have concerning his bishop, when the bishop comes to his home, there is always shown the utmost respect, courtesy and friendliness. When the clergy meet, there is no affectation. We know one another almost inside out, so much so that the corporate judgment of the priest about another priest is generally right. The individual judgment of one priest about another may be wrong or prejudiced, but when the majority agree that one of their brothers is a "good priest," he *is* a good priest. If the general opinion is that he is a bit "flaky" or "far out," he *is* flaky and far out.

I like this description of the greatest fraternity in all the world——that of bishops and priests:

> *It needs no coaxing, no prelude, no ritual. It is subject to no formality. We meet and possess one another instantly. There is not the shadow of a barrier between us, neither age, nor antecedents, nor nationality, nor climate, nor color of skin. Ours is a blunt rough-hewn affection. It almost forgets to be polite. I can sit at his table without invitation; sit in his study and read his books before I've ever met him; borrow his money or his clothes with no security. His home is my home; his fireside, my fireside; his auto, my auto. I can give him my confidence promptly and without reserve. I can neither edify nor scandalize him. We can quarrel without offense, praise each other without flattery, or sit silently and say nothing and be mutually circumvented.*
>
> *And why all this can happen is our own precious secret. It is the secret of men who climb a lonely drawbridge, mount a narrow stair and sleep in a lofty citadel that floats a white flag.*
>
> *Singly we go, independent and unpossessed, establishing no generation, each a conclusion of his own race and name; yet always companioning one another with a strange sympathy, too tender to be called friendship, too sturdy to be called love, but for which God will find a name when He searches our hearts in eternity.*\*

As I reached my seventy-fifth year, I knew I should offer to resign, because this was the wish of the Second Vatican

---

\*Courtesy of Sullivan Brothers, Printers, Boston, Massachusetts.

Council for bishops who headed dioceses. I did not cherish the thought of receiving a letter someday reminding me that, since I had reached the age of retirement, I should do so. And so I prepared for that day by going to Rome for a long audience with the Holy Father, Pope Paul VI, during which I submitted my resignation.

When I resigned, I did not "retire." I *retreaded*. I took on another kind of work. I believe that we spend our last days very much the way that we lived. If we have lived with ease,

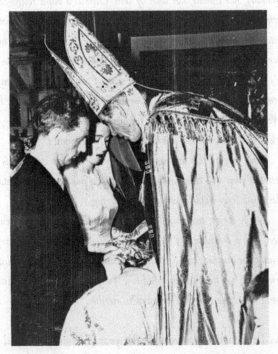

Bishop Sheen officiates at Hapsburg family wedding in Tuxedo Park, New York, 1950s. (*Religious News Service Photo*)

taking our rest, never exerting ourselves, then we have a long
dragging out of our days, like a slow leak. If we live intensely,
I believe that somehow or other we can work up until the day
God draws the line and says: "Now it is finished."

Retirement has many advantages. It becomes a time to re-
make one's soul, to interiorize, to meditate and begin a cram
course for the final exam. In the days of retreading, however,
I was given new opportunities for apostolic work. Two new
titles were given me by the Church. One was appointment as
Titular Archbishop of Newport in Wales. I am often asked:
"What does it mean to be the Titular Archbishop of Newport?" The answer: "It is very much like being made a Knight
of the Garter. It is an honor to have the Garter, but it does
not hold up anything." Being free from responsibilities of a
diocese is like having aspirin without the headaches.

Another honor was being made Assistant at the Pontifical Throne. I could never become very excited about this, although it is an honor, because my heart was always at the
Throne of Peter. This honor merely means that I now can
put my whole body and person where my heart always was.
As the years mount on, I feel that they were meant to be
fruitful—*non recuso laborem.*

## Twelve

# THE HOUR THAT MAKES MY DAY

On the day of my Ordination, I made two resolutions:

1. I would offer the Holy Eucharist every Saturday in honor of the Blessed Mother to solicit her protection on my priesthood. The Epistle to the Hebrews bids the priest offer sacrifices not only for others, but also for himself, since his sins are greater because of the dignity of the office.

2. I resolved also to spend a continuous

Holy Hour every day in the presence of Our Lord in the Blessed Sacrament.

In the course of my priesthood I have kept both of these resolutions. The Holy Hour had its origin in a practice I developed a year before I was ordained. The big chapel in St. Paul's Seminary would be locked at six o'clock; there were still private chapels available for private devotions and evening prayers. This particular evening during recreation, I walked up and down outside the closed major chapel for almost an hour. The thought struck me—why not make a Holy Hour of adoration *in* the presence of the Blessed Sacrament? The next day I began, and the practice is now well over sixty years old.

Briefly, here are some reasons why I have kept up this practice, and why I have encouraged it in others:

First, the Holy Hour is not a devotion; it is a sharing in the work of redemption. Our Blessed Lord used the words "hour" and "day" in two totally different connotations in the Gospel of John. "Day" belongs to God; the "hour" belongs to evil. Seven times in the Gospel of John, the word "hour" is used, and in each instance it refers to the demonic, and to the moments when Christ is no longer in the Father's Hands, but in the hands of men. In the Garden, Our Lord contrasted two "hours"—one was the evil hour "this is your hour"—with which Judas could turn out the lights of the world. In contrast, Our Lord asked: "Could you not watch one hour with Me?" In other words, He asked for an hour of reparation to combat the hour of evil; an hour of victimal union with the Cross to overcome the anti-love of sin.

Secondly, the only time Our Lord asked the Apostles for

anything was the night He went into His agony. Then He did not ask *all* of them... perhaps because He knew He could not count on their fidelity. But at least He expected three to be faithful to Him: Peter, James and John. As often in the history of the Church since that time, evil was awake, but the disciples were asleep. That is why there came out of His anguished and lonely Heart the sigh: "Could you not watch one hour with Me?" Not for an hour of activity did He plead, but for an hour of companionship.

The third reason I keep up the Holy Hour is to grow more and more into His likeness. As Paul puts it: "We are transfigured into His likeness, from splendor to splendor." We become like that which we gaze upon. Looking into a sunset, the face takes on a golden glow. Looking at the Eucharistic Lord for an hour transforms the heart in a mysterious way as the face of Moses was transformed after his companionship with God on the mountain. Something happens to us similar to that which happened to the disciples at Emmaus. On Easter Sunday afternoon when the Lord met them, He asked why they were so gloomy. After spending some time in His presence, and hearing again the secret of spirituality—"The Son of Man must suffer to enter into His Glory"—their time with Him ended, and their "hearts were on fire."

The Holy Hour. Is it difficult? Sometimes it seemed to be hard; it might mean having to forgo a social engagement, or rise an hour earlier, but on the whole it has never been a burden, only a joy. I do not mean to say that all the Holy Hours have been edifying, as for example, the one in the Church of St. Roch in Paris. I entered the church about three o'clock in the afternoon, knowing that I had to catch a train for Lourdes two hours later. There are only about ten days a year in which I can sleep in the daytime; this was one. I knelt down and said a prayer of adoration, and then sat down to meditate and immediately went to sleep. I woke up exactly at the end of one hour. I said to the Good Lord: "Have I made a Holy Hour?" I thought His angel said: "Well, that's the way the Apostles made their first Holy Hour in the Garden, but don't do it again."

One difficult Holy Hour I remember occurred when I took a train from Jerusalem to Cairo. The train left at four o'clock in the morning; that meant very early rising. On another occasion in Chicago, I asked permission from a pastor to go into his church to make a Holy Hour about seven o'clock one evening, for the church was locked. He then forgot that he had let me in, and I was there for about two hours trying to find a way of escape. Finally I jumped out of a small window and landed in the coal bin. This frightened the housekeeper, who finally came to my aid.

At the beginning of my priesthood I would make the Holy Hour during the day or the evening. As the years mounted and I became busier, I made the Hour early in the morning, generally before Holy Mass. Priests, like everybody else, are divided into two classes: roosters and owls. Some work better in the morning, others at night. An Anglican bishop who was chided by a companion for his short night prayers explained: "I keep prayed up."

The purpose of the Holy Hour is to encourage deep personal encounter with Christ. The holy and glorious God is constantly inviting us to come to Him, to converse with Him, to ask for such things as we need and to experience what a blessing there is in fellowship with Him. When we are

first ordained it is easy to give self entirely to Christ, for the
Lord fills us then with sweetness, just as the mother gives
candy to a baby to encourage her child to take the first step.
The exhilaration, however, does not last long; we quickly
learn the cost of discipleship, which means leaving nets and
boats and counting tables. The honeymoon soon ends, and
so does our self-importance at first hearing that stirring title
of "Father."

Sensitive love or human love declines with time, but divine love does not. The first is concerned with the body
which becomes less and less responsive to stimulation, but in
the order of grace, the responsiveness of the divine to tiny,
human acts of love intensifies.

Neither theological knowledge nor social action alone is
enough to keep us in love with Christ unless both are preceded by a personal encounter with Him. When Moses saw
the burning bush in the desert, it did not feed on any fuel.
The flame, unfed by anything visible, continued to exist without destroying the wood. So personal dedication to Christ
does not deform any of our natural gifts, disposition or
character; it just renews without killing. As the wood becomes fire and the fire endures, so we become Christ and
Christ endures.

I have found that it takes some time to catch fire in prayer.
This has been one of the advantages of the daily Hour. It is
not so brief as to prevent the soul from collecting itself and
shaking off the multitudinous distractions of the world. Sitting before the Presence is like a body exposing itself before
the sun to absorb its rays. Silence in the Hour is a tête-à-tête
with the Lord. In those moments, one does not so much
pour out written prayers, but listening takes its place. We do

not say: "Listen, Lord, for Thy servant speaks," but "Speak, Lord, for Thy servant heareth."

I have often sought some way to explain the fact that we priests are to *know* Christ, rather than to *know about* Christ. Many translations of the Bible use the word "know" to indicate the unity of two-in-one flesh. For example: "Solomon *knew* her not," which meant that he had no carnal relations with her. The Blessed Mother said to the Angel at the Annunciation: "I *know* not man." St. Paul urges husbands to possess their wives in *knowledge*. The word "know" here indicates two-in-one flesh. The closeness of that identity is drawn from the closeness of the mind with any object that it knows. No knife could ever separate my mind from the idea that it has of an apple. The ecstatic union of husband and wife described as "knowing" is to be the foundation of that love by which we priests love Christ.

Intimacy is openness which keeps back no secret and which reveals the heart open to Christ. Too often friends are just "two ships that pass in the night." Carnal love, despite its seeming intimacy, often can become an exchange of egotisms. The ego is projected onto the other person and what is loved is not the other person, but the pleasure the other person gives. I have noticed throughout my life that whenever I shrank from demands that the encounter made on me, I would become busier and more concerned with activities. This gave me an excuse for saying: "I do not have time," as a husband can become so absorbed in business as to forget the love of his wife.

It is impossible for me to explain how helpful the Holy Hour has been in preserving my vocation. Scripture gives considerable evidence to prove that a priest begins to fail his priesthood when he fails in his love of the Eucharist. Too often it is assumed that Judas fell because he loved money. Avarice is very rarely the beginning of the lapse and the fall of an ambassador. The history of the Church proves there are many with money who stayed in it. The beginning of the fall of Judas and the end of Judas both revolved around the Eucharist. The first mention that Our Lord knew who it was who would betray Him is at the end of the sixth chapter of John, which is the announcement of the Eucharist. The fall of Judas came the night Our Lord gave the Eucharist, the night of the Last Supper.

The Eucharist is so essential to our one-ness with Christ that as soon as Our Lord announced It in the Gospel, It began to be the test of the fidelity of His followers. First, He lost the masses, for it was too hard a saying and they no longer followed Him. Secondly, He lost some of His disciples: "They walked with Him no more." Third, it split His apostolic band, for Judas is here announced as the betrayer.

So the Holy Hour, quite apart from all its positive spiritual benefits, kept my feet from wandering too far. Being tethered to a tabernacle, one's rope for finding other pastures is not so long. That dim tabernacle lamp, however pale and faint, had some mysterious luminosity to darken the brightness of "bright lights." The Holy Hour became like an oxygen tank to revive the breath of the Holy Spirit in the midst of the foul and fetid atmosphere of the world. Even when it seemed so unprofitable and lacking in spiritual intimacy, I still had the sensation of being at least like a dog at the master's door, ready in case he called me.

The Hour, too, became a magister and teacher, for although before we love anyone we must have a knowledge of

Good Friday at Corpus Christi Church in
Chicago, 1954. *(Eugene J. Nosek)*

that person, nevertheless, *after* we know, it is love that increases knowledge. Theological insights are gained not only
from the two covers of a treatise, but from two knees on a
prie-dieu before a tabernacle.

Finally, making a Holy Hour every day constituted for
me one area of life in which I could preach what I practiced.
I very seldom in my life preached fasting in a rigorous kind
of way, for I always found fasting extremely difficult; but I
could ask others to make the Hour, because I made it.

Sometimes I wished that I had kept a record of the thousands of letters that I have received from priests and laity

telling me how they have taken up the practice of the Holy Hour. Every retreat for priests that I ever gave had this as a practical resolution. Too often retreats are like health conferences. There is a general agreement on the need for health, but there is lacking a specific recommendation on how to be healthy. The Holy Hour became a challenge to the priests on retreat, and then when the tapes of my retreats became available to the laity, it was edifying to read of those who responded to grace by watching an hour daily before the Lord. A monsignor who, because of a weakness for alcohol and consequent scandal, was told to leave his parish went into another diocese on a trial basis, where he made my retreat. Responding to the grace of the Lord, he gave up alcohol, was restored to effectiveness in his priesthood, made the Holy Hour every day and died in the Presence of the Blessed Sacrament.

As an indication of the very wide effect of the Holy Hour, I once received a letter from a priest in England who told me in his own language: "I left the priesthood and fell into a state of degradation." A priest friend invited him to hear a tape on the Holy Hour from a retreat I had given. Responsive to grace, he was restored again to the priesthood and entrusted with the care of a parish. Divine Mercy wrought a change in him, and I received this letter:

> We had our annual Solemn Exposition of the Blessed Sacrament last week. I encouraged enough people to come and watch all day and every day, so that we would not have to take the Blessed Sacrament down because of a lack of a number of people to watch. On the final evening, I organized a procession with the First Communicants strewing rose petals in front of the Lord. The men of the parish formed a Guard

of Honor. The result was staggering; there were over 250 people present for that final procession and Holy Hour. I am convinced that our people are searching for many of the old devotions which many of the parishes have done away with, and this is very often because we priests cannot be bothered putting ourselves out. Next year I hope that our Solemn Exposition will be even better attended because now the word is getting around. These last couple of weeks I have started a Bible study group; this is to encourage our people to read the Word of God. I start with reading of Scripture which we meditate on that evening; we then have a short Exposition of the Blessed Sacrament and meditation on the text until the time of Benediction.

I have also started going around the parish and saying a Mass in one house in every street each week, and inviting all people in that particular street to come and take part. The response has been quite good, especially since I am only starting. I do not wish to become an activist priest, so I rise early and make my Holy Hour. I still have my own personal problems to contend with, but I have taken courage from your words: "you will have to fight many battles, but do not worry because in the end you will win the war before the Blessed Sacrament.

Many of the laity who have read my books and heard my tapes are also making the Holy Hour.

A state trooper wrote that he had my tapes attached to his motorcycle and would listen to them as he was cruising the highways: "Imagine," he wrote, "the bewilderment of a speeder being stopped by me while from the tape recorder was coming one of your sermons about the Eucharist." He found it difficult at first to find a church that was open during the day at a time he could make his Hour. Later on, he found a pastor who was not only willing to open the church, but even willing to make the Hour with him.

Most remarkable of all was the effect the preaching of the Holy Hour had on non-Catholic ministers. I preached three retreats to Protestant ministers—on two occasions to over three hundred in South Carolina and in Florida, and on another occasion to a smaller group at Princeton University. I asked them to make a continuous Holy Hour of prayer in order to combat the forces of evil in the world, because that is what Our Lord asked for the night of His Agony. I addressed them: "You are not blessed with the same Divine Presence in your churches that I believe we possess. But you do have another presence that we do also, and that is the Scripture. At the Vatican Council we had a solemn procession of the Scriptures into the Council every morning as a form of the Presence of God. You could make the Hour before the Scriptures." Many came to me later to inquire about the Eucharist, some even asked to join with me in a Holy Hour before the Eucharist.

Most remarkable of all was a telephone call I received early one morning in Los Angeles. The caller announced himself as Reverend Jack McAllister. He was most insistent that he see me. I told him that I was catching a plane for New York at midday and would be glad to see him at the airport before leaving.

A very distinguished Christian gentleman appeared, Mr. Jack McAllister, who told me that he was engaged in a work of world evangelization, sending tapes on the Gospel to all parts of the world, and also mailing millions of copies of sermons and scriptures to every quarter of the globe: "There is one thing that seems to be missing in my world evangelism, and that is a spiritual practice which will make it successful. What would you recommend?" I recounted how much I depended on a daily Holy Hour before the Eucharist, and then suggested that since he was not blessed with the Eucharist, he could ask all of his people to spend one continuous hour with the Scriptures, in prayer and reparation for the sins of the world.

One year later I received a pamphlet from him entitled: "Jack McAllister writes to ONE HOUR WATCHERS." A paragraph from that pamphlet reads: "Please ... if you are honestly concerned about making Christ known to literally every creature—give God one hour every day. You are needed in God's prayer-force to prepare for work in the totally unevangelized areas of the world. Do you love them enough to pray? Will you 'pay the price' of spiritual battle for one hour daily? Christ asked: 'What, could you not watch with Me one hour?' "

At the end of the first year, he wrote and told me that seven hundred ministers had pledged one hour a day.

As I am now writing this book (about six years after our meeting in the airport) he sends this message: "We have now mobilized and trained over 100,000 One-Hour-Watchers. We are preparing to train an elite army to pray four to six to eight hours daily—'pray ye therefore'—the only solution to the problems related to World Evangelism."

One of the by-products of the Holy Hour was the sensitiveness to the Eucharistic Presence of Our Divine Lord. I remember once reading in Lacordaire, the famous orator of Notre Dame Cathedral in Paris: "Give me the young man who can treasure for days, weeks and years, the gift of a rose or the touch of a hand of a friend."

Seeing early in my priesthood that marriages break and friends depart when sensitiveness and delicacy are lost, I took various means to preserve that responsiveness. When first ordained and a student at the Catholic University in Washington, I would never go to class without climbing the few stairs to the chapel in Caldwell Hall to make a tiny act of love to Our Lord in the Blessed Sacrament. Later, at the University of Louvain in Belgium, I would make a visit to Our Blessed Lord in every single church I passed on the way to class. When I continued graduate work in Rome and attended the Angelicum and Gregorian, I would visit every church en route from the Trastevere section where I lived. This is not so easy in Rome, for there are churches on almost every corner. Fred Allen once said that Rome has a church on one corner so that you may pray to get across the street; the church on the other corner is to thank God that you made it.

Later as a teacher at the Catholic University in Washington, I arranged to put a chapel immediately at the entrance of the front door of my home. This was in order that I might never come in or go out without seeing the sanctuary lamp as a summons to adore the Heart of Christ at least for a few seconds. I tried to be faithful to this practice all during my life, and even now in the apartment in New York where I live, the chapel is between my study and my bedroom. This means that I can never move from one area of my small apartment to another without at least a genuflection and a small ejaculation to Our Lord in the Blessed Sacrament. Even at night, when I am awakened and arise, I always make it a point to drop into the chapel for a few seconds, recalling the Passion, Death and Resurrection of Our Lord, offering a prayer for the priests and religious of the world, and for all who are in spiritual need. Even this autobiography is written in His Presence, that He might inspire others when I am gone to make the Hour that makes Life.

Up to this point a reader may form a very incorrect judgment of the author. While it is true that this practice of sensitiveness to the Eucharistic Presence has been a powerful means of keeping my head above water, it by no means argues to the integrity of my priesthood.

Respect for the Eucharist is not the whole of the priesthood; it is just one of the facets. It is true that many may have seen me in the front of a church, but this is no more guarantee of my love of God than was the presence of the Pharisee in the front of the temple. The Publican in the back, who would not even dare lift his head, was far more acceptable to God. At the Last Supper, Peter boasted to the Lord that though all others denied Him, he would not; and yet in the cold courtyard of Caiaphas, he said to the maid who asked him if he had been with the Master: "I know Him not."

I know thousands of priests who have not had the practice of making frequent visits to the Blessed Sacrament, but I am absolutely sure that, in the sight of God, they are a thousand times more worthy than I. In any case, this is the story of the means I chose in my priesthood to be able just to keep step with my brother priests in the service of the Lord.

## Thirteen

# REFLECTIONS ON CELIBACY

I have been asked a thousand times why priests do not marry. The assumption behind the question is that marriage is less holy in the divine plan than celibacy; it is argued that the mere abstention from marriage suggests that there must be something less perfect about marriage. Both marriage and celibacy are means of communication and have the same goal, namely, a love without satiety, an ecstasy without an end, a surrender to the beloved—God—without ever falling back on egotistic loneliness.

Marriage and celibacy are not contraries in the area of love any more than atomic research and theology are contraries. All love is from God and all truth is from God. Celibacy and marriage both want love. Both are the roadways to that ultimate. Celibacy uses the direct current; marriage uses the alternating current. Celibacy travels by air; marriage by roadway. Celibacy is like poetry keeping the idea ever in mind like a dream; but marriage uses chisel and brush, concentrating more on marble and canvas. Celibacy jumps to a conclusion like an intuition; marriage, like reason, labors through ebb and flow, step by step.

Both celibacy and marriage have the same passion of love except that celibacy is immediate though imperfect, while marriage is mediate and also imperfect. Celibacy is a "passionless passion, a wild tranquillity"; marriage is incompleteness seeking unity and happiness through consuming fires.

Both are good. Celibacy is not higher; marriage is not lower. They are both signs of God's covenant with man. Each has its call to perfection. They are complementary, not competitive, careers. Marriage, however, belongs more to the secular age of this world than does celibacy. "This age passes away." "In the Kingdom of Heaven there is no marriage or giving in marriage." Celibacy is more directly related to the Kingdom of God.

The fallacy in a discussion about celibacy and marriage is the comparison of one vocation with another; it is like arguing about the relative perfection of the right leg over the left. Both want God, and the degree of possession does not depend upon the state of life but on the degree of response to the grace that God gives. The celibate is working for the Kingdom of God by "begetting children in Christ" in Baptism; the married by having children through the profound unity of two in one flesh. God has two kinds of lovers— those who go directly to the ultimate, such as the celibate, and those who go mediately through marriage.

Scripture enjoins: "it is not good for man to be alone." Because the passions of humans are so strong, celibacy would seem like a mutilation of God-given natural desires and instincts. When Our Blessed Lord spoke to the Apostles about the marriage bond being unbreakable, the Apostles because of the risks of adultery said to Him: "It is not advisable to marry." In answer Our Blessed Lord spoke of three kinds of eunuchs. He said: "There are eunuchs born that way from their mother's womb; there are eunuchs made by men; and there are eunuchs who have made themselves that way." Then He spoke of celibates who do not marry "for the sake of the Kingdom of God," finally giving away the secret of how men could be celibate. He called it a gift. He said that celibacy is not for everyone. It is only for those who receive from Him this gift. It is "only for those to whom it is granted. Let anyone accept this who can."

He admitted all the difficulties inherent in weak human nature, but then astounded them by saying that the initiative is on God's side and the response is on ours. Celibacy is not something that a priest accomplishes and fulfills and lives through his own power. No one is bound to receive a gift at Christmastime, but if he does accept it there is at least an obligation to acknowledge it. When God gave the gift of His Son to redeem us from our sins, many did not accept that gift. Calvary was one reaction. For anyone to say that "Christ was forced on us" is just as false as to say that any gift such as celibacy is forced on us; *it is not man's gift to God; it is God's gift to man.*

There are three evangelical counsels: poverty, chastity and obedience. All three are not popular in the same way. Poverty today is "in," chastity and obedience are "out." There is not much reverence generally today for either obedience or chastity. Poverty, however, seems to be rather popular, not so much as a personal dispossession but as helping the poverty of others, which is indeed commendable. The reason why chastity is on the decline is that we live in a sensate culture. In the Middle Ages, there was an Age of Faith, then came the Age of Reason in the eighteenth century; now we are living in the Age of Feeling.

During the Victorian days, sex was taboo; today it is death that is taboo. Each age has its own taboos. I think one of the reasons for sexual promiscuity today is the absence of purpose in life. When we are driving a car and become lost, we generally drive faster; so when there is an absence of the full meaning of life there is a tendency to compensate for it by speed, drugs and intensity of feeling.

Celibacy is difficult because it requires control of the most intense of the three concupiscences: pride, or the affirmation of self; avarice, or the excessive acquisition of property; and sex, or the desire for unity with spouse and prolongation of the human species. The Gospel mentions three "impossibles" but each can be turned into a "possible"—for "nothing is impossible with God." First is the Virgin Birth. The second is poverty; when Our Blessed Lord asked the young man to give up all of his possessions and come follow Him, some of the disciples said: "Then who can be saved?" And Our Lord said:

"With man it is impossible but with God all things are possible." And the final "impossible" was when He was discussing the third class of eunuchs: "those who make themselves eunuchs for the sake of the Kingdom of God." Our Lord went on to say: "And though this is impossible with men, it is not impossible with God," because celibacy is a gift.

We priests too often think that celibacy is something we give to the Church; actually it is something we *receive*, very much as a girl may receive a proposal. The negative aspect of celibacy is the creation of an emptiness. The virgin womb of the Blessed Mother was empty; the Lord filled it. There are two kinds of emptiness in the world: there is the emptiness of the Grand Canyon, which is fruitless; there is the emptiness also of the flute, which can only produce music by human breath. The emptiness of celibacy is of the second kind. There is a surrender on the part of the ego and there follows a gift on the part of God.

Celibacy is hardest when we fall out of love with Christ. Then it becomes a great burden. Once we priests put celibacy in the context of the Church and discuss its history, its sociology, its psychology and the like there is a groaning under the burden. Once we see it in relation to Christ, then it is less a problem and more a matter of love. Celibacy as an ecclesiastical law is hard. Celibacy as a question of discipleship is hard too, but bearable and joyful.

I could draw a curve of my own life, and I am sure any priest could draw a comparable one, and my attitude toward celibacy would be seen always in direct relationship to my personal love of Christ. Once our passions cease to burn for Him, then they begin to burn toward creatures. Celibacy is not the absence of a passion; it is rather the intensity of a passion.

In Toyko, May 1965, with students of the Jesuit Sophia University.
*(Courtesy, Society for the Propagation of the Faith)*

Every passion has an object which excites it; a pile of
gold, a woman, "a hank of hair" as Kipling put it, or Christ.
Why did Jesus accept the Passion of the Cross? Because of
His fiery passion to do the Father's Will. He compared it
even to a fire. A husband who loves his wife intensely has little problem with fidelity, but one who is constantly quarrel-
ing is often in search of greener pastures. All we have to do
is find out what is anyone's supreme object of love, and we
will find a corresponding surrender.

Notable examples of celibacy have manifested themselves
in the modern world. Gandhi, for example, was a deeply religious man. He loved the Untouchables so much for God's
sake that he became a celibate at the age of thirty-one. He
took a vow, with his wife's consent, to practice celibacy the
rest of his life. He claimed he had a "dharma," a life task or
life mission which he was to follow at all costs. That meant

for him the practice of two virtues—poverty and celibacy. As Erik Erikson, the psychoanalyst expressed it: "He gave up sexual intimacy for a wider communal intimacy; not because sexuality seemed immoral." As Gandhi himself explained: "I wanted to devote myself to the service of the community, so I had to relinquish the desire for children and wealth and live the life of 'Vanaprastha,' that is, one retired from the household cares."

Dag Hammarskjöld, late Secretary-General of the United Nations, was another who believed in celibacy because of the passionate love for a goal, namely, peace among nations. As he put it: "For him who has responded to the call of the Way of Possibility, loneliness may be obligatory." On his fifty-third birthday, he penned this line to God: "If Thou give me this inescapable loneliness so that it would be easier for me to give Thee all." Being a normal man, he felt "a longing to share and embrace, to be united and absorbed." But, like Gandhi, he affirmed "the loneliness of celibacy may lead to a communion closer and deeper than any achieved by two bodies."

Some in the United Nations poked fun at him because of his celibacy and accused him of homosexuality. He playfully came at his detractors with the lines:

> Because it never found a mate
> Men called
> The Unicorn abnormal.

So passionate was his love for brotherhood among nations that he saw that much cargo had to be thrown overboard to save the ship.

*I am the vessel.*
*The draught is God.*
*And God is the thirsty one.*

Both of these men, probably without knowing it, were saying the same thing that Paul said about celibacy: "An unmarried man can devote himself to the Lord's affairs. All he need worry about is pleasing the Lord. But a married man has to bother about the world's affairs and devote himself to pleasing his wife. He's torn in two ways." All celibates will be grateful to Dag Hammarskjöld for these magnificent lines: "The ultimate surrender to the creative act—it is the destiny of some to be brought to the threshold of this in the act of sacrifice rather than the sexual act; and experience the thunderclap of some dazzling power."

It all gets back to how passionate a man is, and how high are his flames and how burning his lusts. If a man gives up his freedom for a woman he loves, then it is also possible for a man to give up a woman for Christ. Love in the service of celibacy rises and falls with the love of Him. Once Christ becomes less regnant in human hearts, something has to take over to fill the vacuum. I have received countless letters from my brother priests, who have seen the thermometer of the soul rise and fall. Many of them, without any attempt at self-justification, have returned and have proven that a reconciled love is sometimes sweeter than an unbroken friendship. Christ on the Cross and Christ in the Eucharist forever become the touchstone of the question of celibacy. The more we fall away from response to that gift the less we want to look at a crucifix, the less we want to visit the Lord in His Sacrament. We become like the man who crosses the street when he sees a bill collector on the other side. The Cross, therefore, is where both Heaven and Hell meet. It is a Hell when we see the part we have played in His Crucifixion by our infidelity. It is Heaven when we remain faithful, or when we fly again to His Feet for pardon.

Libido or sex drive is one of the most powerful instincts in a human. One of the great fallacies of some types of sex education is that it is assumed if children know some of the evils that result from excesses they will avoid the reckless use of the libido. This is not true. No mortal, because he sees a sign on a door marked "typhoid fever," has an urge to break down the door in order to contract the disease. But when the word "sex" is written on a door, there is a drive to break down the barriers.

The libido has a much more general purpose than is often assumed; it is not just for pleasure; it is not even just for propagation; it is not only a means of intensifying the unity of husband and wife. It is also a *potential for superiority*. The sex drive is capable of transformation. Carbon may either become fire or it may become a diamond. The libido may be spent or it may be harbored. It may seek unity with another person *without*, but it may also seek unity with another person *within*, namely God.

The soul is not completely the master of itself when solicited, impelled, magnetized or overcome from without. As Carl Jung wrote: "Spiritual transformation always means holding back the sum of libido which would otherwise be squandered in sexuality. Experience shows that when the sum of libido is thus retained, one part of it flows into spiritualized expression while the remainder sinks into unconsciousness. In other words, when the sex drive is withdrawn from an outer object and sinks into unconsciousness, the soul is put in more direct communication with God."

So celibacy is not just the renouncing of the person *outside* but a concentration on the person *inside*. God is not out there. He is in us: "I will abide in you and you will abide in Me." Celibacy is a transformer which multiplies an energy within to concentrate entirely on Christ Who lives in the soul.

Fornicators do not believe that anyone is celibate. They project their own eroticism to everyone. On the other hand, celibates are the ones who most understand the weakness of the fornicators. We priests who have never broken our vow of celibacy are often attacked on the ground: "It is very easy for you; you are not tempted." It is just the contrary that is true. The celibate is tempted perhaps more than anyone else. The apple on the other side of the fence looks sweeter. Who knows better the resistance that a lineman or a tackle or a guard has to put up in a football game—the player or the spectator? Who knows the strength of a wind? The one who is blown over by it, or the one who can stand and resist?

Believe me, the temptations to break the vow of celibacy are multiple and intense; in loneliness it is easy for the imagination to take refuge in the thought "Jezebel understands me." When a celibate breaks his vow and takes on a Jezebel, he very often has to practice many of the same virtues of sacrifice which he had to do before he gave up the priesthood and which, if he had followed in the rectory, would have kept him celibate and happy. When erotomania possesses the means of communication, and sociability is free, it is very easy for sparks to be turned into flames, and for the love of a virtue to become the love of the virtuous as lodged in a particular person. If a priest is popular or well known the keeping up of a love affair with the invisible love of Christ is a real battle. Any slight infraction of the covenant of dedication causes an inner suffering. This may be because of the very close relationship of body and soul as St. Paul suggests. There is certainly less remorse for a sin of pride than for an impure desire. Scripture, therefore, fittingly bids us: "Grieve not the Holy Spirit."

A priest feels sin in its true nature; it is not just the breaking of the law. No one who exceeds the speed limit ever leans over the steering wheel when he drives into the garage and says an Act of Contrition. But when we compromise, in any way, the love of Christ in the soul and belittle our role as His ambassador, we then know sin as *hurting someone we love.* Imagine two men marrying two shrews; one man was married before to a lovely, beautiful wife who died. The other was never married before. Which suffers the more under the shrew? Certainly the one who had the better love. So it is with us; we are tortured, uneasy and sad, not because we have broken an ecclesiastical law—that never enters our mind. But because we have betrayed the best of loves.

If I had to select any scene in Scripture which best depicts the struggle that goes on in the soul of a priest, it would be that of the spiritual experience of Jacob. When he was a young man he had the vision of the ladder—the dream of glory and divine protection, even though he made a kind of a bargain with God. So many of us begin our priestly way of life in peace and pleasantness and green pastures.

Twenty years later life changed as when Jacob faced Esau. Some reach a spiritual crisis when young in the priesthood, but others, either from weakness or defects in their own character, do so at a late age.

Jacob wrestled with someone. He knew not the antagonist, only that it was with a personal will that he grappled. After a while, the adversaries stood out more clearly in the morning light. It was the Heavenly Wrestler who finally touched the nerve of Jacob's thigh and paralyzed it. Then the conflict changed its nature; force gave way to supplication, bidding Him not to depart until he was blessed.

So in our lives, Christ sets Himself up as our adversary in the dark night of the soul in which we are full of shame for what has been done. As we wrestle with the great adversary within us, we shrink from His face, we hang our heads in shame. We are at odds with ourselves and at odds with Him. We grope around in the darkness and forget that even in the darkness He is wrestling with us bidding us to return. When the conscience wrestles with the priest it is always in the form of Christ; He meets us in our silent hours; He speaks even amid the noises; He confronts us with the spectacle of what we might have been.

The Spirit lusts against the flesh and the flesh lusts against the Spirit. It is not so much the wrong that we have done; it is rather how we have smeared the Image. The conscience is most precious when it wounds. C. S. Lewis said: "God whispers to us in our pleasures, He speaks to us in our conscience, He shouts to us in our pain, more than that, in our sins, He uses a megaphone. He is like the voice of God in the beginning of humanity asking Adam: 'where art thou?'

He pleads for future possibilities. He bids us look at our foul raiment and He bids us like one of the returned priests of Babylon to put on new robes."

The preservation of celibacy is a lifelong labor, partly because of the weakness of human nature. Two great tragedies of life are getting what we want and not getting what we want. Birds in cages want to be out, and those outside of cages want to be in. Talking about love is never the same as loving. Talking about onions never makes the eyes run with water.

When the three lawful reaches of the human soul are abused they create an emptiness, though in a varying degree. It is borne out in the experience of any priest, and certainly has been true in my own, that it is most difficult to bring back to Christ souls who have sinned by pride and self-will, because pride inflates. It is also a mountainous task to return to Christ souls who have become avaricious and greedy, because money is a kind of economic guarantee of immortality: "See how much I have. My barns are full."

Celibacy is best preserved and best understood in terms of Christ. We priests are imitating Him. We are carrying a cross to prolong His redemption and any infraction of celibacy is always interpreted by every good priest as hurting Christ. A husband would never say, "I know I gave my wife a black eye; I also gave her a bloody nose; I beat her, but I did not bite her ear." If the husband truly loves his wife, he will not begin to draw distinctions about how much he hurt her. Though a priest in relationship to Christ does not seek fine points as how much he injured Him, the least infraction hurts us because we hurt Him. If I belong to the new humanity which was born originally of a Virgin, why should I not live in exclusivity for the Master? I never felt I gave up love in taking the vow of celibacy; I just chose a higher love. If anyone thinks that celibacy is psychologically harmful to priests, he should sneak into a gathering of priests. I am sure there is more humor among priests than among any other body of professional people in the world.

The more we love Christ the easier it is to be His alone. How do I know I am in rags? By seeing His beauty in the stole and chasuble of his priestliness. How do I know that any pool from which I drank is stagnant? Because I see the fresh flow of waters from His side. So the journey of a priest's life is not to the quagmire and the swamp, but to the ocean of love. I detect all the discords of my life, hearing the music of His voice. He folds me in His arms and I know the depth of my contrition. It is beside His waters that I thirst. It is at the sight of His Eucharistic Manna that I hunger. And it is before His smile that I weep. It is because of His love that I loathe myself. It is His mercy which makes me remorseful. We can have angels to guard us—yes—but not to judge us. It will only be Perfect Goodness that will judge us, and that is our hope. And it is this that saves. So I trust in His mercy and I love Him above all loves, and I can never thank Him enough for having given me the grace of priesthood. I came into it with a deep sense of unworthiness. I end it with a still deeper sense of unworthiness; and though I come in rags, I know that the prodigal son was clothed with the robe of righteousness.

## Fourteen

# RETREATS

If I were asked which of the many activities of my life, outside of the eminently priestly privileges such as offering the Eucharist, appealed to me most, I could not answer.

Teaching would be one response because, particularly in graduate work, it enabled me not only to acquire knowledge, but also to dispense it. Every increase of truth in the mind is an increase of being. One wonders if, among all the professions open to mankind, there is any nobler and purer than that which deals with truth.

The making of converts is also satisfying because, as St. James assures us, "if we save a soul, we help save our own."

Dedication to the missions has been equally gratifying, for it advances the Kingdom of God and it brings one in contact with dedicated souls.

Editing and writing have enabled me to communicate ideas which are bound up with the more general intention to proclaim truth.

Radio and television greatly satisfy me because they give a larger pulpit than any other activity. But they can also be the most dangerous to a priestly soul; of that I have spoken elsewhere.

I have loved every work to which I have been called or sent. But perhaps the most meaningful and gratifying experience of my life has been giving retreats to priests, not only because they brought me into contact with the priesthood, but because the very review one makes of his own spiritual life in order to speak to others helps oneself too. I really wonder if the priests who made these retreats received as much from me as I did from them.

The word "retreat" connotes a series of sermons, exhortations and meditations given over a period of time varying from three days to over a week—the purpose of which is to remind diocesan priests that their own pastoral life, whatever it may be, is intrinsically related to their own sanctification; that the horizontal relationship to neighbor is inseparable from the vertical love of God; that the triple work of the priest is to teach, sanctify and shepherd, for these are three forms in which the holy life manifests itself.

One of the first such retreats that I ever conducted was to the priests of Reno, Nevada, when there were only about twenty-five in the diocese. The Bishop of Reno at that time, Thomas Gorman, had been a classmate of mine at the University of Louvain and he invited me because of our academic bonds. Twice I gave long retreats to the Trappist monks of Gethsemani, Kentucky. On the first retreat, conferences began at four o'clock in the morning. Silence, which was the general rule of retreats in time past, and which is still retained by these monks, made them an extremely receptive audience. The lightest touch of humor to them was hilarious—partly because of the simplicity of their souls. I remember at one morning conference mentioning the name of "Moses" and they broke out in boisterous laughter. On the way from the chapel I asked the Prior the reason for the outburst. He said: "You will find out in due time."

I heard confessions in my room. The monks would line up outside the door, and knock for entrance to make their confessions. They loved to do this because it gave them an opportunity to talk. This particular day when I opened the door, I said to the monk: "Glory be to God, man, where did you get all of this fat in a Trappist monastery?" He said: "What do you mean, 'fat'? I have lost ninety pounds since I have been here." I said: "What is your name?" And he said: "Moses!"

I asked him if he was going to the new foundation the Trappists were establishing in the eastern part of the United States, and he replied that he would be. I then inquired: "But how do you know? You do not speak except infrequently by signs, and I am sure the Superior did not tell you. How, therefore, do you know you are going to the new foundation?" He said: "First of all, I want to go because a new foundation is always more difficult than an established one, and I want to do penance. Second, my laundry number is 423, and the other day as I was passing the laundry room, one of the monks held up his hand—first four fingers, then two, then three—and indicated by a thrust of his hand, a direction; that indicated to me that I was going to the new monastery."

I asked Father Prior afterwards if Brother Moses would be going to the new foundation and the reply was ambiguous, but "If you wish him to go, we shall send him." I said: "Yes, because Brother would love to go to do more penance." Later on I gave a retreat at that monastery, and Father Prior told me: "You are responsible for sending Brother Moses to us, and because of his talent with money, we made him treasurer. We pray for you every day, but we do not think too kindly of you, because it is very hard to get money out of Brother Moses." I am sure that any extra poverty that they felt was kindly accepted in the light of the laughable and lovable character—Brother Moses!

A particularly striking scene at the abbey was Compline, or the night prayers of the monks. Each of them had a small lamp above his choir seat which he would use if he needed to recall the words for reading. But as they came to that part of the prayer which they knew, one by one the lights would go out. The long narrow chapel was then in total darkness, except for the great large window at the far extreme above the main altar, where there was a stained-glass window of the Blessed Mother surrounded by angels and saints. As the evening prayer progressed until finally they came to the hymn to Our Lady, *Salve Regina*, the illumination of the window gradually increased, until at the close of the song and the night prayer it was a veritable blaze of glory. Here were over two hundred strong men as full of passion as and perhaps more full than their fellow men in the world, who all were in love with the same Woman—without jealousy—and in whom they all trusted to make them more like her Son.

Another interesting retreat was to the monks of the Camaldolese Hermitage about twenty-five miles south of Big Sur in California. Here the monks live alone in little hexagonal huts, and have their meals put into a small cubicle. They meet very early in the morning for recitation of the Holy Office and for prayers. They support themselves principally through the making of fruitcake—well seasoned and delectable. Knowing the meagerness of their fare, I brought with me some oranges and cookies to munch on during the nine-day retreat. The Prior called on me the second day and, looking at the unopened meal bucket which I had taken from the cubicle, said: "You have not eaten your breakfast." I said: "I have not been able to open the bucket." They had been hermetically sealed and there was a clasp under the bucket which released the vacuum, making access to the food possible. I, however, was not starving because of the provisions I had brought; but later I learned to open the bucket.

When I had arrived at the hermitage I gave the Prior a large assortment of oranges to give to the monks. As I heard their confessions, each one brought me an orange, so at the end of the retreat I had as many oranges as I had when I arrived. Even to say that one gives a retreat to men like these is like saying that one adds light to the sun. It was I who was edified, inspired and challenged.

When I first began this work of being a retreat master I was embarrassed, knowing that those to whom I spoke were closer to the Lord than I. Later on, I adopted the attitude that we are all weak men, seeking to love the Lord more, and

Byzantine Liturgy at Holy Cross Cathedral in Boston, November 11, 1956, with Rev. George Chegin, Brooklyn, New York, assisting and Very Rev. Daniel P. Maczkov, V.F., Bridgeport, Connecticut, at right. *(Courtesy, Society for the Propagation of the Faith)*

from that time on it was very easy. The priest has an appeal which men of no other profession enjoy, partly because they have a wistful longing for holiness. Even Herod had respect for John the Baptist, and loved to hear him preach; Ahab showed a longing respect for Micaiah, uncompromising though he was; Felix and Agrippa both admitted their fascination with St. Paul. That is why we can give greater scandal than anyone else, because we are messengers from another world. Our status, however, has changed in the last twenty years. It used to be that we were respected always for our office. Because of so many failures, we no longer always receive that automatic response. In other times our status was accepted; today we have to *earn* it; we have to prove we are deserving of it, and that is another reason for retreats.

Since my experience covers sixty years in the priesthood, I saw many changes. Shortly after the Council and in the late sixties, it was possible for a period of about five years to predict those who were about to leave their priesthood. This condition existed only for a short time, but it was so very noticeable that I could not help but moan at its presence, and rejoice when it passed away. If I spoke during a retreat about liturgy or social action, psychology, sociology, sex, there would be no visible or noticeable opposition, but as soon as I began to talk about Christ there would always be one and sometimes two or three of the priest retreatants who would react in a way of which they were totally unconscious, but which was very visible and disheartening to me. One might begin to rub his hand over his face, squirm, twist in the pew, look elsewhere for some source of distraction—in a word, he was annoyed, like someone who has received a third notice for an unpaid bill. In one diocese, I said to the Bishop at the end of the first day of retreat: "You have a priest who is going to leave." I described him, and the Bishop said: "You are mistaken; he is one of the finest young men of the diocese, and I am naming him Chancellor next week." I repeated: "He will not survive the retreat." He did not, though his leaving was as much a blow to me as to his own bishop.

In another diocesan retreat to several hundred priests, I spoke to the Auxiliary Bishop at the end of the second day and told him of someone who was to leave. He asked me who he was and I told him that I did not know him. After describing where he sat in the choir, the next day the Bishop told me his name. He had already given scandal in the diocese and has since left.

In these few instances, from which I trust the reader will

not generalize, it seemed to be Christ Who was at issue. The very mention of His Name, the very appeal to His Words, the most casual word about the Eucharist or Passion caused inner resentment which unmistakably recorded itself on the face. Coming events cast their shadows before them, so that there is a predictability about how some of us priests will react in time. Our Blessed Lord announced the future failure of Judas at the same time that He spoke of the Eucharist. Judas left the Lord the night the Lord gave the Eucharist. In recent years I have seen no more signs of this, but have noted that some of those who left are now, through the Mercy of Christ, on the way back. Once we priests have loved the best, it is hard to love anything else. We have been spoiled by the Perfect Lover.

The method I used in preaching retreats was the same as I used in all speaking. I never sat, since enthusiasm can be shown more in a standing position. I never read or used notes, but tried, through meditation, to absorb the ideas to be communicated and then let the actual retreat be the overflow and outreach of that contemplation. Each conference was limited to thirty minutes, except the last conference, which was a Holy Hour and was sometimes forty minutes in length. The number of conferences was five a day. I need hardly say that all of the conferences were in a chapel, never in a prayer hall, so that we priests would always be in the presence of Our Eucharistic Lord.

I remember one retreat I gave to priests of a diocese, held in a monastery which had a large church that seated about eight hundred. I allowed the people to come to the monastery church and listen to the conferences if they so desired, but the retreat was directed only to the priests. As we made a solemn procession to the foot of the altar in this monastery church, I genuflected. One of the monks reminded me that the Blessed Sacrament was not in the church. I inquired where the Lord was dwelling. He told me that the Blessed Sacrament was kept in the former Prior's room way down the corridor. I walked out of the church, stood in the back until the Bishop of the diocese appeared. He inquired if I was sick, and I told him I would not give a retreat except in the Presence of the Blessed Sacrament. The monks finally led me down a long corridor to an unfurnished room where the Blessed Sacrament was kept. When restored to its proper place on the altar, I began the retreat.

In the course of his life, a priest may make thirty or more retreats. I am sure that most of them could not remember a single resolution they made and kept. This may have been because the retreats were not sufficiently directed to one source of spiritual betterment; it would be like a medical convention in which there was a general recommendation to be healthy but no specific rules about health. For that reason, all of my retreats centered in one general resolution—namely, to make a continuous hour of meditation in the presence of the Blessed Sacrament every day. If this were done, I knew everything else would follow.

I believe we are saved not by our own righteousness, nor by our own good works alone. If I were asked what detail of my sixty years of priesthood I would show to the Lord as a sign I loved Him, I would point to the Holy Hours which have been made by priests in the course of their lives as a result of my retreats. Since these retreats have been put on tape and circulated throughout the world, there is hardly ever a week that goes by without a priest writing me a letter telling me that for nine years, or twenty years, or thirty years he has answered the Lord's request to watch with Him the hour. But it is not only the priests who have practiced this act of adoration and reparation: thousands of laity have likewise been inspired to do so.

I preached retreats not only to priests in various parts of the world, but also to colleges of young men and women, and not least of all, to a few prisons. This calls for a particular

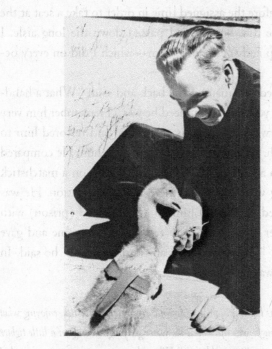

With "Louie" the duck at a priests' retreat
in New York State, 1950s. *(Courtesy, Society
for the Propagation of the Faith)*

approach. Before you, there may be two thousand inmates, all of whom pay you the courtesy of thinking you have on the white hat and they have on the black hats. This is the way I solved the problem: "Gentlemen, there is one great difference between you and me. You have been caught; I was not. In other words, we are all sinners." From that point on, it was very easy to deal with them.

In one prison where there were over 1,700 inmates, I would address them three times a day in a large auditorium. Attendance was not compulsory, but well over 95 per cent were present. Many of them would come to the auditorium an hour before the assigned time in order to take a seat at the end of the row, hoping as I passed down the long aisle, I would stop and speak with them—which I did on every occasion.

I slapped one man on the back and said: "What a handsome man you are," and indeed he was. (I remember him very well. Afterward, I heard his confession and restored him to the Church.) I once received a letter from him. He compared himself to a little flea floating down a river on a matchstick not caring whether or not there was a destination. He was shipwrecked and found himself on an island (prison) with many other fleas. A big flea (retreat master) came and gave him hope. "From now on, I am Jordan-bound," he said. In part, this was his note:

> I was like a flea, floating down a river on a matchstick, enjoying what I thought was life. When the water got rough I hung on a little tighter repeating "it would pass." When the water was running smooth I dabbled my feet and gathered a few other fleas upon my stick—my family. I was especially happy when the river was full of splinters

and other fleas passed by. I joined them in talk and in song. Sometimes I kept them so long and sometimes we enjoyed each other's company so well, they forgot their destinations. I did not forget; I never had one. I never looked for one.

When my little canoe hit rainy weather I took little fleas on board and loaded them on a stick with more shelter. And many times fleas saw me struggling to stay afloat. But one day I hit an iceberg. My "Lusitania" went down. Yes, I could swim. The friendly fleas did all they could to save my stick; it was hopeless. I saw and made it to a little island. [That was the prison.] It was not deserted; in fact it is a place where all torpedoed fleas gather. Last week I met an extraordinary flea [that was I], a sailor who did not go down, whose job it is to patrol the river, stopping at all those little isles, helping all the stranded, giving tools, provisions, but most of all, advice.

The Admiral walked right up to me and says: "You got a handsome face for a flea." This flattery wins me. I'm listening to whatever he says now. Inside, my heart tells me it is more than just that. This Navigator has a million tales; tells us about a place up the river Jordan . . . says it is the home of his Boss. It is a beautiful layout; everybody's welcome. The Boss wants you to bring friends if you can——"the more the merrier" type of Guy. You get a choice of where you want to live. They have many vacancies. I listen real close. I didn't want to miss any tips. He's talked about the river as one's life, using it as a tool to get to the Boss' place. I learned life is just not to follow your dip in the water. So I'm turned on, tuned in and my ship needs a few more necessities. I'm working on them now. I'll catch you on the river.

At another prison one inmate came in for a conversation before Confession. Their introduction was always the same; for example: "John Jones, Number 2835, twenty years to life, murder." I would never ask them about their crimes unless they told me. But this man told me: "I'm in for a meatball rap." I asked him to explain what that meant. He said: "Well, I have been convicted four times and under the Sullivan Law in New York that means life imprisonment. I stole a suit of clothes; I stole an automobile; I forged a check; and once I robbed without violence, and so I'm in for life." "How many years have you been in?" He said: "Twenty-six."

Later on, I wrote to the governor and said: "Papers never change; men do. This man is just the same on paper as he was twenty-six years ago, but he is not the same man inside as the paper man." I asked for consideration of parole. One night I received a telephone call from my friend. He said: "I'm out of prison." "Nick, what did you do in prison?" He said: "I was a cook." "Would you come up and cook my dinner?" He brought a French cookbook with him, containing enough recipes in it to cook for the rest of my life and his.

In another prison, when I was leaving, the men came with me to the gates. I carried my zucchetto in my pocket and decided to give it to the man who was nearest me. He said: "Is this for me?" and started to cry, and went back to his cell. Two months later I received a painting. In this painting there were the crossbars of a cell, but stretching out from the bars were two strong, calloused hands holding the purple zucchetto.

The prisoners all sent Christmas greetings and signed their names to a big Christmas card entitled "These Prisoners' Hands." The greeting read as follows:

> You grasped our souls with your beautiful words,
> you shaped them with pure delight.

*And our spirits soared like angel birds*
*on an upward heavenly flight.*
*You wrapped us up in stardust pride;*
*it was something we've never known.*
*You'll always be there at our side;*
*we'll never walk alone.*

It is easy to give retreats and conduct spiritual exercises for men like this, for they know that they are not so good—and this is always the condition of entering the Kingdom of Heaven. They may have thought themselves prisoners. But I saw among them many saints—actual or potential. No wonder the Lord said that "The first shall be last, and the last shall be first."

*Fifteen*

# PAPAL
# AUDIENCES

*Where Peter is, there is the Church.*

Every afternoon about five-thirty, when I was studying for the priesthood in St. Paul's Seminary, the spiritual director would give us a conference. I was paying the usual amount of attention this particular day, when suddenly I stopped listening. My mind seemed to be suffused with light. I heard not a word he uttered, but during that experience—I don't know how long it lasted—there came to me an illumination of soul, a light that suffused my intellect, bringing with it an overwhelming conviction of the certitude of the Faith.

The Creed and the affirmation "I believe" became not only an intellectual assent: I was momentarily possessed of the absolute and irrefutable character of Faith. As a result of that experience, I never in my life had any doubts about the Faith. My faith centered not just in the Creed, but in the Church, and it became personalized in the Pope as the Head of the Church and the Vicar of Christ.

I can remember as a small boy, about the time when Pius X allowed children to make First Communion, there was a discussion at our family table about its wisdom. A relative who was visiting took a position opposed to that of the Holy Father. How deeply shocked I was at him who, with so little wisdom, opposed the saintly and wise Pontiff! All during my life, attacks against the Church have hurt me as much as attacks against my own mother. The knowledge of a consecrated man of God or a consecrated woman abandoning her vows always caused a heartbreak in my soul.

Having served the Church so many years in mission activities, I could thrill to the famous speech made by a Chinese priest, Tong Che-tche, at Shanghai on June 2, 1951. Summoned by the Communist authorities, he was ordered to deny his Faith. His answer was: "A movement which has grown up outside the Catholic hierarchy is urging us to attack the Pope, who represents Jesus Christ... Gentlemen, I have only one soul and I cannot divide it up; but I have a body which can be divided up. It would seem to me that the best thing to do is to offer my whole soul to God and to the Holy Church, and my body to my country. Since I cannot remedy the conflict, there is nothing I could better do than to offer my soul to one side and my body to the other in the hope of promoting an understanding between China and the Church."

One of the special privileges of my life was to have private audiences with many Pontiffs. The first audience with a Vicar of Christ was when I was a graduate student at the University of Louvain. The Pontiff then on the throne was Pius XI, who had been a librarian at Milan and, therefore, loved books. During the audience he asked many questions about my university studies; turning to the subject of ethics, he inquired if I had ever read Taparelli. I dissolved into an emotional crumble as I answered: "No, Your Holiness, I have never read Taparelli." "What," he said, "you have never read Taparelli!" Taking hold of my hand, he continued: "I want you to promise me that when you leave me, you will go to a bookstore and buy the two volumes of Taparelli and read every line." Later on, I purchased the two Latin volumes and read them from beginning to end.

I knew his successor, Pius XII, before he was chosen as the Vicar of Christ. I had dined with Cardinal Pacelli, spent more than an hour in his office when he was Secretary of State, discussing Nazism and condemning it violently. I met him again when, as Cardinal Pacelli, he visited the United States, and on one occasion had dinner with him in the city of Rome with a mutual friend, Duchess Brady. A private audience was accorded me every year when he became Pontiff, except twice when he refused to see any of the national directors of the Society for the Propagation of the Faith throughout the world when they met at their annual meeting in Rome. When that difficulty was resolved, we returned to our meetings.

Each year I would discuss with him the subjects that I

Sheen, Pope Pius XII, and Msgr. Edward T. O'Meara,
June 1957. *(Courtesy, Society for the Propagation of the Faith)*

would talk about on radio for the coming year. During one
audience this noble, aristocratic Pontiff stood up at his desk;
I, who was seated alongside him, stood up also. He placed before himself a paper in his own handwriting and began reading. I was struck by the unusual nature of the procedure and
was surprised both at the contents and the manner in which
he addressed me. Humility forbids me to reveal all that he said
about my being a "prophet of the times" and that "you will
have a high place in Heaven." Nothing that he said was infal-
lible, of course, but his words gave me much consolation.

The most unusual summons to an audience came one night while dining with some priest friends in the Hotel Bernini of Rome. A telephone call about nine-thirty in the evening brought the message that "Pope John XXIII wants to see you." I thought at first it was a joke, but I decided that once I went to the Vatican at that hour, I would soon find out the truth. On arrival, the Swiss guard said: "Hurry up! His Holiness wants to see you." As I was ushered into his presence, he said: "I hope that I did not disturb you at this hour! But I just wanted to give you a gift." He presented me with a topaz episcopal ring and a pectoral cross: "Now put them in your pocket and hide them for the moment. I do not want to make other bishops envious."

On two occasions I was asked by Pope John XXIII to be co-consecrator with him of a dozen or more missionary bishops. Each ceremony in St. Peter's lasted about three hours. At the conclusion, each of the newly ordained bishops genuflects three times on the altar platform, then proceeds to the Holy Father to embrace him on both cheeks, saying *Ad multos annos* (May you have a long life). On this particular occasion, the last bishop had just made his final genuflection and was about to embrace Pope John when he said to him: "I am tired, kiss me only on one cheek."

I had the privilege of an audience with Pope John XXIII every year during his pontificate. On the very first visit, he asked me if I knew what Malachy had prophesied concerning him. Malachy was a monk of the Middle Ages, a friend of St. Bernard, who prophesied in cryptic terms each Pontiff until the end of history—the last one being Peter II. I answered: "Pastor et Nauta." "That is what I was in Venice," he continued, "a 'shepherd' or head of the diocese, and a 'sailor'

Assisting Pope John XXIII with consecration of missionary bishops.
(*G. Felici*)

because of its waterways. Because you knew that, I am giving you a little special gift—not precious; you need not take it if you do not wish." He presented me with a small silver gondola.

During a visit the following year, Pope John stepped down from his desk, pulled two chairs close together and began: "I want to tell you how I was elected Pope." Papal conclaves, as is well known, are secret. But he proceeded to tell me about the balloting, the number of votes each candidate received and who they were. I kept saying to myself: "This is very interesting material, the world would like to know about it." But when he concluded he said: "Now I impose silence on you for life, in the Name of the Father and of the Son and of the Holy Spirit."

During one audience he asked me to go to his home in northern Italy to meet his brother and relatives. Not only had he alerted his family whom I visited, but the whole town turned out to bid me welcome. It was during that same audience with John XXIII that he spoke of trials in the Church and reflected: "You have suffered much, which will bring you to a high place in Heaven. Is there anything that I can do for you?" I told him there was nothing I wanted except to do the will of God. He answered: "That makes it very easy for me."

I have in my study a photograph of John XXIII and myself standing alongside a very large circular map of the world. His eyes were wide open with interest as I pointed to some mission countries. I was actually saying: "Your Holiness is the commander in chief of all the missionaries of the world. Why not develop some kind of papal logistics for the distribution of missionaries? Instead of allowing each particular community to choose its area and the number it will

With Pope John XXIII in the Pope's study. (*G. Felici*)

send, why should not Your Holiness mobilize an army of two or three thousand missionaries and direct them to an area that seems most responsive to grace?" He asked if I had mentioned this to Cardinal Agagianian of the Congregation of the Propagation of the Faith. When I assured him I had, he continued: "I shall speak to him about it." Good Pope John never lived long enough to implement that idea.

On another occasion he said with a chuckle: "I am a prisoner in the Vatican. I cannot do as I please. I want to take you up to my private quarters on the next floor. Let us sneak into this small corridor." When he opened the door, he saw a papal guard, and with a laugh said: "See! I told you I am a prisoner in the Vatican." The guard directed us to the elevator, which took us to the private quarters of the Holy Father, where he showed me his desk. On it was a photograph and some books which he had authored. "I autographed this picture for you at five o'clock this morning, and also these books. Come into the chapel." I was surprised at its simplicity. As we came out after a prayer, he reflected: "This is where I received my inspiration to hold Vatican Council II. I knew very well that if I told the cardinals they would say, 'Oh, you are too old to hold a Council,' or 'There are too many conflicts in the Church,' so I called my secretary, Monsignor Capovilla, and said: 'We will go out to the Church of St. Paul Outside the Walls and announce the Vatican Council and then no one can stop it.' " As we returned to his office downstairs, he called in a photographer. "Come, let us have our picture taken. It may make some in the Church jealous, but that will be fun."

His successor in the Chair of Peter was the former Cardinal Montini, Pope Paul VI, on whom fell the burden of continuing Vatican Council II after the death of Pope John XXIII. The Lord granted me the continued privilege of making obeisance to him almost every year of his pontificate. As many others had done, Pope Paul VI brought up the subject of suffering in the course of one audience. Quoting St. Paul's letter to the Colossians that "we fill up the quota that is wanting to the sufferings of Christ for the sake of His Body, the Church," he reflected that the Kingdom of Heaven is won only by some tribulation. He took a blank sheet of paper and wrote on it: *nolo sine cruce crucifixum* (I do not wish to be crucified without a cross). He threw it in the wastebasket. I asked His Holiness if I might retrieve it from the wastebasket and keep it. I have it framed, and it is preserved above my bed so I may remember that audience.

Another year, I observed that he was well named "Paul" because he had been crucified with Christ. "Yes," he observed, "every night about midnight I open my mail of the day. Almost every letter has a thorn in it. When I put my head on my pillow at night, I really lay it on a crown of thorns." Then he continued: "But I cannot tell you what an ineffable joy it is to suffer all this for the sake of the Church. The other day I had some visitors from Yugoslavia. One of them was a priest who had been under torture for twenty years. He was so overcome with awe at being free and having an audience, that he did not say a word; but I could see in his face the heavenly joy at standing before the Vicar of Christ whom he would not deny even under extreme torture."

Another year when granted an audience, I seated myself in an outer room very near the Holy Father's private office. During a wait of about fifteen minutes, I made a quick review of my life, asking: "Have I really served the Church as well as I should? Have I used the many talents the Lord has given me? Have I cast fire upon the earth as the Lord asked His bishops to do?" I finally came to a negative conclusion. I had done little. At that moment the door was opened; I was ushered before His Holiness. I said: "Your Holiness, I have just discovered how easy Judgment is going to be." "Oh," he said, "tell me, I would like to know." "While I was waiting to come into your presence I had come to the conclusion that I had not loved the Church as much as I should. Now that I come before Your Holiness, I see the Church *personalized*. When I make my obeisance to you, I make it to the Body and to the invisible Head, Christ. Now I see how much I love the Church in Your Holiness, its visible expression." He said: "Yes, Judgment is going to be that easy for those who try to serve the Lord."

As I mentioned in an earlier chapter, I went to Rome just a few months before retirement time, and submitted my resignation to Pope Paul VI. I made that known to him as soon as I entered his study. He said nothing, but discussed another subject for about ten minutes, after which I brought up the resignation again. "Your Holiness, I have offered you my resignation as Bishop of Rochester. Is it your pleasure to accept it?" Some minutes more passed in which we discoursed about another aspect of Church life, but still no answer. I knew the audience would not last much longer, so I finally said: "Your Holiness, you have not answered my question. Will you graciously accept my resignation as the Bishop of Rochester since I have reached the age limit to be an active bishop?" He said: "What date would you like to resign?" "September 20, which was the anniversary of my Ordination." He wrote on

In audience with Pope Paul VI when
Sheen offered his resignation as Bishop of
Rochester, 1969. *(Courtesy, Society for the
Propagation of the Faith)*

a pad: *September 20th?* I said: "Your Holiness, why do you put
a question mark after September 20?" "Well," he said, "it
may not be that date, but it will be around that date that I
will accept it." As a matter of fact, it was about a month
later.

I received this letter from His Holiness commemorating the
twenty-fifth anniversary of my episcopal consecration:

To Our Venerable Brother
*FULTON JOHN SHEEN*
Titular Archbishop of Newport

*We have the most happy remembrance of you, Venerable Brother; We cherish with the highest esteem your life and manifold activities, and We seek at this present moment to amplify that most sweet joy We bear toward you. Willingly are We impelled, speaking with you for a little while at a distance by letter, to harmonize with one mind, before God and the Church, the providential goodness and largesse of the Merciful Redeemer in your behalf. For no other than the Lord Jesus Himself is the One Who has poured out to others, through your ministry, such an immense abundance of graces. It is this same Lord, Whom you love most intimately, Whom you venerate so eminently in the Sacrament of the Eucharist, Whom you have followed so assiduously in the Sacred Scriptures, and Whom you never ceased to glorify and proclaim in your teaching, your writing and your speaking.*

*Nor could We ever omit to mention the countless thousands of souls who, through you as an author, as a leader and a preacher——either came to know Christ the Saviour better, or looked more favorably upon His Church on earth, or more ardently loved divine and human truths. We also know that within that vast multitude there are those whom you have significantly helped, taught and influenced. Because of that, at this very moment, We pause to allow Ourself gratuitously and willingly to pay you honor on the anniversary of your Episcopacy.*

*Twenty-five years have quickly passed since that day when you in this very city of Rome, near the Tombs of the Apostles, received the plenitude of the Priesthood and were constituted a Bishop of the Titular Church of Caesariana, together with all its rank and dignity. But that eleventh day of June was neither the beginning nor the end of your remarkable industry in every field of Catholic Apostolate; rather, it im-*

posed a meritorious crown on the thirty-two years of your Priesthood and gave a new impulse to follow, without interruption, new and singular undertakings and works for Jesus Christ, for His Church, and for souls thirsting for salvation and heavenly light.

You gave yourself totally to promoting the missionary works of Catholics in your country, as you most vigorously directed The Society for the Propagation of the Faith. For a long time before that, you taught with great success the truths of Philosophy and the doctrines of Sacred Theology. Then—God willing—you were made a Bishop and you intensified that ministry by a program of preaching and writing, which, because of its wide diffusion and the knowledge of the Gospel which it spread, helped in the salvation of souls and added to the glory of the Church. It is truly impossible to describe the number of those who read your books, heard you on radio and saw you on television.

All these testimonials and achievements are before Our eyes to see as you commemorate the Silver Jubilee of your Episcopacy. In virtue of this, Venerable Brother, We wish to offer you Our heartfelt praise for each and every one of these, and to honor you and congratulate you for these and all your magnificent works. We greatly rejoice and give thanks to God, for neither age nor state of health has impeded you, but always with a joyful spirit, with pastoral devotedness and good manners, even now you draw many men to Christ and to the Church; particularly to priests you have given spiritual admonitions and help; to vast assemblages you have sown the truths of the Gospel.

We beseech the Most Benign Redeemer to invigorate and strengthen you in your fruitful work, and rejoice you with the consolation of a strong faith. Then, when it pleases Him, may He make you happy in the clear vision of Himself in Heaven. May this letter of Ours be a sign of Our fraternal gratitude to you, Venerable Brother, as We lov-

*ingly impart to you Our Apostolic Benediction on your eighty-first
birthday.*

> *Given at the Vatican, the 8th day of May, 1976,
> the 13th of Our Pontificate*

*Paulus PP. VI*

I never met John Paul I, for it almost seemed as if he
came to say goodbye with a smile. I had the pleasure of
meeting Pope John Paul II when he came to New York. I narrated his visit on national television as I had done years before when Pope Paul VI visited New York.

I was greatly honored to receive this letter from John Paul
II on the occasion of my sixtieth anniversary in the priesthood:

*To my venerable Brother*
**FULTON J. SHEEN**
*Titular Archbishop of Newport*

*I am one with you in giving thanks to God for your sixty years in the
priesthood of our Lord Jesus Christ.*

   *God called you to proclaim in an extraordinary way his dynamic
word. With great zeal you accepted this call, and directed your many
talents to spreading the Gospel of Jesus Christ. Thus, in these six
decades of your priestly service, God has touched the lives of millions of
the men and women of our time. They have listened to you on radio,
watched you on television, profited from your many literary achievements and participated in spiritual conferences conducted by you. And so
with Saint Paul, "I thank my God whenever I think of you; and every*

*time I pray for . . . you, I pray with joy, remembering how you have helped to spread the Good News" (Phil 1:3–4).*

*Beloved Brother in Christ, united as we are in prayer and the ministry of God's word (cf. Acts 6:4), which Christ in a special way entrusted to the Apostles and their successors, I ask you to pray for me and for the success of my ministry as universal pastor of the Church. And I shall pray for you, asking our Lord Jesus Christ to give you deep peace and to sustain you in his love.*

*I commend you to the intercession of the Blessed Virgin Mary, Mother of God and Mother of priests. And with fraternal affection I impart to you my Apostolic Blessing.*

*From the Vatican, October 11, 1979*

*Joannes Paulus PP. II*

I responded as follows:

500 East 77th Street
New York City
November 26th, 1979

*Your Holiness:*
*After the greeting extended me by Your Holiness at Saint Patrick's Cathedral, and the beautiful letter on my Sixtieth Anniversary, were it not for the renewed strength the Lord gave me, I should have sung my "Nunc Dimittis."*

*But I am still, thank God, blessed with the Psalmist's promise— "Vigorous in old age like a tree full of sap." (92:14)*

*I bow in humble gratitude for the Pontifical approval of my ministry of the Word, saying with Saint Augustine:* Nisi fideliter praecederet Piscator, Non humiliter sequeretur Orator.

*Pray for Your Holiness? That I always do for the Vicar of Christ, but in this fourth cycle of a crisis which strikes the Body of Christ every five hundred years, I pray for Your Holiness as for another Gregory the Great, Gregory VII, Pius V, and for our times as the poet Slowacki put it: "A Slav Pope will sweep out the Churches and make them clean within."*

*Every night when silence gives vision scope, I pray to Our Lord in the Blessed Sacrament for the Chief Shepherd of our souls, and the only moral authority left in the world.*

*On the one hand, my heart bleeds for Your Holiness, for like Peter knocking at our doors, some of us like Rhoda hear your voice but do not admit you into our hearts.*

*On the other hand, there is being fulfilled in the Vicar what was said of the Lord: "Why the whole world has gone after Him!" (John 12:19)*

*I wish I were younger to enjoy the blessings to come, for as one of our poets put it:*

*Lift up thy head and hark*
*What sounds are in the dark,*
*For His Feet are coming to thee*
*On the waters!*

*In prayerful gratitude for Your Blessing, I remain,*
*Obediently yours in Christ,*

*Titular Archbishop of Newport*

*His Holiness,*
*Pope John Paul II*

I believe that John Paul II will go down in history as one of the great Pontiffs of all times. As one looks over the history of Christendom, it seems that there is a crisis about every five hundred years. The first cycle of five hundred years was the fall of Rome, when God raised up the great Pontiff Gregory the Great, who had been a senator in Rome. He became a Benedictine monk and then set about conversion of the barbarians and prepared the way for a Christian Europe. The second cycle of five hundred years brings us roughly to the year 1000, when there was the Eastern schism, but also the decline of holiness in the Church. Three dominant evils prevailed—clerical concubinage, simony or the buying and selling of ecclesiastical offices, and the naming of bishops by princes and kings. Gregory VII, who was a Benedictine, was raised by God to heal that crisis against much opposition from within and prepared the way for the great medieval civilization.

In the third cycle of five hundred years, there was a breakup of Christian unity. Clergy again became corrupt, nuns became secular and everyone recognized the need of reform. Some undertook to reform the Faith. There was nothing wrong with the Faith. What needed reformation was behavior. The great Dominican Pontiff, Pius V, saved the Church by applying the reforms of the Council of Trent and by establishing missionary activity throughout the world. Now we are in the fourth cycle of five hundred years, with two world wars in twenty-one years, and the universal dread of nuclear incineration. This time God has given us John Paul II, who has drawn the attention of the world to himself as no human being has done in history.

The explanation, I believe, must be sought in what is

the characteristic note of the twentieth century, which is mysticism—not true mysticism rooted in God, but a pseudo-mysticism. In the language of Charles Péguy, "false mysticism ends in politics." Our times have seen the rise of the Red mysticism of class and party in communism, the Black mysticism of the state under fascism, and the Brown mysticism of the race under Nazism. In other parts of the world, a false mystique uncoiled like a serpent suffocated freedom of speech and suppressed opposition and assassinated those who differed.

Into this world of a false *mystique with a politique* comes Pope John Paul II, who has a *mystique without a politique*. He has no armies, no publicity directors, no propaganda machine and comes from the smallest state in all the world. The *mystique* that he preaches is the *mystique* of human freedom, which does not mean the right to do whatever you *please*, otherwise only the strong are free; which does not go to the opposite extreme of totalitarianism of defining freedom as the right to do whatever you *must*, otherwise there is only freedom of a party. The freedom that he preaches is the freedom to do whatever you *ought*, and oughtness implies a goal, a purpose in living and a meaning. His *mystique* affirms the sacredness of life, the right to worship God according to the light of conscience, and the commitment to human rights which is very like that which is written in our own Declaration of Independence: that all of our rights and liberties come to us from our Creator.

His *mystique without a politique* has an unheard-of appeal to the people of the United States partly because our nation is becoming a kind of *politique without a mystique*. We have been split up into parties, groups, factions and cliques ever since we split the atom. Each one wishes to strike his own note; not one wants to sing a song of patriotism and unity. Our hands are full, but our hearts are empty; we suffer from hunger of the spirit while much of the world is suffering from hunger of the body. As sheep without a shepherd, we suddenly began seeing the value of the spiritual in a man dressed in white. To all who have found their way, he has become their guide in faith and morals; to all who have lost their way, he has become a beacon of hope.

Over a century ago, a Polish poet by the name of Slowacki wrote these prophetic lines:

> God has made ready the throne for a Slav Pope,
> He will sweep out the Churches and make them clean within,
> God shall be revealed, clear as day, in the creative world.

A Polish woman who died in 1972 at the age of ninety-two knew Father Wojtyla as a young priest. Among her effects at death there was found in her prayerbook this prophecy of Slowacki under which she had written the lines: "This Pope will be Karol."

During my life I have seen the papacy move gradually out into the world from the Church within which it had somewhat locked itself. This can be described in terms of the places where each Pontiff in the course of my lifetime was crowned. If one calls to mind the inside of the Basilica of St. Peter's, the story of this growing relationship with the world can be told. Pope Benedict XV of World War I was crowned at the altar of the Blessed Mother, at the very *rear* of the Basilica of St. Peter's—about as far from the front door as he could get. His successor, Pope Pius XI, moved about a hundred feet forward and was crowned at the main altar of the basilica under the great dome. Pius XII, after he was crowned, walked down the nave of St. Peter's and mounted a small stairway to the balcony *outside* of St. Peter's. With that motion he literally stepped into the world. He was not yet in it, but the papacy was advancing toward it. John XXIII not only stepped onto the balcony, but he threw out his great arms like the columns of Bernini, and bade the whole world come to himself.

Pope Paul VI celebrated his Mass of Coronation outside of St. Peter's in the great piazza open to the world. So did John Paul I. Pope John Paul II not only stepped outside of St. Peter's, was not only crowned in the presence of the world and spoke several of the world's languages at his coronation, but he began walking into the world—into Poland, to Mexico, to Ireland, to the United States—and he has not stopped walking yet.

When I say that recent Popes have sought to narrow the gap between their "goings into the world," I am immediately open to confusion. The word "world" in Scripture has two meanings. First of all, it stands for the cosmos and the development of it through man. In this sense it is "good." "And God saw that it was good." But the word also has another meaning, i.e., a "spirit of the primacy of the self," the pursuit of pleasures of the body over joys of the mind, the domination of human personality by pride, lust or avarice. This "world" is summarized in: "I gotta do my thing," or "I am my own master." Of this world Our Blessed Lord warned His Apostles: "I have taken you out of the world, therefore the world will hate you."

Immediately after the Second Vatican Council, which had

prepared a brilliant document on the *Church in the Modern World*, some turned the Church's interest in the development of humanity in the world into secularism, with the result that there was a decline of spirituality, the breakdown of religious life and the loss of the sacredness of vocations.

The task before John Paul II is to restore the divine balance between the Kingdom of God being *in* this world, but not *of* it. Because "world" is ambiguous, it is possible to fall into abysses on either side of the roadway of truth, thus producing psychotics and neurotics. A psychotic believes that two and two make five; a neurotic believes that two and two make four, but he is mad about it. The neurotics hold to the real, and forget the ideal. In Scripture the Church is symbolized as the rock that was struck and from which came living waters. The rock is permanent, the waters represent the change and dynamism of the Church. The psychotics hold to the rock and forget the waters; the neurotics swim in the waters and forget the rock. The psychotics want only the bed of the river; the neurotics only the flowing water. The psychotics would isolate the Church from the world; the neurotics would identify the Church with the world. For the psychotics religion is cultic; for the neurotics it is activistic.

When Goethe's devil started translating the Gospel of John: "In the beginning was the Word," he hesitated because he could not subscribe to the primacy of the Word of God. So he wrote instead: "In the beginning was action." I believe John Paul II is healing this divorce of things that God willed should be kept together.

This close association with so many Pontiffs was only the coming to a head in my life of that experience of faith which occurred in the seminary. I had such reverence for the Vicars of Christ because I saw in them the visible head of the Body of Christ, the Church. It has always grieved me to see little candles spluttering in contempt at the corporate and garnered wisdom of the Church. The self-conquest of the ascetics, the endurance of her martyrs, the holiness of all the long line of Pontiffs, except a few, both exalted and abashed me. As I saw how each Pontiff respected the Scripture, tradition and the Magisterium of the Church, it was to me a kind of a trinity through which the Word of God reached us; and I realized what a joy it was not only to think "with the Church," but "in the Church." Our Lord said to Peter: "Simon, son of John, feed *My* sheep." He did not say: "feed *your* sheep." We are always Christ's sheep. And when it comes to being fed, I have always been well cared for spiritually by Peter and every other Vicar of Christ.

# Sixteen

# MAKING CONVERTS

A priest never touches reality until he touches a soul. The Lord balanced the universe against a soul and the soul won: "What will a man gain by winning the whole world, at the cost of his true self?" Or: "What can he give that will buy that self back?" St. James assures us that "any man who brings a man back from his crooked ways will be rescuing his soul from death and canceling innumerable sins." St. Paul pronounced a woe against himself if he did not save souls: "It would be misery for me not to preach." The world is in a tragic state when salesmen do not believe in their products and soldiers are not on fire with their cause.

But the subject of making converts and saving souls is a very difficult one, for it is so easy to believe that we are the agents who cause the results, when actually all we are at best are instruments of God. As it has been said—He can write straight with crooked lines. Pius XII once asked me: "How many converts have you made in your life?" I answered: "Your Holiness, I have never counted them. I am always afraid if I did count them, I might think I made them, instead of the Lord."

"Conversion" in Greek is *metanoia*, or a complete turning around from the direction which we are facing. Talking once to a group of drug addicts in Harlem, I gave this example: Suppose I took a ball and rolled it down the center of this hall; it would evidently go in a straight line, unless it was diverted by some outside force. When we are living our lives in the direction of selfishness and lust and pride, there will be a continuity in that way of life unless some superior force intervenes from the outside, and that is *grace*—to know things which we did not know before.

It is possible for a human being to live on any one of three levels—the first level is the *sensate*, in which one cares for the flesh and its pleasures. Man can live also on a second or higher floor, and that is the *rational*. Here he will pursue the good pagan life and practice natural virtues with enthusiasm. Under the inspiration of reason he may be tolerant, contribute to the needy and to community enterprises, but he refuses to believe that there is a Knowledge above that which he possesses and a Power above that which he experiences. To invite a person who lives on the second floor of reason to the third floor above is often to invite ridicule of what is called supernatural order. These critics are willing to admit an evolutionary process on a horizontal plane until man is produced but they refuse to mount to the third floor, sometimes denying its possibility. Two tadpoles were discussing the possibility of any kingdom above their own. One little tadpole said to the other: "I think I will stick my head above the water to see what the rest of the world looks like." The other tadpole answered: "Don't be stupid; don't try to tell me that there is anything in the world besides water!"

Conversion is an experience in no way related to the upsurge of the subconscious into consciousness; it is a gift of God, an invasion of a new Power, the inner penetration of our spirit by the Spirit and the turning over of a whole personality to Christ. If I begin to recall some instances of con-

In Rome, with Cardinal Pietro Fumasoni-Biondi, Prefect of the Sacred Congregation of the Society for the Propagation of the Faith, April 1952. (*Courtesy, Society for the Propagation of the Faith*)

version during the course of my life, it will not be to shed any glory upon myself, for I could no more make someone else a Christian by my own influence than I could turn a sawdust doll into a pretty little child of six. I am, nonetheless, grateful that the Lord used me to bring others to Himself. I have always had a deep passion for helping others find faith.

When I was stationed in Washington I would go to New York almost every weekend to instruct converts on Saturday and to preach on Sunday, in either the Paulist Church or St. Patrick's Cathedral. Because I was on national radio at this particular time, many wrote asking for instructions. These classes were first held in the rectory of the cathedral, in St. Patrick's Cathedral School and later on in a small auditorium. I was constantly warned by my fellow professors at the university that I was shortening my life. It was universally agreed that I would never live to reach the age of forty-five. During holidays I would accept engagements throughout the country. I once spent seven consecutive nights on "sleepers" and I can testify that those were the only moments I ever doubted that man was made to the image and likeness of God—for that resemblance is forfeited as he tries to take off his trousers in an upper berth!

During this period when I would hold two convert classes annually (one in New York City, and the other in Washington), there would be an average attendance of between fifty and one hundred who would eventually become members of the Mystical Body of Christ. The period of instruction either for an individual or for a group would be at least twenty to twenty-five hours. A very noticeable change would come over a group as the instructions developed. At the first meetings, each would seek out the best seat and was reluctant to allow another to take his place. But once an instruction was given on Christ, the group immediately changed—offering a place to one another, helping each other with coats and accepting everyone in the group as all bent on a common purpose: an encounter with Christ.

Though I give here a few examples of *metanoia*, I must remind you that there were hundreds of others besides these whom I recall: housekeepers, flight attendants, ministers, beggars at the door, businessmen, housewives, alcoholics and college students. Some few cases, however, will illustrate the following three points:

First, many are seeking God without being aware of it. As Newman said: "I knew the Church was the true Church, but I did not know that I knew." Pascal noted: "Console thyself, thou wouldst not seek Me if thou had not found Me."

Second, some may acknowledge the existence of God, but He is on the circumference of their lives. As Voltaire said of God: "We nod, but we do not speak." Though a convert may be described in the last stages as a rose that bloomed, it must ever be kept in mind that the one who explains the Creed and commandments is nothing more than the gardener with a hoe and a rake.

Third, the one who receives enlightenment always experiences in his soul a sense of repentance or a discovery that life as lived until now was not right in the sight of God. I recall what Tertullian said: "Penitence is a certain passion of the mind which comes from disgust at some previous feeling." Christ becomes not just the agent of repentance to the convert, but also the agent of forgiveness. I have never known a convert who did not say two things: "I am a sinner" and "I am forgiven."

The following recollections about those who embraced Christ in His Church prove the truth of the above statements.

Bella Dodd was the lawyer of the Communist party, and had considerable influence in the labor unions of New York City. She was testifying one day before the Un-American Activities Committee in Washington, and Senator McGrath of Rhode Island asked her to pay me a visit. "What has he to give me?" Senator McGrath answered: "He teaches communism at the Catholic University, that is to say, he knows the philosophy of Marx and Lenin." The senator then asked her if she was afraid to visit me. She accepted the challenge and telephoned me that she was on the way.

We met in a small outer room at my residence and exchanged generalities, after which I observed: "Dr. Dodd, you look unhappy." She said: "Why do you say that?" I said: "Oh, I suppose, in some way, we priests are like doctors who can diagnose a patient by looking at him." When the conversation came to a dead end, I suggested that she come into the chapel and say a prayer. While we knelt, silently, she began to cry. She was touched by grace. Later on, I instructed her and received her into the Church. With Marx behind her, she began teaching law first in Texas and later at St. John's University in Brooklyn.

My first convert as a young priest was in Washington, D.C., and it illustrates how much Divine Light in the soul, rather than the efforts of the evangelist, produce the harvest. When I went to the Catholic University to begin graduate studies, an aunt of mine asked me to visit a relative of hers who was ill. She was a fairly young, married woman with two children. I had been warned, however, that she was not well disposed to Catholics. When I introduced myself at the front door, she spit in my face and told me to leave. That was in the month of September. Every single morning in Holy Mass I begged God to give her the grace of conversion.

In February I received a telephone call from her. I asked: "Why did you send for me?" She said: "I do not know. I went to the doctor yesterday and he told me that I would be dead in two weeks." She drew her two young children to herself and wondered who would care for them. I assured her that she was not going to die in two weeks and told her of the prayers I offered for her conversion. "The Lord, I believe, is frightening you into the Church." The next day I began explaining the teachings of the Church, baptized her in May and continued to keep in touch with her for many years.

I remember the first convert I made in France, after two years of graduate study in Europe. In preparation for the University of Louvain in the autumn, I spent the summer at the University of Paris to train my ear to French. I lived in a French boardinghouse in the Latin Quarter: rue Jules Chaplain. There were about five or six other boarders in the pension, most of whom were American. After a week, Madame Citroen, who managed the boardinghouse, knocked at my door and said something in French which I could not understand. I called two schoolteachers from Boston who were residents in the pension, and asked them to interpret. Madame had said that she was baptized a Catholic, married in the Church, but after marriage and World War I, her husband left her. One daughter, who was born to them, became a woman of the streets. She added that the boardinghouse was a financial failure, and she felt no reason to live. Then, pulling a small bottle out of her pocket, she said: "This is poison; I intend to take it and do away with my life. Can you do anything for me?" I said, through the interpreter, "Madame, I cannot do anything for you if you intend to take that stuff." I asked her, however, to postpone her suicide for nine days.

I then began a novena to the Sacred Heart at the Church of the Notre Dame des Champs. Kneeling before the statue of the Sacred Heart, I pleaded: "If you really love souls—and you do—then save this one." Every evening of the novena, I would take a dictionary in my left hand, thumb it with my right, and with a contemptuous disregard for tenses, would attempt to stammer out some simple, elementary Christian truth in French. However, knowing that she could not be brought back to the Faith by my poor instructions in French, I had recourse to the confessional. I reasoned that if she would humble herself, and go to Confession, the Good Lord would give her grace.

Two nights before the novena ended, I took her to the St. Joseph Church near the Etoile and asked one of the Irish priests there who spoke French to hear her confession. But she did not receive the gift of Faith. In the meantime, I asked one of the servant girls in the house how long *she* had been away from the sacraments. I then begged her to go to Confession the final day of the novena with Madame. During the confession, the night before the novena ended, she received the gift of Faith, and the following day I gave her Communion; the French maid also received Communion.

In the fall, I went to the University of Louvain. Madame wrote to me, telling me that her daughter was seriously ill in Chartres. She was willing to give up anything, provided God would spare her daughter. I asked her to make an offering of her daughter; it might be a means of reconciling her and her husband. So it happened. Her husband, whom she had not heard from in years, came to visit the sick daughter. The husband and wife were reconciled at the sickbed. The daughter recovered. In the end, grace triumphed as the mother and daughter restored the husband to the Church. The following summer on my way to Lourdes, I stopped at Dax and was driven away to a beautiful chateau in the mountains where, for three days, I enjoyed the hospitality of Monsieur and Madame and Mademoiselle Citroen. When I visited the village priest I asked if the Citroens were practicing the Faith. He did not know the story but answered: "They are the most wonderful Catholics in the

Pyrenees. Isn't it beautiful when people keep the Faith all during their lives!"

Then there is the beautiful story of the conversion of Fritz Kreisler and his wife. I received a letter from a stranger who asked me to call on her uncle. His wife had committed suicide a short time before by throwing herself out the window. The writer asked that I try to bring some consolation to the uncle. The apartment house in Manhattan alongside the East River was the type that had only two apartments to a floor. I went to the apartment where I expected to visit the man in question, but he was not at home. I asked the elevator man who lived in the other apartment, and he told me—Fritz Kreisler.

I rang the bell, introduced myself to Fritz and Mrs. Kreisler, and after a short conversation, asked them if they would like to take instructions for the Church. Fritz Kreisler was one of the finest and noblest men I ever met in my entire life. When I would quote a text from the Old Testament, he would read it in Hebrew; when I would quote a text from the New Testament, Fritz would read it in Greek. One evening during an auto trip together, I observed: "Fritz, tomorrow you are playing your violin on 'The Telephone Hour.'" "Yes." "Will you practice?" "No." "Will you practice before the concert?" "No." With that, Mrs. Kreisler said: "I always contended that if Fritz had practiced, he would have been a great violinist."

When I began my television series, I asked Fritz to write me a theme song for my programs. He gave me about forty or fifty manuscripts that had never been copyrighted. He told me to choose from any one of these, and he would give me the copyright. The one that I chose, as I remember it, was the "Vienna March." I took it back to Fritz. "This is the one that I like, but I cannot march on the stage. Can you change it to waltz time?" Fritz said: "It cannot be put in waltz time." I said: "Fritz, you can transpose anything; please sit down at the piano and try it." "No," he said, "it can't be done." I begged him and he sat down at the piano, played one measure and said: "See, I told you; it cannot be done." With that, Mrs. Kreisler said: "Fritz is in his 'no' mood tonight." She then took him by the hand, walked him down the corridor to another studio at the other end of the apartment. A short time later I heard the strains of my theme song coming from the piano in waltz time. It later became my theme song on television.

I was a very close friend of the Kreislers from the time of their reception into the Church, and it was tragic to see Fritz in his last days, blind and deaf from an automobile accident, but radiating a gentleness and refinement not unlike his music. I visited them every week for some years until the Lord called them from the Church Militant to the Church Triumphant, where I am sure the music of Fritz Kreisler is in the repertoire of Heaven.

Heywood Broun was one of the most distinguished newspapermen in America. Often he had been described

as "looking like an unmade bed," or a "one-man slum."
One Sunday I was passing the Plaza Hotel in New York
with Fulton Oursler. In the main dining room of the
Plaza Hotel we could see Heywood Broun. Fulton Oursler
said: "Did you ever try to make a convert of Heywood?"
When I answered in the negative, he said: "Try it." The
next weekend when I came to New York from Washington, I phoned Mr. Broun: "I should like to see you." He
said: "About what?" "Your soul." "When?" "Three o'clock
Saturday at the Navarro Hotel on Fifty-ninth Street." Mr.
Broun explained: "Yes, I am interested in the Church for
the following reasons: I am convinced that the only moral
authority left in the world is the Holy Father; second, I
made a visit to Our Lady of Guadalupe in Mexico and
was deeply impressed by the devotion to the Mother of
Christ. Finally, and most important, I do not want to die
in my sins."

While I was instructing Mr. Broun he would often
say: "Do not go into detail; I am not going to live long,
just long enough to be absolved from my sins." Inciden-
tally, he was the first person to receive Confirmation from
Archbishop Spellman when he came to New York from
Boston. About a month after I received him into the
Church, I phoned him and said: "Heywood, you have run
about a thousand miles; you had better come in and let
me service you." He came in for Confession and a short
time after that, he died. I preached his eulogy at St.
Patrick's Cathedral, and in the course of the sermon told
the reasons he gave for wanting to become a Catholic.
The next day the Communist *Daily Worker* carried the

headline: "Monsignor Sheen reveals the secrets of the confessional." What were given, of course, were the reasons Mr. Broun gave me when I first met him.

Herbert Hoover and Al Smith were the principal candidates in the 1928 campaign for President. The Hoover campaign was directed by Horace Mann. Bigots during the campaign warned Americans that if a Catholic were elected President, the Pope would sit in the White House. Al Smith answered the bigotry, which he attributed to Mann, in a famous speech delivered in Oklahoma City. In the meantime I was very friendly with Al Smith, and for years took dinner with him every Sunday night. Sometime after the election, I called on Horace Mann and proposed instructions. He said that he could not accept the authority of the Church, for his authority was the Bible. I told him the Bible is not a book, but a collection of books. Someone had to gather them together and authenticate their authorship as inspiration. As the Supreme Court interprets the Constitution, so the Church safeguards the Bible. Furthermore, the Church was established throughout the Roman Empire before any book of the New Testament was written. Later on, Horace Mann and Mrs. Mann were both received into the fullness of the Lord, and Al Smith sent them both a telegram of congratulations on the day of their First Communion. Horace Mann told me that he was in no way responsible for the anti-Catholic side of the Hoover campaign.

Many letters were received in the course of one week asking me to visit friends and relatives in various hospitals in New York. I spent one afternoon and evening making the visitations. The last patient whom I saw this day was on the eleventh floor of Memorial Hospital. I was very happy that the evening was over, for I was hungry and tired. When I descended to the first floor, the elevator man said: "Oh, I forgot to tell you, there was a nurse on the eleventh floor who wanted to meet you." It was one of those moments when you wonder whether or not you should trouble yourself. But I went back. The nurse said: "Oh, I saw you on television, and I just wanted to meet you." "Are you a Catholic?" I asked. "No." "Are you engaged?" "Yes." "Is he a Catholic?" "Yes." I said: "What does he do?" "He is a doctor studying a speciality." I said: "Very well, you and the doctor come to my home tomorrow night for dinner, and begin instructions." I finished instructions for the nurse and later went to Canada to witness their marriage, and in the course of the years, baptized their six sons: Matthew, Mark, Luke, John, Peter, and Paul.

I was told about a leper in New York City. Being interested in that work, on account of visiting leper colonies and because of my association with the Society for the Propagation of the Faith, I spent about six months searching for him. He was put out of his home by his parents when they discovered the disease. His hands and feet were badly twisted and his face bore the marks of the disease. It took several months to drive hatred out of his soul, but then, under the inspiration of grace, he was received into the Church and it has been the happiness of my life to help support him ever since. I had him to my table very frequently and we became close friends.

One evening a well-dressed woman with a rather affected accent called on me. She explained: "I would like to become a Catholic, but I would not want any ordinary priest to instruct me, for I am an intellectual. Knowing your background, would you intellectualize your faith for me?" "Madam," I answered, "I am willing to instruct anyone who comes to me. As a matter of fact, a young man with leprosy who just finished instructions sat in that very chair on which you are seated now." She literally flew out of the house and I never heard from her again.

I put in a telephone call one day to Congresswoman Clare Boothe Luce and invited her to dinner. After dinner, as we got into the subject of religion, I said: "Give me five minutes to talk to you about God, and then I will give you an hour to state your own views." About the third minute, when I mentioned the goodness of God, she immediately bounded out of the chair, stuck her finger

At annual meeting of national directors of
the Society for the Propagation of the
Faith, in Rome, with Pius XII, late 1950s.
*(G. Felici)*

under my nose and said: "If God is good, why did he
take my daughter?" Her young daughter, a short time before, had been killed in an automobile accident. I answered: "In order that through that sorrow, you might be
here now starting instructions to know Christ and His
Church."

Never in my life have I been privileged to instruct anyone who was as brilliant and who was so scintillating in
conversation as Mrs. Luce. She had a mind like a rapier.

If I added up all the summers I spent in St. Patrick's Church, Soho Square, in London, they would amount to six or seven years. Being an American, I opened the church in the morning, for the Americans rose earlier than the English did. This particular Epiphany morning in January, a limp figure fell in—that of a young woman about twenty-four or twenty-five years of age. "How do you happen to be here?" "Well, where am I, Father?" "Oh, 'Father'?" She said: "Yes, I used to be a Catholic, but not any more." I said: "Were you drunk?" She admitted she was. I added: "Men drink because they like the stuff; women drink because they do not like something else. Who are you running from?" She said: "Three men—and they are beginning to find out, so I got drunk."

It was one of those typically cold January mornings in London; she had been exposed to the cold all night long; I made a cup of tea and asked her name. I pointed to a billboard across the street, asking: "Is that your picture over there on the billboard?" "Yes, I am the leading lady in that musical comedy." I invited her to come back that afternoon before the matinee. She agreed on one condition: "that you do not ask me to go to Confession." I said: "I promise not to ask you to go to Confession." She said: "I want you to promise me faithfully not to ask me to go to Confession." I said: "I promise you faithfully not to ask you to go to Confession." That afternoon before the matinee, she returned. I then told her that we had a Rembrandt and a Van Dyck in the church: "Would you like to see them?" As we walked down the side aisle, we passed a confessional. I pushed her in. I did not ask her to go, for I had promised not to *ask* her to go. Two years later I gave her her veil in a convent in London, where she is to this very hour.

Mr. Louis Budenz was the editor of the Communist *Daily Worker* in New York City. He had written a series of articles in the paper attacking me. Many of the articles asked rhetorical questions. I answered all of them in a booklet entitled "Communism Answers the Questions of a Communist"—but not in my own words, only by quotations from Marx or Lenin. When Budenz would lecture in Union Square, New York, many would use my pamphlet to refute him. But a short time after the publication of the pamphlet, he asked to see me. I did not know until years later that the Central Committee of the Communists asked him to contact me in the hope that they could win me over to their cause.

The conversation at dinner opened by his saying: "I tell you what we have against you; you do not believe that Russia is a democracy." I answered: "How can you say that Russia is a democracy in light of Articles 118 to 124 in the Soviet Constitution?" He retorted: "What are those articles?"

I told him I was not interested in discussing communism; I wanted to talk about his soul. Six or seven years passed. Then he wrote and asked to see me again, and returned to the Faith. Only recently did I learn from Mrs.

Budenz that he would not allow any radio in the house to be turned on to me while I spoke—so much did he detest me. Later she asked him why he chose to contact me since he bore such animosity. His answer was: "He told me that he was interested in my soul."

Instructions had to be conducted by stealth. I would drive at night to his home in Westchester and sit around the table with him and his wife. She was a graduate of the University of Pittsburgh and also was willing to take instructions. The instructions went on for several months and were held in the greatest secrecy. Then came the night of his reception into the Church and the eve of his Communion. About seven o'clock that night, I sent word to the Associated Press that Louis Budenz had been received into the Church. A short time afterward, one of the members of the Communist party called me and asked: "Is it true that you have received Louis Budenz into the Catholic Church?" I said: "Don't tell me that the Communist *Daily Worker* is at last interested in the truth?" His retort cannot be found in any manual of prayer. The following morning, Budenz and his wife and children were received into the Church at St. Patrick's Cathedral. It might be added that the conversion of Louis Budenz took the Communist party so much by surprise that the masthead of their *Daily Worker* had his name as editor in chief the day of his coming to Christ.

Continuing other historical incidents of the spirit of God in souls, I recall a surprise visit made one day from a German who told me that he had been with his country's Army in World War I. During a heavy bombardment he said that he jumped from shell hole to shell hole to escape. Immediately after leaving one, a shell exploded in the hole he had left. Most of his companions in the shell hole were Catholics who recited the Rosary. He heard them recite the Rosary so often that he knew the prayers by heart. He promised God that he would become a Catholic if he were preserved safe from the war. That was the reason for his visit to me. Later on we gave him instructions, and he became a professor in one of our American universities.

When I was hearing confessions in a church on the eve of the first Friday each month, a young woman entered and began: "I am not here to go to Confession; I am here to kill time." I asked: "How much time would you like to kill?" She said: "About five minutes." Again I inquired about whom she was trying to fool besides God. "My mother," she said; "she thinks I am going to Confession. She is waiting outside for me." I asked her if she were afraid to go to Confession and she said that she was. I said: "Well, if I could see you, I could probably make your confession for you. Will you let me take down this veil between us and turn on the light?" She agreed. I said to her: "You are a streetwalker." "Yes," she answered. "Well, that is your confession, is it not?" "No," she said, "there is something else." I begged and pleaded with her for twenty minutes or more to tell me—but to no avail. I

then asked her to kneel at the Communion rail for a few
minutes before leaving church. She said that she would
think it over.

On leaving the church, I met her on the steps. I
pleaded with her again for a half hour to tell me why she
would not go to the Sacraments. "I will tell you," she said,
"and then I will leave. Because I was arrested for street-
walking, I was put into the home of the Sisters of the
Good Shepherd. I promised the devil that I would make
nine sacrilegious Communions if he would get me out of
the home. On the ninth day I escaped." With that she ran
away.

When I went back that evening for confessions, I
asked every penitent to recite the Rosary for the conversion of a sinner. All agreed except one. I finished hearing
confessions about nine o'clock, went to the Communion
rail and knelt there from nine until twelve-thirty praying
for her. At twelve-thirty the front door opened. I was almost afraid to look, thinking it might be a policeman
worried about lights in the church after midnight. It was
the girl, who walked immediately into the confessional, to
make her peace with God.

Working in a parish in New York in what was known
then as "Hell's Kitchen," I remember two little girls came
into the rectory with exciting news. "Kitty is sick." I asked
for more details. They were amazed: "Have you never
heard of Kitty? Everybody knows Kitty." The address was
along the Hudson River, fifth floor back. Since they told

me she was seriously ill, I brought the Viaticum, and the Holy Oils. On the fifth floor of this slum apartment, I found in one of the dirtiest rooms that I had ever been in a girl about twenty-one or twenty-two. Scraps of old papers and uneaten food were thrown about the floor. "Are you Kitty?" "Yes, everybody knows me." I asked her about her physical condition and then her spiritual condition.

In regard to the latter she said: "I cannot go to Confession because I am the worst girl in the city of New York." I assured her: "You are not the worst girl in the city of New York; the worst girl in the city of New York says that she is the best girl in the city of New York." She did not understand the paradox. I begged and pleaded with her for a half hour to hear her confession, which she finally made. Her mother, who had been waiting outside the room, and a friend of hers named Anne then came into the room. At this moment she began to lose consciousness. She told me that her husband used to beat her if she did not bring in enough money, since she worked the streets.

A poison administered by her husband was beginning to affect her brain; as it touched the area of senses, she would have the impression of losing that particular sense, which explained her statements: "Here, Anne, is my ear; you keep it when I am gone," "Mother! Here is my eye," and "Father, you take the other eye; this is for you." Not having anointed her, I immediately gave her the Sacrament of the Sick and she began to recover at once. I said: "Kitty, you are back in this world," and she agreed: "Yes, in order to prove that I can be good." From then on she worked to help the same people she had been with on the streets. Every Saturday as I would hear confessions in the parish, I would hear when I opened the slide: "Father, I am the boy Kitty told you about," or "Father, I am the girl Kitty told you about."

One night Kitty came to the rectory, breathless: "I have a girl with me who committed murder." "Where is she?" "She is in the church." "But the church is closed." "Well then, she is across the street on the stoop." She gave me her name and I went to the front door and called her. Pretending that I knew nothing about what troubled her conscience, I merely told stories about God's mercy; they were sufficient for the Good Lord to pour grace into her soul. She later on went to Confession. Kitty continued to be an apostle for as long as I stayed in the parish, and long afterward.

While I was teaching at Catholic University, I used to receive letters almost every few weeks from a baroness in New York. The name was in big letters on the outside of the envelope. Each letter invited me to dinner. I had made it a rule practically never to accept social engagements. The more you become known in the world, the more you have to stay away from it. In any case, having despaired of the invitations that were not accepted, she wrote stating that she was interested in becoming a Catholic.

Each weekend I would go up from Washington to instruct her. About the fifth visit, she inquired: "Are you always going to give me instructions?" I said: "Yes." "You know, I have no money." "I am not giving you instructions because of money; I am only interested in your soul." She pointed to a bracelet around her wrist: "This is not gold; it is made out of thorns that are gilded. You see this necklace about my neck; it is not gold, it is made out of seashells that are gilded." It was probably her intent to convince me that she had no money that prompted her to show me these trinkets.

I finished the instructions and received her into the Church. That summer she invited me to visit her in Paris. Another priest friend and I went over to visit her. She was living in a chateau that once belonged to Louis XV, located about fifteen miles outside of Paris. It was a tremendous edifice with a moat around it and white deer grazing in the park. She was quite elderly when I received her into the Church, and I had the pleasure of supporting her soul with sacraments and prayers at her death.

Not every soul that is instructed remains faithful to the grace. Our Blessed Lord said in the parable about the seed falling in among stones on the roadway: "Sometimes the grace does not fructify unto perseverance." One who came very close to it, and I hope someday finds grace, was a Mr. G. in Paris—a diamond merchant. I had gone from Louvain to Paris to preach on the first Sunday of February. I stayed in a small hotel near the Opéra-Comique. In the parlor an Englishman was playing the piano.

I invited him to dinner that evening. He admitted: "I have never met a priest in my life." "Well, we are just like anyone else," I told him. "If you prick me with a pin, I will jump too." We went to a restaurant near the hotel, and during the dinner he asked me if we priests ever had to answer moral questions.

His moral problem was this: "I have never met one good man or one good woman in my life." I thanked him for the compliment, and he then continued: "This past eleventh of January over at that table there, a woman was trying to break a lump of sugar into a cup of coffee. As she could not do it, I broke the lump for her. She told me how cruel her husband was to her. I asked her to come and live with me, which she did." Continuing his story, he said: "I get tired of these women in about a year, so this morning I bundled up all of her clothes and left them with the concierge. She anticipated my move and left me this note," which he proceeded to hand to me. It read: "Dear Puppy: If you refuse to continue to live with me until the eleventh of February I shall throw myself into the Seine." He asked: "May I continue living with her to prevent her suicide?" "No, you may not do evil that good may come from it; and secondly, she will not commit suicide."

After dinner, he offered to walk me back to the hotel, but I told him: "I am not going back to the hotel; I am going to Montmartre." He said: "I was just beginning to think you are all right, and now you tell me you are going up to that hellhole of Paris." "Yes, but there is something on the hill of Montmartre besides 'dives.' On that hill is the Basilica of the Sacred Heart, where for night and day over fifty years there has been continuous adoration of the Blessed Sacrament." I begged him to go with me. He

refused at first, and then relented—probably out of curiosity.

On the way up to Montmartre on the subway, I told
him: "I have a thousand and one reasons for believing
Christ is present on that altar tonight. You have only one:
because I tell you so. There will be at least a thousand
men in adoration during the night. They are good men
and if they have wives, they are good women, and if they
have children, they are good young men and women.
There *are* good people in the world." As a matter of fact,
when we entered, I recognized in the front row Jacques
Maritain, the philosopher, and also the Romanian Prince
Vladimir. "What shall I do—stand, sit, kneel?" "Do just
as you please." "How long?" "Well, I intended to stay until the sun comes up over Paris tomorrow morning. But,"
I added, "I will leave whenever you care to go." He made
no move to go and the next morning I offered Mass in
the basilica.

As we descended the hill of Montmartre, he asked me
if I would stay in Paris for a few days to teach him to be
good. I promised to meet him that night at his apartment.
At the appointed hour he came into the courtyard with
another woman, not the woman he had mentioned the
previous night. She could speak no English and he could
speak little French. He said to me: "The three of us will
go out to dinner." And I said: "No." Punning on the
French word for crowd, which is *foule*, I said: "Two is
company and three is a *foule*. Furthermore, I have made an
appointment with Mr. G. and I want to see him alone." I
took Mr. G. aside and said: "Tonight you are either go-

ing out with that woman, or you are going out with me."

He walked up and down the yard a few times and then came up to me saying: "Well, Father, I think I will go out with her." Two years later I saw him on the streets of Brussels. He did not recognize me. He was with another woman still—not the woman in the courtyard that evening. I have always had hopes that the good inspiration that he received during the night he spent with the men of prayer will eventually save his soul.

I was giving a Lenten course in the Paulist Church in New York City. After the talk, a young woman came into

13th Mission Assembly in Cebu City, at the ceremony commemorating the 400th Anniversary of the arrival of Christianity in the Philippines, when Sheen spoke to a half-million men at a midnight Mass, 1965. *(Courtesy, Society for the Propagation of the Faith)*

the rectory with a challenge: "I am an atheist; what are you going to do about it?" I answered: "I'll bet you a dime you cannot give me three good arguments for atheism; if you do, I will find three answers in a book that was written seven hundred years ago. She was not able to give three arguments, and so I collected the dime. "You ought to be ashamed not knowing them." I then began instructing her. The instructions lasted for almost a year.

On Easter I gave her First Communion in St. Patrick's. About six weeks after her First Communion, I phoned her: "Are you going to Mass every Sunday?" She replied: "Yes, I go to Mass every day." "Do you go to Communion?" "No." "There is a reason for that. Are you going with a married man?" "Yes," she admitted. That particular evening I bumped into her and this man in the Waldorf-Astoria. He walked on ahead. She said: "I am marrying him before a justice of the peace, for he is not free to marry. He is a Jew and very well known in the theater. Tomorrow we will leave on our honeymoon, which will take us around the world." I said: "L., you will never be happy." Her last words were: "Well, maybe not."

Every Good Friday as I preached the Three Hours in St. Patrick's Cathedral this girl would be under the pulpit, standing the entire three hours. One day I said to her: "Happy?" She said: "Yes, I would be"—pointing to the crucifix—"if it were not for Him." A year or so later, she asked me to give her husband instructions. The husband had been married before to a Jewess. If he came into the Church he would be eligible for the Pauline Privilege. I was reluctant at first to give him instructions, but I finally entered upon them, and he proved to be one of the truest friends of my life. The chapel in my apartment was designed by this celebrated designer—a memorial to his skill and faith.

We made application to Rome for the validation of the marriage because of the Pauline Privilege. In due time it was received. He phoned her, for she was on a ranch in Wyoming, telling her the news to come home and be married in the Church. She said: "Sorry, I am divorcing you; I am marrying a cowboy." She married a cowboy who worked on a summer ranch three or four months a year, and lived three or four miles off the nearest passable road. He was heartbroken and gave up hundreds of thousands of dollars' worth of contracts in the theater and went to Arizona to ride horses and forget his troubles. As I gave him Communion one Christmas night in the Church of the Blessed Sacrament in New York City, tears were streaming down his cheeks. After Mass he brought me a small golden crucifix. He said: "This was the wedding ring L. gave me when she married me; I told her I would never take it off. But when I phoned her in Wyoming and she told me she was divorcing me, I found the ring in the palm of my hand. I had it made into a cross. This was her gift to me—the gift of Faith and the cross of Christ."

This was his second marriage and a failure. I said to him: "You are still free to marry. Since you have had such a failure in picking a woman, I think you should allow me to court the woman and then you marry her." However, he did not pursue the courtship of the young woman I proposed, but married an actress who was received into the Church and I witnessed their marriage in Washington. His wife became an alcoholic and he spent the rest of his life alone, always loving, faithful and devoted to the Church. God gave me the grace to assist at his funeral.

A few years later, I received a telephone call from L., who told me that she was leaving the cowboy and wished to be received back into the Church, to which she is faithful to this day. As Augustine observed: "Late have I loved Thee, O Beauty, so ancient and so new. Late have I loved Thee."

A Jewish jeweler in New York whom I had known for twenty-five years or more was always very kind to me. When I would ask him the price of anything, he would always say: "It cost me . . ." Then he would check through his filing cabinet and be sure of the cost price; that would be the price for me. One year he went to Europe and during the trip at sea, as he was seated at the captain's table, I sent him a cablegram which read: "This cost me $7.87." He said he lost his soup in the reading of that cablegram.

One day he phoned me and said: "Would you like a large number of silver crucifixes?" I went down to see him, and in a little brown bag he had many dozens of silver crucifixes about four inches high. I said: "Where did you get these?" He said: "From Sisters. They brought them in to me and said they were not going to use them any more—wearing the crucifix separated them from the world. They wanted to know how much I would give them for the silver." The jeweler said: "I weighed them out thirty pieces of silver. What is wrong with your Church?" I answered: "Just that! The contempt of Christ and His Cross which makes it worldly." Those words became the channel of the Spirit working in his soul. I explained to him the cost of Redemption, the blood of Christ; he embraced the Faith and died in it.

In the parish where I worked in the early days of my priesthood, I took a census. Instead of knocking only at the doors of Catholics, I went to visit every single house in the poor parish. In a rather poor and tumbledown house, I was met by an elderly woman who told me that she had been a Catholic when she was a young girl. She invited me in and while I was urging her to return to the Church, her son, who was evidently an automobile mechanic (which I gathered from the way he was dressed, and which I later learned was true), came in the back door. He was carrying a monkey wrench in his hand. He saw me in the chair and let the monkey wrench fly at my head. I had to dodge quickly to escape it.

He then went to the stairs and called his wife. The two of them standing over me, he said: "Look what the cat brought in." I said: "I would like to ask you a question or two about how much it would cost to put a new carburetor into a Hudson." He said: "A Hudson is no good, and it is not being made any more." Nevertheless, I insisted upon talking about prices, installation and service. After fifteen or twenty minutes he became rather normal. I said: "My good man, I do not have a Hudson; I am not interested in fixing up an old car." "Why, then, did you tell me you had a Hudson?" "I did not tell you I had a Hudson;

I merely asked you how much it would cost to put a carburetor into a Hudson. I got on this particular subject just to prove that you could be kind." All of them afterward became devout members of our parish.

The pastor told me that he was given a gift of $10,000 to build a shrine altar to Our Lady. I expressed amazement that there was $10,000 in the entire parish. He said: "Well, it was given to me by such and such a woman." My eye ran down that street, and it seemed that none of the houses could be sold for $10,000. I inquired where she could possibly have gotten the money. He said: "Her brother was a bank robber, and I think that she probably was given this money, and is now returning it to the Church in reparation for his soul." I asked if he had ever tried to retrieve the robber, but he said he had not.

That afternoon, I called on the woman and her brother. He sat in an armchair, a very handsome, benign old man with a full head of white hair. I said: "How long has it been since you have been to Confession?" He said: "Seventy years." I said: "Would you not like to make your peace with God?" "No. That would be cowardice. Do you know my record? I have robbed banks and post offices to the tune of a quarter of a million dollars. I have spent over thirty years of my life in jail, and have killed two men. Why should I now, at the end of my life, be a coward and ask God to forgive me?" "Well," I said, "let us see how brave you are tomorrow morning. I will come here to your door at eight o'clock. I will not be alone; I will bring the Good Lord with me in the Blessed Sacrament. I am sure that you will not turn us both away." When I returned in the morning, he opened the door. I heard his confession and gave him Communion—which proved to be Viaticum because he died the next day. He was not the first thief the Lord saved on his last day.

Among the souls who have been treated during my days of "retreading," it just happened that two of them were associated with opera. One of them was a singer; and the other one, a vocal coach. When the coach first came to see me, she said that she was not sure that she would enter the Church. She began by laying down a condition. She said: "There is one thing that you must not talk about because if you do, you would prejudice me against the Church, and that is the crucifix." I said: "Very well, we will now begin with the crucifix because you do not understand it; otherwise you would love it."

When she was received into the Church, she would go backstage at the Metropolitan always holding a crucifix in her hand, reaching it out to singers who were a bit frightened to walk onto the stage, fearful of not fully playing their part. She encouraged them, and now some of them are also carrying the crucifix.

In conclusion, let no one make a false estimate of me and give me undue credit for being a convert-maker. As I said before, just as the tin soldier that a little boy plays with on a carpet before Christmas cannot with a touch of the hand be made into a flesh-and-blood soldier, so neither can I by myself make a Christian. I am only a porter who opens the door; it is the Lord Who walks in and does the carpentry and the masonry and the rebuilding on the inside. I have merely narrated cases where for the most part I had some success as a porter. I did not mention many in which I failed nor those who came into the Church and fell away, nor the occasions I had for bringing others closer to the Light when I failed to take advantage of the opportunity.

Years ago souls were brought to a belief in God by the order in the universe. Today souls are brought to God by disorder within themselves. It is less the beauty of creation and more the coiling serpents within the human breast which bring them to seek repose in Christ. Oftentimes what appears to be a doctrinal objection against the Faith turns out to be a moral objection. Most people basically do not have trouble with the Creed, but with the commandments; not so much with what the Church teaches, as with how the Church asks us to behave.

I remember a stewardess on an international airline who began instructions. When we came to the subject of confession and sin, she said that she could not continue. I begged her to take one more hour of instruction, and then if she did not like what was said, she could leave. At the end of the second hour on that subject, she became almost violent and shouted: "Now I'll never join the Church after what I have heard about confessing sin." I said to her: "There is no proportion whatever between what you have heard and the way you are acting. Have you ever had an abortion?" She hung her head in shame and admitted that she had. *That* was the difficulty; it was *not* the sacrament of Penance. Later on I received her into the Church and baptized her first child. From my experience it is always well never to pay attention to *what* people say, but rather *why* they say it. So often there is a rationalization of the way they live.

*Seventeen*

# THE SECOND VATICAN COUNCIL

In the almost two-thousand-year history of the Church the Second Vatican Council was only the twenty-first that convened. To have been present at that Council and to have had a part in it was one of the great blessings the Lord bestowed on my life. The first Ecumenical Council was held in 325 at Nicaea, now a part of Turkey, and there were only 318 persons participating. The last previous one, the First Vatican Council, was held over a hundred years ago. The definition of ecumenical or general council is a solemn assembly of the bishops of the world called by the Pope to consider and decide, under the leadership of the Vicar of Christ, matters concerning the whole of Christendom. In the speech delivered by Pope John XXIII on the eve of the Council's opening on October 11, 1962, he said: "The coming Ecumenical Council, by virtue of the number and variety of those who will participate in its meetings, evidently will be the greatest of the Councils of the Church held so far." In previous Councils the members mostly came from Europe in general or from the Mediterranean area, but here bishops from every part of the world came to mingle their feet with the dust of the tomb of St. Peter.

The First Vatican Council in 1870 had only 737 attending its opening session; it was held in the right transept of St. Peter's, which had been closed off to accommodate such a meeting. At Vatican Council II, the bishops who numbered about 2,600, along with theologians and expert consultants and representatives of other faiths, swelled the number to over 3,000. The Fathers of the Council—as they were called—were seated on both sides of the large nave of St. Peter's on banks of chairs ten rows high. Since they were dressed in their choir robes, an onlooker would have seen a cascade of color stretching 360 feet from the inner doors of the basilica to the Tomb of St. Peter under the dome.

Every advantage of the electronic age was used. Sometimes small churches have difficulty with their loudspeakers; but there was not a spot in that vast basilica where the voice of the speaker could not be heard. Telephones, typewriters, electronic machines for tabulating ballots, rooms for the press with different language sections, radio and television studios—all the world came to the Church as the Church prepared to go to the world.

Each general meeting of the Council began at nine o'clock sharp every morning, except Saturday and Sunday. The Holy Eucharist was offered as each day's work was begun and was read in a different Rite every day—which meant that there were many non-Latin chants used in the Eucharistic sacrifices, chants peculiar to different parts of the world. After the Mass a fifteenth-century New Testament would be carried to the main altar through the nave and was solemnly enthroned in a place of honor. The bishops then recited a prayer together and intoned the Creed, which was one of the most moving of the daily events of the Vatican Council. In a world torn by a diversity of creeds it was a daily affirmation for all of us in the faith of the centuries.

The official language of the Council was Latin. All documents were in that language and all speeches were spoken in that language though there was the diversity of pronunciation and accent for which I suppose the bricklayers of Babel are to be blamed. Several documents would be passed out to the Council Fathers each day. One of the unrecorded marvels of the Council was the Vatican press, which was able to publish these documents so quickly in such volume and without ever the discovery of a misprint. Material that was presented for discussion had been prepared by special commissions before the Council. It was my honor to have been named to a preconciliar commission—namely, the Catholic Action Commission. I recall that several of the members of this commission were very anxious to introduce a chapter into the Council on tourism. I was about the only one who

could see no value in such a chapter unless it was to remind
the faithful about attendance at the Holy Eucharist on Sun-
days and Days of Obligation. In order to convince me, the
Cardinal who was in charge one day brought a list of the
speeches that Pius XI had given in the course of his Pontificate. He pointed out that he had addressed tourist groups
four times; if the Pontiff thought such a subject was so important why should not I? That night I took home a review
of the talks that the Pontiff had given to other groups and I
found that he had addressed urologists five times. The next
day I argued that inasmuch as the Holy Father had spoken
more to urologists than he had on the subject of tourism, we
should therefore have a chapter on urology. I am sure it was
the only time there was a defense of urologists given in Latin
in a Council. It will be recalled that there was no chapter on
tourism in the Council documents.

Later on, the Holy Father named me to a task with which
I was more familiar: I was named to the Conciliar Commission on the Missions. I pleaded before the commission that
the Congregation for the Propagation of the Faith change its
name because the word "propaganda," as it was known in
Latin, had a bad connotation. My suggestion was rejected on
the grounds that it showed little respect for a congregation
whose name had endured for three centuries. It was interesting to note, however, that after the Council—and certainly
not on account of anything I said—the name of the congregation was changed to the Congregation for the Evangelization of Peoples.

Bishops were asked to send in recommendations before
the Council and I wrote several Latin documents on the missions. I wonder if I was the only Conciliar Father who, be-

fore the Council, asked that there be a chapter on women. I had a strong conviction that the feminine principle in religion had been neglected. Many world religions were without the feminine principle and we were beginning to live in an age when women were coming into their own. I still feel that it would have been well to have included a chapter on women—it certainly was far more important than tourism!

In the Council itself total freedom of speech was granted, the only restrictions being that the discourse be in Latin, that it be limited to ten minutes and that it be relevant to the subject under discussion. If any of these limits was exceeded, Cardinal Felice, who presided over the sessions and who could say anything in Latin, and say it well, would ring a bell. Many a speaker heard these words: *"Habe excusatum, Pater, sed tempus jam elapsum est"* (Excuse me, Father, but your time is up). Or *"Non pertinent ad rem"* (You are getting away from the subject). I believe that I was the only speaker in the Council who was allowed to exceed his time. That was because I was the last speaker during the Council to speak on the subject of the missions. In order to speak at the Council the request had to be handed to Cardinal Felice at least three days before the expected time of speaking. On each of two days I was told that I would be called to speak that day but I was never called. On the third and last day, Cardinal Agagianian, who was the head of the Congregation for the Propagation of the Faith, asked Cardinal Felice to cut short the proceedings just before I spoke. Why he did this, I have no way of knowing. I do know that Cardinal Felice told him: "Sheen will speak." And Sheen did, the report of which is to be found in the Council Daybook, Vatican II, Session 3, pages 233 and 234 (Bishops' Conference, Washington, D.C.).

During the Council, which lasted from October 1962 to December 8, 1965, there were 168 general meetings and 10 plenary ones. One hundred forty-seven reports were made and there was 2,212 speeches. Applause followed some discourses of the Fathers and this was permitted.

I would be in my seat early each morning in the Council and my interest generally was riveted on those who had suffered for the Church. I delighted in seeing Bishop Thomas Quinlan, the Columban bishop from Korea, of whom an American general said that every time he saw him during the war he had a man on his back. Forty-nine bishops from Red-ruled countries received permission to attend the Second Vatican Council. The greatest number came from Poland and Yugoslavia; other bishops were from Cuba, Hungary, Czechoslovakia, Bulgaria and East Germany. Only one of the three cardinals whose nations had been taken over by communism was present, namely, Cardinal Wyszynski, the Primate of Poland, the Archbishop of Warsaw. One of the most striking of all those from Red-dominated countries was a Yugoslav bishop who had had gasoline poured over him and then had been set afire. His appearance almost resembled that of a walking ghost. But to those of us who came from the affluent countries of the West, and I am sure from other parts of the world, the greatest inspiration came from those dry martyrs who died a thousand deaths to testify to the Faith that was represented by all in that Council.

Each of the major subjects discussed in the Council—thirteen in all—was introduced by a *relator*. Every member was permitted to speak and to hand in (in Latin) observations concerning suggested changes. These were called "interventions," and would pass into the hands of commissions and ultimately a theological commission. In the course of the entire Council there were 4,361 written interventions. The voting cards permitted three options—*placet* (yes), *nonplacet* (no), and *juxta modum* (with reservations). As an example of the way the voting changed as debates and discussions went on, the following sample is the voting on the Decree on Religious Life. After preliminary discussions and debates and presentation of *modi*, the voting was as follows:

| ARTICLES | PRESENT | YES | NO | YES WITH RESERVATIONS | INVALID |
|---|---|---|---|---|---|
| I–3 | 1955 | 871 | 77 | 1005 | 2 |
| 4 | 1960 | 1049 | 64 | 845 | 2 |
| 5–6 | 1949 | 883 | 77 | 987 | 2 |
| 7–10 | 1950 | 907 | 66 | 975 | 2 |
| II–13 | 1946 | 940 | 56 | 947 | 3 |
| 14 | 1844 | 1676 | 65 | 103 | 0 |
| 15–17 | 2122 | 1833 | 63 | 226 | 0 |
| 18–19 | 2117 | 1936 | 50 | 131 | 0 |
| 20 | 2112 | 1639 | 50 | 419 | 4 |

Many votes after this one were taken and finally after more debates and discussions the solemn juridical and decisive vote was taken with 2,321 Fathers present, of whom 2,317 voted yes, with 4 against the decree—but there were 4 who voted against every chapter because they believed that the Vatican Council should not have been held.

One aspect of the Council that has been rarely touched upon is the humor. The amount of humor that anyone gets out of the world is the size of the world in which he lives. Materialists have only this cosmos as the raw material for their humor. Not so with 2,500 bishops, who are using time only for the sake of eternity and who, therefore, live in the heavens by hope as well as on the earth. There is a greater raw material for humor when one expects another life than this one; then there is no burden to take the world too seriously. The humor of the Council came out of the various characterizations that were printed and spoken about those in Council. For example, Cardinal Ottaviani had as his motto *Semper Idem* (Always the Same). Because he was generally opposed to any changes by the Fathers, stories soon became current that one day he asked the taxi driver to drive him to the Council but the driver took him to Trent, a town in northern Italy where a Council was held in the sixteenth century.

Under the two great tiers which seated about 1,200 bishops on each side of the basilica, there were two coffee bars. It was not long before the Fathers found names for them. One was called Bar-Jona, which was part of the Hebrew name for St. Peter.

Referring to the camaraderie that prevailed among the bishops, this rhyme was composed by a bishop from Australia's great desert at the beginning of the Council:

> *Call us comrades, or cobbers or mates,*
> *Or even buddies, the term in the States.*
>> *Secure in the knowledge*
>> *We belong to the College,*
> *With the Pope we're to have tête-à-têtes.*

Cardinal Suenens, when he addressed the Council on the subject of women, inspired this humorous reflection:

*Said Suenens, in one Congregatio:*
*I'm weary of this Segregatio.*
*The Patres are churls,*
*Let's bring in the girls,*
*Though there's sure to be some admiratio.*

The theologians and other experts or *Periti* were not allowed to mingle among the Council members. Several of them were conspicuous for slipping into the restricted area, which prompted a jingle ascribed to Cardinal Felice reminding them to remain in their proper places:

*Our Secretary's not sympathetic*
*To an expert who's peripatetic.*
*He thinks a Peritus*
*Should remain in his situs*
*Unless he's rather dyspeptic.*

Bishop Stephen Leven of the Diocese of San Angelo, Texas, gave a speech in the Council in which he was rather critical of bishops of a certain nationality. The next day these verses were circulated:

*From Texas came young Bishop Leven*
*Where the six-shooters are six and not seven,*
*Saying "They give me the pip,"*
*He blazed away from the hip,*
*Sending numerous bishops to heaven.*

Cardinal Cushing of Boston did not speak often but when he did it was in loud tones:

> *Cardinal Cushing of Boston avows*
> > *Though he's not a Latin scholar*
> > *He can certainly holler,*
> *At the Council he brought down the house.*

With regard to the sacredness of life and the discussion on the limitation of birth, these lines appeared:

> *Some moralists claim that the Pill*
> *May be used even though you're not ill.*
> > *It gives the ability*
> > *To banish fertility*
> *But I can't really think it's God's Will.*

Finally, when the time came for the bishops to leave at the closing of the Council, this last rhyme came from Bishop John P. O'Loughlin, who had so delighted the Council Fathers:

> *As we bishops depart from old Roma*
> *We can proudly display our diploma*
> > *At the Council's finale*
> > *We say "buon natale"*
> *And "goodbye" to Bar-Jona's aroma.*

Bishop O'Loughlin is still the Bishop of Darwin, Australia.

The Vatican Council was held at that period of history when it was necessary to strike a balance between two extremes both in the world and in the Church: *individualism* and *social-ism*. By individualism I mean the emphasis on the right of the individual either to develop his own spirituality or econom-ically to increase his own capital without much concern for the social good. By socialism I mean the stress on social wel-fare with little concern for either the individual's religion or his morals.

I am sure that many priests have had the same experience that I have had—that previous to the Council one hardly ever heard of a sin against social justice, for example, paying shamefully low wages to a farm laborer or a maid or an em-ployee. Then quickly under the impact of Marx and commu-nism, the whole emphasis was thrust to the social order, to the care and service of the poor, to the defense of environ-ment, care for the inner city and the refugees.

What the Council did was establish equilibrium or bal-ance between these extremes—between evangelization and human progress, between soul-winning and society-saving, between divine salvation and human liberation. It made both inseparable. The Council decided that we must beget children of God through evangelization but not without giving witness to fraternal love and a sensitiveness to hu-manity's desire for freedom and justice. For the first time in the history of all the Councils of the Church, there was a chapter on "The World" in which there was stressed *the unity of creation and redemption*; and the truth that the dignity and freedom of the human person is inseparable from sal-vation. It was a master stroke under the inspiration of the Holy Spirit, that bishops gathered from all over the world could see the new direction the Church must take—which actually was nothing else than the old direction that Christian salvation has an earthly and historical dimension, namely, the relation of the love of God and love of neighbor.

Once the Vatican Council was over and even before it had finished, bishops became sensitive to two extremes that were springing up in their dioceses and among the priests, religious and people, and it all came about by misunderstanding the word "world." One of the very famous interventions delivered in the Council was made by a Belgian bishop who made a very clear distinction between the world as the cosmos which God made and which is good, and the world as a spirit which is inimical to the Church and which is guided by the primacy of the world and the flesh and the devil.

Those of us who were at the Council knew the balance that was being struck between being *in* the world and not *of* it, but it was very difficult to convince either of the two ex-

At St. Peter's during the Second Vatican Council. *(Courtesy, Society for the Propagation of the Faith)*

tremes—the conservatives and the worldlings—of how the spiritual and social were to be combined.

The document on "The Church and the World"— brought forth some of the most balanced thinking from the Council. Cardinal Journet noted that man is a member of two societies—one spiritual, the other temporal. He added that man's relation with God transcends the temporal order, that a man in error in matters of religious truth within the temporal order *is still a human being* and must not be coerced by civil society unless the public welfare is involved.

Despite the fact that several of the speakers, such as Cardinal Silva of Santiago, Chile, and Cardinal Bea, the distinguished Jesuit ecumenist, found fault with the document's Latin, the Council bishops generally followed the American bishops and their stress on religious liberty.

Paragraph 30 formed with great clarity the balance of the personal and the social, and declared that "no one ignoring the trend of events or drugged by laziness contents himself with merely individualistic morality. It grows increasingly true that the obligations of justice and love are fulfilled only if each person, contributing to the common good, according to his own abilities and the needs of others, also promotes the public and private institutions dedicated to bettering the conditions of human life ... Let everyone consider it his sacred obligation to esteem and observe social necessities as belonging to the primary duties of modern man."

No one adverts today to the many delicate issues that were considered in this chapter. It is remarkable that the final vote was 2,309 in favor and only 75 against. No one who attended that final session will ever forget the moving words of Paul VI as he described modern man as

*. . . the tragic actor of his own plays—as the superman of yester-*
*day, and today, ever frail, unreal, selfish and savage; man unhappy with*
*himself as he laughs and cries, man the versatile actor ready to perform*
*any part; man the narrow devotee of nothing but scientific reality; man*
*as he is a creature who thinks and loves and toils and is always waiting*
*for something—man sacred because of the innocence of his childhood,*
*because of the mystery of his poverty, because of the dedication of his*
*suffering, man as an individual and man in society, man who lives in*
*the glories of the past and dreams of those of the future; man the sinner*
*and the saint.*

The tensions which developed after the Council are not
surprising to those who know the whole history of the
Church. It is a historical fact that whenever there is an out-
pouring of the Holy Spirit as in a General Council of the
Church, there is always an extra show of force by the anti-
Spirit or the demonic. Even at the beginning, immediately
after Pentecost and the descent of the Spirit upon the Apostles, there began a persecution and the murder of Stephen. If
a General Council did not provoke the spirit of turbulence,
one might almost doubt the operation of the Third Person
of the Trinity over the Assembly.

After an early Council there were a dozen or more pseudo
Councils held throughout the Christian world trying to re-
establish Arianism, which at one time was in danger of
swamping the Church. In the Second Vatican Council it was
not schism or heresy that was at issue, but rather the Church
and the world. The world pouring into the Church and the
Church rushing into the world. Man was becoming the center and reference point of everything; this the Church could

not accept, for it was the Church's mission to affirm a divine intervention in the world. The Church could not pull up all the drawbridges, lock all the doors, close all the highways which united herself to the world. The answer was not to be found either in an isolation from the world by erecting a red "STOP" light outside of St. Peter's Square; neither could the Church answer the same challenge the world hurled at its Head on the Cross: "Come down and we will believe." "Come down from your belief in the sanctity of marriage." "Come down from your belief in the sacredness of life." "Come down from your belief; the truth is merely what is pleasing." "Come down from the Cross of sacrifice and we will believe."

It was this world the Vatican Council had to deal with, and every one of the bishops who went into that Council had in his heart a love for the Vicar of Christ. To be a part of that Council, to mingle with more than two thousand bishops from different nationalities and cultures, and to sing the Creed together with them each morning is a Council of Nations which would make the United Nations blush for want of a common commitment.

The Council of Trent, which was held four hundred years ago, was a Mediterranean Council; it was Latin; it was European. Vatican Council I was equally Mediterranean. There was not one single bishop in that Council in 1870 from Africa or Asia. In Vatican Council II, 60 per cent of the bishops were from Asia, Africa and North and South America. I remember when I started as National Director of the Society for the Propagation of the Faith, there were only 2 native bishops in all of Africa. As I write these lines, there are over 250 and they are multiplying every month. For the first time in the history of the Church, the dust of the world mingled with the dust of Peter. If there was any one word that came out of the Second Vatican Council that would symbolize change it was that word—"world."

Those who read the Documents of Vatican Council II have no idea how much care and preparation went into every word they contained. Having been on several commissions both prior to the Council and after it, I can testify to how we would discuss various Latin words for a day in order to arrive at a precise meaning. Then, after a chapter was prepared, printed and given to the Council Fathers, the debates on each subject went on for months until finally there were hammered out documents that were acceptable to all except a very few who voted against them, either because they felt there should never have been a Council, or because a pet idea of theirs had not been incorporated.

Here is an example. One of the most sacrifical bishops in the Church, whose life is totally identified with the oppressed, is Dom Helder Camara of Brazil, who spoke with enthusiasm about calling the Church "the Church of the Poor." The Council floor heard all the arguments advanced by him and Cardinal Lercaro. The Theological Commission set up a special subcommission to study the text and the expression "the Church of the Poor" was rejected because of its ambiguity. One of the grave dangers in any discussion is to take a simplistic point of view and divide all mankind into two classes—the rich and the poor, or the oppressors and the oppressed. It seems to have a divine approval, for St. Paul wrote: "For your sake He made Himself poor though He was rich so that you might become rich by His poverty."

With Cardinal Spellman and Pope Paul VI in Rome during the Council, mid-1960s. *(G. Felici)*

But when a study was made of the Greek in the New Testament it was found that the Greeks had two words for "poor." One word is *penes*, which describes a man who has to work for a living, and who never has a surplus but exists from hand to mouth. The other Greek word is *ptochos*, which means absolute and abject poverty—a poverty that is beaten to its knees, a poverty that has nothing at all. The First Beatitude does not use the word *ptochos* but *penes*, the man who has no earthly resources whatever and *therefore must put his whole trust in God.* When Our Lord spoke that Beatitude He did not mean that living in slums is a blessed state, or not having enough to eat, but rather it is a *poverty of spirit* which realizes utter lack of resources to secure pardon and mercy and forgiveness. That is why it is followed by the Second Beatitude in Matthew of weeping because of a broken heart. Blessed is the man who is intensely sorry for his sin, the man who is heartbroken for what sin has done to His Christ, and who is appalled by the havoc that is wrought by sin. The text from Qumran uses the expression "poor in spirit" which leaves no doubt about the Gospel understanding of the poor.

Furthermore the Fathers of Vatican Council II later on, in speaking of the Blessed Mother, said: "She stands out among the poor and humble of the Lord who confidently await and receive salvation from Him." This certainly does not mean liberation from material poverty or social oppression. The Council Fathers were willing to admit that the economically poor had a greater subjective inclination to the Kingdom of Heaven; but they are not the only ones—for there are humble, rich people as there are also proud, poor people who resist the grace of God and, therefore, the Council Fathers settled on the definition of the Church as the "visible instrument of Christ" or the "universal sacrament of salvation." She was meant to be the Church of all men or "of the people." "Among the people" the Church may have a preference, though not an exclusive preference, and still less a "class option" for the poor, the slum dwellers, the abandoned, the destitute and the orphaned.

I wonder if it was not a reading of the media rather than the reading of the decisions of the Council which made so many Sisters abandon the classroom for the inner city. And was it not the failure of many priests to read the Council's distinction of the world as a theater of redemption and a spirit which is anti-Christ which prompted so many to abandon pastoral activities and to be more concerned with management as imitation and the industrial life of the world.

Added to this is the number of meetings called by the bishops of various heads of departments which keep priests and religious away from their assigned duties, to enter into fruitless prolonged dialogues which manifest little light but much heat.

# Eighteen

# THE
# LIGHTER SIDE

By nature I am a rather serious person. But in a paradoxical kind of way, I am very fond of humor and laughter. I have had several discussions with Milton Berle on this subject and he has attributed humor to me though I have never claimed to possess it as a gift. There may be incidental flashes of it here and there but it is not one of God's gifts to me. However, there is a close relationship between faith and humor. We say of those who lack a sense of humor that they are "too thick"; that means they are opaque like a brick wall. Humor, on the contrary, is "seeing through" things like a windowpane. Materialists, humanists and atheists all take this world very seriously because it is the only world they are ever going to have. He who possesses faith knows that this world is not the only one, and therefore can be regarded rather lightly: "swung as a trinket about one's wrist." To an atheist gold is gold, water is water and money is money. To a believer everything in this world is a telltale of something else. Mountains are not to be taken seriously. They are manifestations of the power of God; sunsets are revelations of His beauty; even rain can be a sign of His gentle mercy. I remember once meeting a doorman at the Great Southern Hotel in Killarney. I said to him as I came out of the hotel door: "Oh, it's raining." He put out his hand and said: "You call that rain, Father. That's holy water from Heaven and it's blessing yourself you ought to be doing with it," as he signed himself with the sign of the Cross.

All the parables of Our Blessed Lord are tokens of something eternal. Camels, eyes of needles, patches on clothing, seed on a roadway, the quickness of the lightning flash, redness of the western sky—all these reminded Him of moral and spiritual lessons in the Kingdom of God. That is why He began each parable with: "The Kingdom of God is like . . ." The only thing He ever took seriously was a soul. He did not take even death seriously, for death is a condition of life.

In the early days when I was on national radio, a man came into St. Patrick's Cathedral one Monday morning and, not recognizing me, said: "Father, I want to go to Confession. I commute from Westchester every day. I had three friends with me—all Protestants. I became very angry and spoke most disparagingly and bitterly of that young priest that is on radio, Dr. Fulton Sheen. I just cannot stand him. He drives me crazy. I am afraid that I probably scandalized those men by the way I talked about a priest. So, will you hear my confession?" I said: "My good man, I don't think you committed a serious sin. There are moments in my life when I share exactly the same opinion about Dr. Sheen that you do. Go to Communion and reserve your confession for another day." He left very happily, saying: "It certainly is wonderful to meet a nice priest like you."

I gave many Advent sermons in Blessed Sacrament Parish in Manhattan. During World War II, a woman came into the rectory before Mass and said to me: "Every time I cross Seventy-sixth and Broadway on my way to Mass I get a pain in my left ankle. At that moment, the Blessed Mother speaks to me and says: 'Tell Monsignor Sheen that I want him to go

Sheen with Milton Berle and Mayor Vincent R. Impellitteri of New York at a telethon, 1950s. (*Courtesy, Society for the Propagation of the Faith*)

to Germany at once to convert Hitler.' " I said to her: "My dear lady, it's very peculiar that every time I cross Seventy-sixth and Broadway, I get a pain in my right ankle. The Blessed Mother appears to me and says: 'Do not pay any attention to what I told that lady this morning.' " She went away satisfied.

For many years I preached the Easter Sunday sermon at the ten o'clock Mass at St. Patrick's Cathedral. Admission was by ticket only. One Easter morning about an hour before Mass, a gentleman came in and said: "I will give fifty dollars for a ticket to hear Bishop Sheen." I said to him: "You can have the pulpit for fifty." That was clue enough for him to recognize me.

On a train trip from New York to Boston, I sat next to an Episcopalian clergyman. We began a friendly discussion on the validity of Anglican Orders. He contended he was a priest as much as I was, that he could offer the Holy Sacrifice of the Mass and that he could forgive sins. He was well versed in history and in theology and our discussion proved to be so interesting that many passengers gathered around us to listen to the friendly debate. He got off the train at Providence. He advanced several steps, then turned around and, facing the audience which we both enjoyed, thought he would give me the last telling challenge by saying: "Remember, Bishop Sheen, I can do anything you can do." I just had time to answer: "No you can't. I can kiss your wife, but you can't kiss mine."

On the occasion of the Emmy Awards every recipient thanked producers, directors, friends, colleagues and assistants. When my name was called out for an award, I was momentarily lost for words and then it struck me: since everyone was thanking others, I should say a word of thanks, too. "I wish to thank my four writers, Matthew, Mark, Luke and John." Milton Berle later on claimed that line as his own. But he made up for it by giving me credit for many humorous remarks which I had not the talent to make.

A good retort is always enjoyed by an audience. One of the brilliant ones that I recall was that of the great Methodist preacher John Wesley. In the sermon he quoted a word of Greek and then of Hebrew to explain a text. Someone in the audience shouted: "God does not need your learning." To which Wesley retorted: "He doesn't need your ignorance either." This reminds me of a lecture I was giving to a group of university students in Minnesota. In the question period that followed, one asked me how Jonah was in the belly of the whale for three days. I answered: "I have not the vaguest idea, but when I get to Heaven, I will ask Jonah." He shouted back: "Suppose Jonah isn't there." I said: "Then you ask him."

In the course of my life I have given hundreds of lectures on different subjects. When one lectures an audience for an hour, even though one uses no notes, as I never did, an audience naturally becomes tired. I always thought it well, therefore, to have a few good stories to tell to change the pace of the lecture and to give the audience a bit of mental repose or, better, a moment of laughter.

The following story always went over well before the end of a lecture and was helpful in holding the audience's attention—and so, I have often told it: "A family moved from Dublin to Boston. One of the sons later on moved to Chicago. The father died in Boston. The son in Chicago wired his brother inquiring: 'What were Father's last words?' A telegram came back: 'Father had no last words. Mother was with him to the end.' "

Another story which changes the pace for an audience is an incident that happened in San Francisco. The speaker who preceded me on the platform that day was handed a program by his wife, who was immediately below the dais at a nearby table. It was very easy to read her message. Scribbled across the program were the words K-I-S-S PHYLLIS. When he finished speaking, I said: "Wasn't that nice of your wife to give you that message." He said: "Oh, it doesn't mean what you think it does. It means 'keep it short, stupid.' "

Once a taxi driver in New York who recognized me said: "I never had much of an education—not beyond the third grade. But I pick up many people who use big words, so I have learned to speak, too." He then went on to say how much he enjoyed me on television. "What I enjoy particularly is your voice. You have a wonderful voice. It has so much *animosity* in it."

During one of the thirty visits I made to Lourdes in my lifetime, there was a pilgrimage from Leeds, England. At the same time, there was a pilgrimage from Uganda. Some black priests from Uganda went to the English Bishop and said: "We have no bishop. Therefore, we cannot have a Pontifical Mass of our own. But we would like to share yours. May we supply all the ministers at the altar, the choir and the altar boys?" So it was agreed. I was to be the preacher. As I approached the Bishop on the throne surrounded by his black assistants, he leaned over to me and whispered: "Dr. Livingstone, I presume."

Coming back again to Ireland and that same hotel in Killarney, I once hired a jitney driver to show me a view of the lakes. When we finished the drive and we returned to the hotel, I said: "How much do I owe you?" He said: "Father, I have a wife and ten children. I leave it to you." I pride myself on being a good tipper. This time, I gave him what I thought was a very generous fee. And then, in addition to that, what I believed to be a generous tip. Whereupon he took the blanket from off the horse and threw it around the horse's head and said: "Father, I'd be ashamed to let the horse see you giving me this."

Countless are the stories that came to me as a result of television. It is unfortunate that I have not kept the letters of mothers whose children revealed a lighter side of life. A Canadian mother once told me that her two young children, six and three, seemed to be extraordinarily quiet. She suspected something was wrong, found the boy, aged six, in the attic with a suitcase and dressed in hat and coat. "Where are you going?" the mother asked. He said: "I am going to New York to see Bishop Sheen." "But where is your sister?" "She's in the suitcase."

Another mother wrote that her son was under her feet in the kitchen and she said to him: "Go into the parlor, turn on the television, listen to Bishop Sheen. He's smart. You will learn something." He did as he was told and at the moment I appeared on television, I was writing the word "sex" on the blackboard. He ran out to his mother and said: "He is not so smart. He doesn't know how to spell six."

Another handy story I've often told during lectures to stir up an audience is about a Scripture professor who was lecturing on the twelve minor prophets of the Old Testament. He had finished about four of them in an hour and a half.

Sheen with George Gobel, both honored at Sylvania Television Awards Foundation dinner, New York City, mid-1950s. Gobel, whose show aired on Saturdays in those days, recently recalled that at the award presentation Bishop Sheen quipped: "I trust the Lord will forgive me for being a little fast with my last few penitents. But I wanted to get home from church in time to watch George Gobel on TV." *(Wagner International Photos)*

Realizing his audience was getting tired, he introduced the next prophet with some degree of histrionics. Throwing out his hands he shouted: "And now where shall I place Habacuc?" Someone got up in the back of the hall and shouted out: "He can take my seat."

One Sunday, preaching in a parish church in Ohio, a mother in the front seat got up with a crying child and quickly made her exit down the middle aisle. I stopped the sermon and said: "Madam, do not worry, the child is not disturbing me." She said: "No, but you're disturbing the child."

In the very beginning of my lecturing and after-dinner talks, I had the privilege of addressing New York schoolteachers at the Waldorf-Astoria in New York. That very morning an article had appeared in the *New York Times* by Einstein, saying he could never accept a religion of love or a religion of law, but only a religion of the cosmos. In the course of my talk to the teachers, I reflected on that: "I doubt very much whether Dr. Einstein gets any satisfaction out of worshiping the cosmos. I do not believe that a man can love anything he cannot get his arms around. The cosmos is too big and too bulky. That is why God had to become a child in order that we might embrace Him to our heart." Among the protests for saying a word against Einstein was a letter from a woman in Washington. "How dare you say I cannot love anyone unless I can get my arms around him?" I answered her: "Madam, that is not my problem, that is yours."

During my student days at the Catholic University as a young priest, I was chaplain at St. Vincent's Orphan Asylum. I would read Mass every morning about six o'clock for the Sisters and the young girls. The orphanage was about a mile from the university and I would spend the time on the journey preaching to the telephone poles and the trees. There was a good-natured black lady who helped the Sisters in the kitchen. She seemed to have many men friends and always called upon the good Sister who did the cooking to write her love letters. One day the Sister said to her: "Now, what do you want me to say in this letter?" The woman answered: "I don't care what you say as long as you use the word 'notwith-standing.'"

I gave many lectures in Philadelphia and each year for a number of years, one was given at the Town Hall. One evening I lost my way and I asked a few boys for directions.

They told me where it was and then they asked: "What are you going to do there?" I said: "I'm going to give a lecture." "On what?" they asked. I did not tell them the title of the lecture but simplified it by saying: "Boys, I'm going to talk on Heaven and how to get there. Would you like to come and find out?" They said: "You don't even know the way to the Town Hall."

On a train trip from Washington to New York in the days when I was a professor at the university, I sat at a table in the dining car directly opposite someone who was using very crude and broken English. I looked up at him and he said: "I know you." I answered: "I know you. You are Tony Galento." He bade me sit with him. I said: "Tony, are you boxing tonight?" He said: "Yes." "Will you win?" "I always win." I said: "Tony, I have never talked to a professional boxer before. I wish you would give me some insights into this sport or showmanship, whatever you call it." He said: "No, I would rather talk to you about a novena." I pressed for information on boxing, and Galento pressed for communicating to me his views about a novena. In order not to scandalize him, I said: "All right, Tony, tell me the story." He said: "My father was very sick and dying. Some nuns who live near us came over to visit. They brought a small statue, put it beside his bed and said to him: 'Mr. Galento, we're going to pray for you for nine days and you are going to get better.' At the end of the nine days, my father recovered." In order to show proper interest in this felicitous answer to prayer, I said: "Tony, whose statue was it?" He hesitated a moment and then said: "Is it a mortal sin to say 'Jesus'?"

Here is a true story which I attest to on my word of honor. But because a brother bishop is involved, and in order that he might have a greater immortality than this story gives him, I will leave him anonymous. The scene took place during Lent in a cathedral in a large city. The priest in the pulpit was conducting the Way of the Cross. He was interrupted by a totally naked man running down the center aisle of the cathedral, then making a left turn and running down the side aisle out of the church. This elderly bishop, who by this time was getting to be a little senile, saw the naked man, clapped his hands loudly and shouted at him as he went by: "Young man, in this cathedral, we walk, not run."

This incident also really and truly happened in Chicago. This particular evening a husband and wife were looking at my television show. A knock at the door; a man came in and said: "Oh, I see you have Bishop Sheen on television. May I sit down with you and look at him? I enjoy him so much." When the show ended, he tied them up and ransacked the house. That's how much influence I had on his life.

One day on a New York subway when the door opened at Forty-second Street a drunk got in and threw himself alongside of me and began reading a paper which I doubted very much he could see in his condition. Then he said to me: "How does a man get diabetes?" I said: "Oh, by getting drunk and paying no attention to his wife and children." A moment later I was sorry for having made that quick diagnosis. I asked him: "Why did you want to know how a man got diabetes?" He said: "I was just reading that the Pope had diabetes."

While National Director of the Society for the Propagation of the Faith, I did not have far to walk from the residence on Thirty-eighth Street near Park Avenue to our office near the Empire State Building. But each day going and com-

Sheen and Ed Sullivan for Look Award, Sunday, December 30, 1956.
*(Courtesy, Society for the Propagation of the Faith)*

ing I would pass the old home of John Pierpont Morgan.
The Lutherans had bought it and now they were making an
addition, a five-story building. This particular day one of the
hardhat workers recognized me and said: "What do you
think of us Catholics putting up a building for these lousy
Methodists?" I said: "They're not Methodists, they're Lutherans and they are friends of ours." One of them looked
up to another hardhat standing on a rafter on the fifth floor
and shouted out: "All right boys, put in the rivets."

One of my converts was a Jewish woman, jolly and fat. I
hesitated for a time about receiving her into the Church, for
she found it difficult to learn. But finally convinced of her
deep faith, I baptized her. Six months later she wrote me that
she went down to Laurel, Maryland, to marry a divorced
man. After getting the preacher out of bed, who had to pre-

pare himself for the ceremony, she said to her prospective husband and the preacher: "I don't think Bishop Sheen is going to like this." She walked out, unmarried. She then wrote to me and told me how ashamed she was of what she had done. A few years later, I met her and she had lost dozens and dozens of pounds. "My dear Mrs. M.... how did you happen to lose so much weight?" She said: "I keep a picture of the Sacred Heart on the inside of the refrigerator door." She was spending her time taking care of cancer patients without remuneration, thus proving that she deserved the gift of Faith.

Having gone to Los Angeles to give a few sermons and lectures, I packed my full regalia. Arriving at the hotel in the morning, I went out for the day. When I came back I found that the maid had completely unpacked my bag. One of the vestments which a bishop wears is called a rochet. The rochet is linen from the shoulders down to the waist, and lace from the waist down to the knees. To my surprise, when I got back that night I found my pajamas on one bed and the rochet on the other.

In upstate New York, I cannot remember which city, a new auditorium had been built. For two years it had not been filled, although to draw crowds they had tried dancing, wrestling, boxing and theatricals. One usher said to the other: "Well, it's going to be filled next Thursday night." The other asked: "Why, who's coming?" He said: "Bishop Sheen." The other usher said: "Who's he wrestling?"

*Nineteen*

# THINGS LEFT UNSAID

Every full life is like a triangle. Not only are we made in the image and likeness of God Who is triune, but we are remade in the three purifications mentioned in Scripture: crosses, cups and tensions.

    I. Crosses come from without. The burden laid on the shoulders of Christ: "His government is on His shoulders" was not tailor-made. It comes not from His people but from Caesar. A cross in life is unrelated to the way we live. The Jews in the fiery furnace at Auschwitz and the starved and beaten in the Gulag Archipelago did nothing to deserve a cross except commit the crime of believing in God.

2. Cups filled with bitter dregs come from God. "Shall I not drink the cup My Father gave me?" Was it not from Pilate, or Judas, or Caiaphas or the people? No, they were only the hands through which the Father passed the cup filled with the world's sin, and which the Son had to drink even to the last dregs, lest one drop of the world's iniquity fall to the earth and like Abel's blood cry for further redemption.

3. Tensions between persons come from within the Church, as with the believers Paul and Mark. Both were pillars of the Church, one carrying the Epistle, the other the Gospel. But they had a difficulty. And it was so sharp that Paul took Silas in one direction while Barnabas went with Mark to Cyprus. But all is forgotten when they were united in a reconciliation "profitable to the ministry."

Elsewhere in this book I have written about sufferings from outside the Church, and about cups from the Father, but here a brief word about tensions. Two men of God, both with a vivid sense of the world's need of the Christian Gospel, know in their hearts that difficulties between them are unworthy of the One Who forgave the crucifiers.

The curious would like me to open healed wounds; the media, in particular, would relish a chapter which would pass judgment on others, particularly because, as a French author expressed it: *hous vivons aux temps des assassins*—"we live in days of assassins"—where evil is sought in lives more than good in order to justify a world with a bad conscience. Father Tabb once compared fighting clerics to fighting cats and highlighted the stupidity of it all in:

*They fought like demons of the night*
*Beneath the shrunken moon,*
*And all the roof at dawning light*
*With fiddle strings was strewn.** 

In any case, the greatest wars any person has in life are not found without, but from within. When Racine read his play *Esther* to Louis XIV, he came to a passage describing the civil war between higher and lower natures. The monarch answered: "I know that war very well."

Silence about tensions behooves us. As Euripides observed: "Silence is wisdom's first reply."

Silence is recommended because any discussion of conflicts within the Church diminishes the content of the Christ—love within the Mystical Body—as the hand excessively rubbing the eye diminishes vision. Impatience and blame is a blight to humanity; rebellion against having one's own will crossed is a plague to obedience. If we are right in a conflict the Lord bids us absorb any wrongs like a sponge; if we are wrong, we are to see others as the instrument of working His Will. A dog when he is struck with a stick bites the stick, not discerning that the stick only moves as the hand directs it. The dog never learns the lesson and most of us never learn it until the end of life.

*From "Cats," *The Poetry of Father Tabb.* Copyright © 1902, 1923, 1928 by Francis A. Litz. Used by permission of the publisher, Dodd, Mead and Company, Inc.

A moment of meditation before a lecture,
Palm Beach, Florida, 1971. *(Palm Beach
Newspapers)*

Silence is also imperative in order to avoid the danger of
self-justification. As C. S. Lewis put it:

> When we see how all our plans shipwreck on the characters of peo-
> ple we have to deal with, we are, "in one way," seeing what it must be
> like for God. But only in one way. There are two respects in which
> God's view must be very different from ours. In the first place, He sees
> (like you) how all the people in your home or in your job are in various
> degrees awkward or difficult; when He looks into that home or factory
> or office He sees one more person of the same kind—the one you never
> do see. I mean, of course, yourself. That is the next great step in wis-

Speaking at the Mayor's Prayer Breakfast at the St. Francis Hotel, San Francisco, February 4, 1975. *(Joseph Rosenthal; San Francisco Chronicle)*

*dom—to realize that you are just that sort of person. You also have a fatal flaw in your character. All the hopes and plans of others have again and again shipwrecked on theirs.*

*It is important to realize that there is some really fatal flaw in you; something which gives the others just that same feeling of despair which their flaws give you. And it is always certainly something you don't know about—like what the advertisements call 'halitosis' which everyone notices except the person who has it.* *

---

*Lewis, C. S., *God in the Dark* (William B. Eerdmans Co., Grand Rapids, Michigan), p. 153.

Finally, silence is recommended because if I judge not, I will not be judged. As we hope the Good Lord will throw our sins in the wastebasket, may He not justly expect that we throw our self-righteousness into it also. As the prophet observed: we receive fewer blows than we deserve, for "Our God has punished us less than our iniquities deserve."

During one of his journeys King David was approached by a member of Saul's family whose name was Shimei. Seeing David he began showering stones on him. Though Shimei might have been justified in his own conscience, the stones were nonetheless bruising to David. One in the company of David, Abishai, asked David if he should not retaliate by cutting off Shimei's head. David answered: "If the Lord has told him to curse David, who can question it . . . for the Lord has told him to do it." The Almighty can use others as instruments of retribution. If the stones are not due to us while they are being thrown, or for a particular act, they may be for something else we've done or will do at some other time. In the course of many a life God bids a Shimei to use a stone and then the stone is really thrown by the Hand of the Righteous and Merciful God. In punishing us for our sins, God often mercifully uses gloves, that is, human instruments. He does not use His bare Hand; the penalty would be too great. The less we connect the Providence of God with all that happens, the more we are upset with the smallest annoyances of daily life.

I am certain that it was God Who made certain people throw stones at me, but I am just as certain that I have thrown stones at other people, and for those stonings I beg His mercy and pardon.

*Twenty*

# THE WOMAN
# I LOVE

I think one of the major defects in world religions has been the absence of the feminine.
The absence becomes more striking in a
study of Christian sects where so little attention is paid to the Mother of Christ. It
would be strange to visit a friend's home and
yet never hear him speak of his mother. Why
are pulpits which resound with the Name of
Christ, so silent about His Mother, who was
chosen for such a dignity in the agelessness of
eternity? Hymns abound in praise of her
Son, but not a verse to her who brought

timelessness into time. True, in the course of history, there have been exaggerations in devotion to Mary, but it was not the Church that made her important; it was Christ Himself. The Church has never adored Mary, because only God may be adored. But she, of all creatures, was closest to God. Without her as the key, it is difficult to discover the treasures in the vault of Faith.

God Who made the sun also made the moon. The moon does not take away from the brilliance of the sun. The moon would be only a burned-out cinder floating in the immensity of space, were it not for the sun. All its light is reflected from that glowing furnace. In like manner, Mary reflects her Divine Son, without Whom she is nothing. On dark nights we are grateful for the moon; when we see it shining, we know there must be a sun. So, in this dark night of the world, when men turned their backs on Him Who is the Light of the World, we look to Mary to guide our feet while we await the sunrise.

"It is not good for man to be alone." That verse of Genesis applies just as much to a priest as to the laity. There must be a Woman in the life of a priest. That Woman came into my life at birth. When I was baptized as an infant, my mother laid me on the altar of the Blessed Mother in St. Mary's Church, El Paso, Illinois, and consecrated me to her. As an infant may be unconscious of a birthmark, so I was unconscious of the dedication—but the mark was always there. Like a piece of iron to the magnet, I was drawn to her before I knew her, but never drawn to her without Christ. When I received my first Holy Communion at the age of twelve, I made the conscious dedication of myself to Mary. Though I cannot recall the exact words of my prayer, it was certainly similar to the motto which I chose for my coat of arms as bishop: *Da per matrem me venire* (Grant that I may come to Thee through Mary). My First Communion book with its mother-of-pearl cover contained the Litany of the Blessed Virgin, which I began reciting every night as a boy and have continued to this hour.

The call to the priesthood was always in my mind; it was her intercession I sought, to make myself worthy and to be protected from great falls. While I was still in the first grade, a suggestion was made by a good nun that we put at the top of every page the initials *J.M.J.*, standing for dedication to "Jesus, Mary and Joseph." In the course of my life I have written tens of thousands of pages. I do not believe I ever set my pen or pencil to paper without first having put that seal of dedication on my work. The practice continued even automatically when I was on television and used a blackboard. I did not so much advert to the fact; it was already a lifetime habit. Thousands of letters poured in asking for the explanation.

When I was ordained, I took a resolution to offer the Holy Sacrifice of the Eucharist every Saturday to the Blessed Mother, renewing my feeble love of her and invoking her intercession. All this makes me very certain that when I go before the Judgment Seat of Christ, He will say to me in His Mercy: "I heard My Mother speak of you."

During my life I have made about thirty pilgrimages to the shrine of Our Lady of Lourdes and about ten to her shrine in Fatima. One of the first pilgrimages to Lourdes was while I was a university student at Louvain. I had just enough money to go to Lourdes but not enough to live on once I arrived. I asked my brother Tom if he had any money, but he was a typical university student too—no money. I said to him: "Well, if I have faith enough to go to Lourdes to celebrate the fifth anniversary of my Ordination, it is up to the Blessed Mother to get me out."

I arrived in Lourdes "broke." I went to one of the good hotels—though by no means would any hotel in Lourdes ever be considered in the luxury class. I decided that if the Blessed Mother was going to pay my hotel bill, she could just as well pay a big one as a little one. I made a novena—nine days of prayer—but on the ninth morning nothing happened, the ninth afternoon nothing happened, the ninth evening nothing happened. Then it was serious. I had visions of gendarmes and working out my bill by washing dishes.

I decided to give the Blessed Mother another chance. I went to the grotto about ten o'clock at night. A portly American gentleman tapped me on the shoulder: "Are you an American priest?" "Yes." "Do you speak French?" "Yes." "Will you come to Paris with my wife and daughter tomorrow, and speak French for us?" He walked me back to the hotel; then he asked me perhaps the most interesting question I have ever heard in my life: "Have you paid your hotel bill yet?" I outfumbled him for the bill. The next day we went to Paris and for twenty years or more after that, when I would go to New York on weekends to instruct converts, I would enjoy the hospitality of Mr. and Mrs. Thomas Farrell, who had become the agents of the Blessed Mother to save me from my creditors.

When I finished my university studies, I made another pilgrimage to Lourdes. I was deeply concerned that perhaps I would not be permitted to return to Mary's Shrine again, for I knew not to what task the Bishop would assign me. I

asked the Blessed Mother to give me some sign that despite
the odds of returning to Lourdes, she would do what seemed
impossible. The sign I asked for was this: that after I offered
the Holy Sacrifice of the Mass and before I would reach the
outer gate of the shrine, a little girl aged about twelve, dressed
in white, would give me a white rose. About twenty feet from
the gate I could see no one. I remember saying: "You had
better hurry, there is not much time left." As I arrived at the
gate a little girl aged twelve, dressed in white, gave me the
white rose.

When I was assigned to a parish in Peoria, I told the pastor I would be going to Europe the following year to visit
Lourdes. He justly retorted: "I have been a pastor for fifteen
years and have not been to Europe once; as a curate, you expect to go at the end of the year?" "Yes, but I do not know
how it is going to happen, except that it will happen." At the
end of a year's service in the parish, the Bishop told me I was
assigned as a teacher to the Catholic University and that I
could go to Europe to begin immediate preparations for my
course. So I visited the shrine of Our Lady again that summer.

If anyone thinks that prayers are never answered, let him
offer a prayer to the Lord that some suffering be sent to save
a soul. At the end of this particular pilgrimage to Lourdes, I
had made reservations to take a night train back to Paris, the
train leaving about 9 P.M. As lovers are reluctant to say goodbye, I sought to prolong my visit until the last minute. At
about eight in the evening, I hurried to the grotto and asked
the Blessed Mother to send me some kind of trial and suffering or a splinter from the Cross to help a soul. I hurried
to the hotel and ran up three flights of stairs, two steps at a

time, to my room. I noticed someone was running up the stairs after me. I paid little attention to it until the third floor as I went down the corridor to my room. I turned around and saw a young Dutch girl of about twenty-one. "Are you following me?" "Yes," she said, "but I do not know why. I saw you in the procession this afternoon and decided that I should talk to you." When asked if she was in Lourdes to make a pilgrimage, she said: "No, I am an atheist." "You are not an atheist," I insisted, "otherwise you would not be here. More likely you have lost your faith." I then told her: "I believe you are an answer to my prayer. I asked for some trial and suffering to save a soul; you are that soul."

I purposely missed my train and stayed in Lourdes three days until she made her confession and was restored again to the life of the Church. Then my troubles began. It took me three more days to get back to Paris. Though I could speak the language, conductors told me my tickets were inadequate; they put me off the train at odd stops; and it was impossible to find a restaurant or an inn. After seventy-two hours and multiplied inconveniences, sleeplessness and inadequate food and rest, I finally arrived in Paris. There is a price tag on every soul—some are cheap, others are expensive. As it is possible to transfuse blood from one member of society to another to cure an anemic condition, and as it is possible to graft skin from one part of the body to another to restore pristine elegance, so it is also possible for any cell-member of Christ's Mystical Body to apply his splinter of the Cross to some other soul in need.

Spiritual aid to needy souls has not kept pace with the material aid we gather for needy bodies. No want of collections exists to help those in body need, but there is a lessened sense of reparation for the spiritually starving. "If one member suffers anything, all the members suffer with it." If there are eye banks for the blind and blood banks for the anemic, why should there not be prayer banks for the fallen and self-denial banks for sinners? Many a spiritually wounded traveler is without the Good Samaritan to pour the oil of intercession and the wine of reparation into his weary soul.

Devotion to the Blessed Mother brought me to the discovery of a new dimension in the sacredness of suffering. I do not believe that I ever in my life said to the Good Lord: "What did I do to deserve all these trials?" In my own heart I knew that I received fewer blows than I deserved. Furthermore, if Christ the Lord had summoned His Mother, who was free from sin, to share in the Cross, then the Christian must scratch from his vocabulary the word "deserve." When she brought her Divine Child to Simeon she was told He would be a "sign of contradiction" and "a sword would pierce her heart too." His Mother was the first to feel it—not in the sense of an unwilling victim, but rather one whose free act of resignation made her united to Him as much as a creature could be united with Him in the act of redemption. If I were the only person who had eyes in a world full of blind people, would I not try to be their staff? If I were the only one in a battlefield who was unwounded, would I not try to bind sores? Then shall virtue in the face of sin be dispensed from cooperation with Him Who even paid in advance for her gift of being immaculately conceived?

When I had open-heart surgery, only gradually did it dawn on me during my first four months in the hospital, that the Blessed Mother not only gives sweets, but she also gives bitter medicine. Too striking to be missed was that on three

*Above and opposite:* At the famous shrine of
the Blessed Mother at Lourdes in southern
France, May 1957. Archbishop Sheen
would never visit Europe without making
a pilgrimage to Lourdes. *(Courtesy, Society
for the Propagation of the Faith; Photo Lacaze)*

feast days of Our Lady I was brought to the door of death,
and endured great suffering. The first was the Feast of Our
Lady of Mount Carmel, July 16, when the doctors stayed
with me all day and night trying to preserve the small flick-
ering spark of life. Then came another operation on the
Feast of her Assumption, August 15, and the implanting of
a pacemaker. By this time I was beginning to feel a kind of
holy dread of what might happen on September 8 when the

Church celebrates her birthday. Sure enough, a kidney infection developed which, over a period of several weeks, made me feel some new tortures.

As I reflected on this concomitance of the Church festivals of Mary and my enforced solidarity with the Cross, I took it as a sign of the special predilection of Mary. If the

Lord called her, who "deserved" no pain, to stand at the foot of the Cross, why should He not call me? If I had expressed a love for her as the Mother of the Priesthood, why should she not, in maternal love, make me more like her Son by forcing me to become a victim? If she did not despise this conformity with Him on Calvary, why should she, whom I recognize as Heavenly Mother, be less solicitous about seeing the image of her Son stamped more indelibly on my soul? If my own earthly mother laid me on her altar at birth, why should not my Heavenly Mother lay me at His Cross as I come to the end of life?

When I was in the second year of high school, the Brothers of Mary who were our teachers asked us to say three Hail Marys every day to St. Joseph for the grace of a happy death. I have continued that practice daily, but in the last twenty years have added a prayer to the Blessed Mother that I would die on a Saturday which is dedicated to her, or on one of her feast days. In a recent conversation with Malcolm Muggeridge, the famous British journalist and former editor of *Punch*, he told me that it was wrong to pray for death on a certain day. He said: "I so long for death that I welcome it at any time. Whether we live long or short on this earth is merely a nuance." I do not know whether the Blessed Mother will grant me my wish, but it really is not important. I trust in her intercession to provide as direct a route as is possible to Christ, my Saviour, for "she knows the way."

Devotion to the Mother of Christ has been one of the principal safeguards of celibacy in my priesthood. Celibacy is surrounded on every side by hucksters of an erotic civilization where even automobiles are advertised as having "sex appeal." The celibate is bound to feel lonely in that atmosphere, but it is a different kind of loneliness that plagues the erotic. The former is tempted because, in the natural order, he is without a partner; the other is lonely even when he has his partner, for as St. Augustine reflected: "Our hearts were made for Thee, O Lord, and they cannot rest until they rest in Thee." The loneliness of one who seeks the Infinite is different from the loneliness of him who seeks the finite as the Infinite.

The role the Mother of Christ plays in this drama of the incompleteness of man is that she is the ideal *Woman*. As she was loved in the Eternal Mind before she was ever born in time, the celibate is bidden to love an ideal before he loves in fact. How often the young meet hundreds of friends until one day there comes the certitude: "Here is the one I have been looking for," or "She satisfies my ideal." Every person carries within his heart a blueprint of the one he loves; what appears to be "love at first sight" is often the fulfillment of a desire and the realization of a dream. Life becomes satisfying the moment the dream is seen walking and the person appears as the incarnation of the one that is loved. Whether that always is true of man, it is certainly true that God loves an ideal before He loves in fact.

An act of love is not only an affirmation, but a negation. When a husband affirms love of his wife, he negates his love of other women. Respect for womanhood increases with the love of the ideal. Furthermore, because there has been a dedication to this Beautiful Lady, she protects her lovers—even when they fall. Though sinless, she knows what sin is, namely, separation from God. She had lost her Divine Son for three days and thus came to know vicariously the alienation and separation which tortures the heart of a sinner. Besides, she chose as her companion at the Cross Mary Magdalen, adding merit to her title as the "Mother of Sinners." Above all else, Christ the Son of God on the Cross commended to her all His disciples and faithful in the world as He said to John: "This is your Mother."

Though Mary is the ideal Woman in every truly Christian life, I cannot express how *real* she has been in my life. As a mother carrying a child often feels the kicks of the young, so Mary has felt my rebellion, but still sought to form Christ in my soul as she formed Him in her womb. Despite the unglutted beast that strains in the body of every priest, she held onto the leash to tame its madness. Even the beast has a heart and by mysterious and intangible touches of love, she kept that inner immured plot for God. She changes *eros* to *agape*, the water of my life into wine, and helped provide those tears to wipe Blood from wounds that gaped on the Cross. In my mind's eye I have gazed on her beauty, a beauty which leaves all other beauty plain. My heart thrilled a thousand times at her gentle hand's caress, knowing full well that she was content with the little I had to give, for at the Cross she took the son of Zebedee as a son for the Son of God. After many years of courtship, the deep conviction pervades my soul: she really loves me—and if she can love me, then Christ is with me.

For years in sermons and often in lectures I quoted a poem about this Ideal Lady who became so real to me. The poem is about a child's thoughts concerning her. Since we can enter the Kingdom of Heaven only by reversing age and becoming like a child, I fittingly close this chapter about "The Woman I Love" with child-talk.

*Lovely Lady dressed in blue*
    *Teach me how to pray*
*God was just your little Boy*
    *Tell me what to say!*

*Did you lift Him up, sometimes*
    *Gently on your knee?*
*Did you sing to Him the way*
    *Mother does to me?*

*Did you hold His hand at night*
    *Did you ever try*
*Telling Him stories of the world?*
    *O, and did He cry?*

*Do you really think He cares*
    *If I tell him things—*
*Little things that happen? And*
    *Do Angel's Wings make a noise?*

*Can He hear me if I speak low?*
    *Does He understand me now?*
*Tell me, for you know!*

*Lovely Lady dressed in blue*
    *Teach me how to pray!*
*God was just your little Boy*
    *And, you know the way!* *

*"To Our Lady" reprinted with the permission of Macmillan Publishing Co., Inc. from *The Child on His Knees* by Mary Dixon Thayer. Copyright © 1926 by Macmillan Publishing Co., Inc., renewed 1954 by Mary D. T. Fremont-Smith.

# Twenty-One

# THE THREE
# STAGES OF
# MY LIFE

I wonder if every bishop is not in some way related to one of the twelve Apostles. Since we are theologically their successors, may there not also be a psychological or character lineage which relates us to one of the twelve whom the Lord has chosen? If this be so, I have always believed that I was related to Peter, having the same combination of his love of Christ and his weakness. Even the title of this book—*Treasure in Clay*—is the story of the contrast of the mountain of dignity to which I am called and the valley of the human nature where that treasure reposes. The same contradiction that existed in Peter is in my very name—Fulton Sheen. In Gaelic, *Fulton* means "war" and *Sheen* means "peace." Here already was an indication of conflicts, trials and tribulations, in the sense of "I have come not to bring peace, but the sword." Julius Caesar tells us that "All Gaul is divided into three parts." Looking back on my life, I find it also is divided into three parts:

1. The first look—the call.
2. The profession with staurophobia (fear of the Cross).
3. The second look.

As the graph of Peter's life was not an upward climb, so neither was mine. I have a cartoon in my office which I once asked Dik Browne, the cartoonist, to draw for me. It shows me seated at my desk, looking at a large graph on the wall which indicates receipts for the missions during the year. Under each month, the line on the graph is toward the bottom of the page, except for the month of June, when it rises to the top. I am on the telephone, looking at the graph and saying: "Oh, that's right, I was away in June."

# THE FIRST STAGE: THE FIRST LOOK

Since I was baptized "Peter," I will try to summarize my life in terms of Peter. The First Look was immediately after Andrew and John met Our Lord at the Jordan and told Simon—for his name was not yet Peter—that they had found the Messiah. Then "Jesus looked at him closely." It was one of those deep penetrating looks that bore into the very soul. Immediately Our Lord, Who has chosen us in the divine councils from all eternity knew him and changed his name: "Your name is Simon; from now on you will be called Cephas—or Rock." In other words, your horizons stop at the other side of Lake Genesereth, your hope is to beget another generation of fishermen, but I tell you that from now on you will be a fisher of men. You will even lose your name and become a rock.

A vocation is a particular task that God assigns to each of us, and it is especially true of priests: "You must be called by God as Aaron was. No man takes the vocation unto himself." That calling comes from the infusion of a spirit which has to be cultivated in order that it may grow in the sun of His grace. Peter's vocation was not changed automatically with his name. If his faith was to become as strong as a rock it was still housed in a personality that could only be sometimes called by the Lord: "a stone in his path." When God makes a man a great musician He does not dispense him from study and practice. When God calls an apostle, He places the seed in the nature that has to be cultivated. A "vocation" is only the free response of a free creature of the summons of God. God only proposes; He does not impose. The call to follow Him does not occur only in the interior of the soul; it occurs in the body which can be impetuous and full of errors of judgment and beset with weaknesses.

It is purely incidental that my name was changed, not by the Lord, but by circumstances mentioned elsewhere in this book. There is no doubt whatever that as the Lord looked on Peter, so He looked on me and on every priest whom He ever called to be "another Christ." My calling was not as distinct as Peter's, but it emerged in the earliest recollections of childhood. There were times when I wished that God would confirm the urge that I had in my soul by shaking my bed vigorously as He shook Paul and made him an apostle. But it was an undatable, persistent, silent summons that gave no rest, and the more I thought of doing anything else, the more uncomfortable I became inside. The more I had moments of peace and the more I prayed, the more pressing were the solicitations of that loving Host of our Hearts: *dulcis Hospes animae*.

Hidden in the vocation of Peter was the lesson: "Never despair. If you fail, start again. Launch out into deep waters." *Duc in altum*. Peter and his companions had toiled all the night and had caught nothing, but the Lord, Who had just come to the shore, had told Peter to go back where he came from and start again. Begin again, not by repeating old lapses, but by correcting former imperfections. Peter tries many designs before he finally finds the reality which corresponds to his ideal. The Lord told Peter to go out again to the sea and cast nets, and behold he was blessed with a great catch of fishes.

Vocation is not immune to failures. We pray and do not become more spiritual; we mortify and still are tempted; we take a resolution and still return to backbiting. When we have labored "all the night and have taken nothing" we are summoned to recommence our response to vocation. There is not a priest in the world who has not had in his life a long chain of generous beginnings, the rowing out again into the very sea we thought was barren. Even the Church itself is in the process of beginning again. She is persecuted, sometimes driven out of a country, but she comes back, as from persecuted Poland came the successor of Peter.

Another incident in the life of Peter was his reaction to the miraculous draft of fishes. It was when Peter obeyed the words of the Lord to row out again into the sea that he found his nets full. From the point of view of nature, why should he go out at noon when fish are not biting? When the night experience had proven there was nothing to be taken, Peter learned that obedience is the key to blessing. We inquire not into the reason why the Lord orders us to do something; but when we find success because we have done His bidding, we learn that the most successful moments of our priesthood are when there is a deep personal relationship between Christ and ourselves. It takes a long time for us to learn as we do social work, preaching, and evangelization: "Without Me you can do nothing." When Peter returned to the shore with his boat filled with the silvery slime of a catch, the Lord told him that He would make him a fisher of men—not taking men as fish to be consumed, but rather to give them a new life. In the full consciousness of that summons and the nakedness and sinfulness of his own heart, Peter cried: "I am a sinful man, O Lord." When the boat left the shore, Peter had called Him "Master"; when the boat returned laden, he called Him "Lord." His feelings were something like those of Job when the Divine Glory shone on his soul: "I have heard of Thee by the hearing of my ear but now my eyes see Thee whereupon I abhor myself and repent in dust and ashes."

The sense of unworthiness is always the immediate reaction to the certitude of the vocation. This unworthiness comes as it did from Peter, not just from a sense of one's own sins, but rather because of the favors and graces with which the Lord honors us. The seeming contrarieties of humility and affection seem to meet.

*He is my Maker—dare I stay?*
*He is my Saviour—dare I turn away?*

I knew what Peter felt. As a young man I would always approach the Communion rail with the words: "O Lord, I am not worthy." This is always the attitude of a creature before the Creator. The lover is always on his knees; the beloved is always on the pedestal. Though I would try to drive the vocation out of my mind on many occasions because I felt myself unworthy to respond, and though I knew the Lord had plenty of reasons for ignoring me, I also knew that He came to this world not to save the just, but the sinners. At one moment I am saying: how can Christ, Who has unfallen angels in His service, ever choose me? The inflamed eye may cause a person no pain when screened from daylight, but exposed to the midday sun the anguish becomes almost too great to be endured. So it is with the soul confronted by its own weaknesses in the glory of Him before Whom the seraphim hide their faces. Yet I knew that Christ wanted free men who were not the best or the noblest; otherwise success would be in *us* and not in *Him.* How often I read that verse in the Epistle to the Hebrews: "For every high priest is taken from among men and appointed their representative before God, to offer gifts and sacrifices for sins. He is able to bear patiently with the ignorant and erring, since he too is beset by weakness; and because of this he is bound to make sin-offerings for himself no less than for the people." *Homo peccator sum.* I knew I was not superior to those to whom I would preach, nor as learned as some whom I would instruct, but I had to learn the rule of the apostolate: "Everything is done by God and nothing is done without us."

Insufficiency is no longer an excuse. I began to see that the Lord was always asking people to loan Him something, for we creatures cannot give; all that we are belongs to Him. He borrowed a crib in which to be born; He borrowed Peter's boat in which to preach; He borrowed the sponge of a soldier to slake His thirst; He borrowed the spear of a Roman centurion to reveal His loving heart. Why, therefore, should He not take a loan of this lump of clay and put a treasure in it?

## THE SECOND STAGE: PROFESSION WITH STAUROPHOBIA (FEAR OF THE CROSS)

In the first stage there was the dichotomy of the call with a sense of unworthiness; in the second stage there is the tension of the profession of Faith and the practice of that Faith. None of these stage have exact time spans, for they are rather spiritual conditions. But the second period of the priesthood is the way it was practiced; its apostolate, preaching, and caring for the sick. Here I return to Peter to describe this second stage. Peter made an eloquent profession of the divinity of Christ, but a fear of the Cross diminished his full understanding. The Lord had all of His Apostles gathered around Him and asked the most important question that men ever had to answer—What am I? Peter gave the right answer: "Thou art the Christ, the Son of the Living God."

Peter knew the truth only by the illumination of Heaven—"It is only by faith that we know Christ is the Son of God." Now comes the other side of the picture. Once the Apostles, through their leader whom He made the rock of His Church, understood His divinity, the Lord went on to say that "Since I am your Christ as you confess, I must suffer death even on the Cross."

Peter's face was afire as he proclaimed the divinity of Christ and as he saw the keys of the Kingdom of Heaven swing from his fisherman's cincture. But no sooner had the Lord displayed His Cross than he shouted: "God forbid!" in amazed indignation. "I am willing to have a Divine Christ, but I am not willing to have a suffering One. What is the use of be-

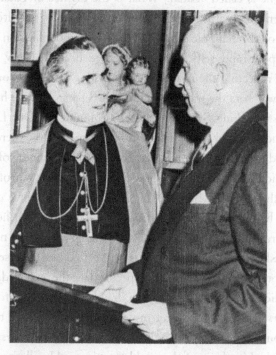

Sheen receiving "Man of the Year in TV" award from Frank Burke, editor of a television trade paper, January 1953. *(United Press International)*

ing Christ if You are not going to use all of Your tremendous power? Why all this waste? What place is there for defeat and contradiction and disgrace in Him Who is God in the flesh?" There is no doubt that it was Peter's love for Our Lord that inspired this reaction to some extent; but it was also indicative of how little he understood God's way in dealing with a sinful world. He was asking the Lord to find a more popular way than the Cross.

The reaction of Our Lord was like a thunderbolt: "Get behind Me, Satan." A moment before he was called a "Rock"; now he is called "Satan." What is the essence of Satanism? When the devil is stripped of all his trappings, the ultimate goal of the demonic is to avoid the Cross, mortification, self-discipline and self-denial. As George Bernard Shaw once said, reflecting the mood of the world: "The Cross on the highway bars the way." Peter was called Satan because he did the same thing Satan did at the beginning of Our Lord's public life. The three temptations against Christ were the worldly ways of escaping the Cross. At the beginning of His public life, Satan tried to show the Lord another way of saving the world except by dying for its sins. The three offers that he made were: first, satisfy every "id" of fallen human nature; never mortify an instinct; if hungry, You may miraculously produce bread; if passionate, find sex. The second temptation was to use the spectacular, the extraordinary, publicity, emotion, anything to draw a crowd, like throwing Yourself off the top of a temple unharmed. The third temptation was probably the only true words the devil ever spoke: "All the kingdoms of the world are mine and I will give them to You if falling down You will adore me." Identify Yourself with the world, do what is popular, for I am its prince.

Peter's sin reveals how it is possible in the same person to have infallibility and to be without impeccability. Peter was told he would be without error if he would use his power of keys, but the Lord gave him no assurance that he would be without sin. That goes for every priest in the world. It is one thing to say the Creed; it is quite another to obey the commandments. It is easy to proclaim the Divinity of Christ from a pulpit, but hard to see the same Christ when He sends a cross. It is so facile to mount a professor's platform, but so difficult to descend to the rubbish heap of Golgotha. To make Christ out to be a moral teacher, a social activist, a defender of the poor is so satisfying to social instincts; but to see in Him a Saviour Who takes on the burden of the world's guilt and Who says: "Take up your cross" is a frightening specter.

*I was a priest without being a victim.* The priest is one who offers to God; the victim is what is offered. In the Old Testament and in all pagan religions, what was offered was something distinct from the priest himself—a lamb, an ox, a bullock. But when Our Blessed Lord came to this earth He changed all this. He, the Priest, was also the Victim. He did not offer something *apart* from Himself; He offered Himself. During His trial He spoke to Pilate seven times as a Priest, and He was silent seven times as a Victim—silent, for what defense can sinners make for their sins? On the Cross He spoke first as a Priest: "Father, forgive them, for they know not what they do," and as a Victim He feels that awful alienation and loneliness which is the lot of sinners: "My God, My God, why hast Thou forsaken Me?"

When I was a priest I thrilled at being called "Father." I found the title "Monsignor" mellifluous, but was I a victim?

I enjoyed the prestige of being a university professor, and of appearing on radio and television not only at home, but abroad; I was popular, I was sought after, I was loudly applauded after lectures and banquet talks, I was a friend of both royalty and the masses, my features became so recognizable that I would be identified by a passerby in a revolving door, my face appeared in millions of homes. I made the right kind of enemies, namely, the Communists. But... but... how close was I to the Cross? I was the priest; was I the victim? I offered the Eucharist, saying: "This is My Body; This is My Blood" indicating the Body and Blood of Christ. But was I saying of myself: "This is *my* body; this is *my* blood"? While many young priests sought ways to imitate the way I preached, was I inspiring anyone to imitate Christ in the daily carrying of His Cross? I knew it was not right. I

Alfred E. Smith dinner at the Waldorf-Astoria, New York City, October 8, 1953. (L. to r.) Mr. Charles H. Silver, president of Beth Israel Medical Center; Hon. Vincent R. Impellitteri, former mayor of New York; Hon. Thomas E. Dewey, former governor of New York; Gen. Alfred M. Gruenther, U.S.A., S.H.A.P. chief of staff; Bishop Sheen. *(The Catholic News)*

knew I should be giving away more than I gave. I should have resembled more closely Christ, Who had nowhere to lay His head. I should have fled from some applauding mobs as the Lord fled from the enthusiasms at Capharnaum after the multiplication of bread; maybe I was like Peter, who at one point "followed the Lord far off."

I loved creature comforts. I dressed well and I excused myself for this, saying that the ambassador of Christ should always present himself as a gentleman to the people and one of whom they could be proud. But this can be overrationalized. I drove a Cadillac for more than twenty-five years of my life. How that came to be is interesting. I was driving my Chevrolet by a Cadillac agency in Washington when I was stopped by the owner of the agency, Floyd Akers, who did not know me, but who just wanted to talk to a priest about conditions in his shop. At that time there were sitdown strikes throughout the world. He complained that the workers were not giving an honest day's work for their pay. He asked what the Church would recommend. I explained to him that workmen are willing to sit down on someone else's tools, but not on their own. "Why not give the workers a share in your profits since in addition to their daily labor for which they receive a salary, they also serve the general good and add to your capital for which they receive no remuneration." I proposed, therefore, that he give about one half of the profits every year back again to the workers.

He accepted the plan; the following Christmas I went down to the agency and announced profit-sharing to all the employees of the Cadillac agency. There was not much reaction to it until the checks were distributed. A black woman who simonized cars received, over and above her salary, a check for $1,800. The amount each employee received was in proportion to the number of years he had worked at the agency. The result was a considerable increase in profits and a dedication among the workers. A mechanic one day backed up a car over an electric light which had been protected by a wire guard. Another worker forced him to go into the office and pay for the damage because "it comes out of our profits." Mr. Akers was so pleased with the proposal that every year after that he gave me the loan of a Cadillac. When the new models appeared he would ask me for the old one to be serviced and then would send back a new one in its place.

No great mortifications ever stand out in my life. The laws of fasting and abstinence which the Church enjoined were indeed followed, but except for one or two rare occasions, there was not a taking on of the burdens and sins of the world as a priest is supposed to do as a co-victim with Christ. Granted that I never liked money and gave it away as soon as I received it. Nevertheless, it would be very true to say that outside of fulfilling the law of the Church in essentials there is no great evidence I could be called a mortified priest, nor could I ever say with Paul that "I have been crucified with Christ." I have never preached on fasting although I have among my undelivered sermons one on that subject which I have shrunk from giving because I never fasted beyond what was required by law.

Looking at both the ideal and the reality, I wonder if I would ever really be pleasing to the Lord if He had not intervened. I did indeed pick up a chisel and a hammer and, here and there, knock off some blocks of egotism, but if the Divine Sculptor Himself had not come to complete the work He would never be able to see in me His image. I believe that when we priests die the Lord will show us His Scars as He promised to do to all mankind at His second coming. He will look at our hands to see if they have been scarred from giving, our feet to see the calluses from travel to preach His Gospel, and our side to see if we have loved to a point of sacrifice. Woe to us who come down from Calvary with hands unscarred and white.

God does not like unfinished symphonies, or unfurled flags. In His mercy He will finish the temple we have left unfinished and clean and polish that which has remained unadorned. What we may regard as an evil may be actually a hidden good like the surgeon's use of a scalpel. He does not ask us if we will accept the finishing of the work His Father sent Him to do. He drafts us into His service as Simon the Cyrene that we might not be unripe and unplucked wheat in His Eucharistic sanctuary. He has many ways of tightening the violin strings that the priesthood may give forth a better harmony.

Since I would not take up the Cross, the Lord would lay it on my back as He laid it on Simon of Cyrene, who later came to love it. The cross took two forms: trials *inside* the Church and *outside* the Church. Eventually I came to see that the Lord was teaching me not only to be a priest, but also to be a victim. This explains why two of the books which I authored are on this very subject.

I can remember when, after four months in the hospital, I began to recover; I was reading Mass on an altar constructed over the bed before a few priests and friends. I spontaneously gave a sermon, which I remember so well. I said that I was glad that I had open-heart surgery because when the Lord comes to take us all, He will look to see if we have any marks of the Cross upon ourselves. He will look at our hands to see if they are crucified from sacrificial giving; He will look at our feet to see if they have been thorn-bruised and nail-pierced searching for lost sheep; He will look at our heart to see if that has been opened to receive His Divine Heart. Oh what joy is mine just to have endured the minuscule imitation of His suffering on the Cross by having a wounded side. Maybe He will recognize me from that scar and receive me into His Kingdom.

## THE THIRD STAGE: THE SECOND LOOK

"The Lord disciplines those whom He loves."

As Paul had to learn, "there was a thorn in the flesh" which after three prayers to God was not removed; as Peter had to learn, he would have to stretch out his hands to go where he would not go; as I learned, with an apostolate there was to be a Golgotha. The Lord did with me what Michelangelo did with a piece of Carrara marble that he had found hacked and ruined by some cheap artist. He brought it to his studio, applied his chisel and his genius and brought out his immortal statue of David. So, too, I had to be brought through trials both inside and outside the Church before I could understand the full meaning of my life. It was not enough to be a priest; one also had to be a victim.

When Peter had been told that to deny the Cross was to enroll in the army of Satan, he was given another chance. The first time the Lord "looked at him" was when he was called. Now came the second look—"The Lord turned and looked upon Peter." Jesus had been in the courtroom of

Caiaphas, being unjustly tried, while Peter stood outside by a fire "warming himself," still making himself comfortable as the Lord began His agony. As the door opened and the Lord advanced, what did Peter do? It is very likely that he did what any of us would do after a weakness and a fall, namely, turn one's back on the Lord—not because he despised Him, but because he could not bear His eyes. Evidently the Lord passed him by and then turned quickly. As the Vulgate put it: *Conversus Dominus*. The Lord turned quickly around and thus faced Peter. Judas got His lips; Peter got His eyes, for as the Gospel states: "And the Lord looked upon Peter." The Lord was bound, He had been accused, He had been struck in the face, but His thought was of wandering Peter. He did not speak; He just looked. I am sure that what was written on the Master's face was: "Peter, I love you still. You have denied Me, but I will not deny you. I cannot give you up." The grace which saves a soul is not a noisy thing. No one saw that look except Peter himself. That look was like an arrow of the Divine Huntsman wounding a stag. And as the stag seeks the thicket to bleed and die alone, so Peter went out to draw out the arrow. But that look opened the sluices of Peter's heart, for "he went out and wept bitterly."

That face many times haunted John on the isle of Patmos, and after half a century he spoke of it: "I saw a great white throne, and Him Who sat upon it, from Whose face the earth and heaven fade away." The face that Peter saw that night was a look of the mildest reproof along with the tenderest pity. Above all, that face had upon it a forgiving look, for the Lord knew how deep would be Peter's self-reproach and anguish of soul when he came to himself. So this look would inspire him with hope. Not a word was spoken, only

Archbishop Sheen accepts a Catholic Actors Guild Award in his first public appearance after open-heart surgery, November 1977, at the New York Hilton. (*Chris Sheridan, The Catholic News*)

a glance was sufficient for Peter to know himself in his weakness and his shame. One look of Divinity is enough to convict us of sin, and with that one look Peter, under the eye of God, became Peter the penitent. Sin is not just a transgression of the law; no one cries because he has broken a speeding law. Every sin beats against Love. It was enough to make Peter say: "He still counts on me, and I am sure I can make good in spite of the fact that I have failed Him so miserably."

Our Lord had told both Peter and Judas that they would fail. Judas did what he wanted to do—what he planned to do—what he was paid to do. Peter did what he did not plan to do—what he did not wish to do—what he had been warned against doing—what he declared he would never do. And they were both brought face to face with their guilt. Judas had only remorse, but Peter showed sorrow. If Judas had returned to the Lord he would have been saved by that second look, but in him there was a total and final rejection of Christ; in Peter, a loving return. The only difference between a sinner and a saint is found in their attitude toward their sins—the one persisting in them; the other weeping bitterly.

And so there was in my life and also in the life of every priest, a Second Look, and despite any failings or any discouragement as we measure our finitude against His Infinity, the love of the Lord continues. One of the beautiful hymns of St. Ambrose invites us to beg Christ for the gentle look which merits His continuing love:

*Jesu, labantes respice,*
*Et nos videndo corrige.*

"Jesus, look on us when we are succumbing, for Your look sets us right again."

*Si respicis, labes cadunt*
*Fletuque culpa salvitur.*

"When You look at us, our stains disappear, tears dissolve our faults."

The experience of the Second Look is not unique in life;

it happens many, many times, for we are always falling down and picking ourselves up. The Second Look meant to me what it has always meant to all my brother priests—the joy of beginning again. Seventy times seven, you can always begin a new chapter, start a second mile, catch a second wind, launch out into the deep, excavate new layers for untold spiritual wealth. There is always, in the Church, that wonderful Land of Beginning Again. These prodigal robes can be thrown into the pile of our spiritual nakedness, our spiritual nakedness clothed and new trails found.

The Vulgate describes the divine chiseling as *Foris pugnae, intus timores* ("Trouble at every turn, confrontation all around us, forebodings in our heart").

I have had a measure of discipline from the Lord in the course of my life. Discipline in the sense of pain and suffering and conflicts is of two kinds—both pure and impure. Pure discipline is naked suffering and pain without an explicit reference to guilt or to the action of others. Impure discipline is that which comes from others, deserved or undeserved, deliberate or accidental. Since I have resolved in this book not to touch on any suffering that came to me from others, I shall combine both the pure and the impure under a general title—sufferings, trials and "the slings and arrows of outrageous fortune." The impure sufferings would have had a time span of about ten years and the pure sufferings of an intense kind most directly related to the open-heart surgery and consequent complications in which I came to a new dimension of pain.

I discovered that pain and suffering can be *outside* us and also *inside* us. When pain is outside, such as a toothache, a wound, a hurt, one is in the position to "offer it up." Pain can become so intense that it possesses us like being drowned by the sea; no possibility exists of laying hold of it as one does an object outside of the hand. Sequence of thought is impossible; memorized prayers are never finished, they are so invaded by this crucifying assault.

What is important is not details of "my operation," but rather what I learned from suffering. Knowledge is of two kinds: *intellectual,* such as a doctor may have of a disease he treats in the patient; and *existential,* which is the knowledge that comes from living through an experience. Thomas Aquinas says there are two ways of knowing chastity. One is to know it as a moral theologian, and the other is to know it through living it out of love for the Kingdom of God. It is one thing to see the movie of *Holocaust* on the television screen and quite another to have lived through Auschwitz.

The first lesson I learned, but only gradually, is that all sufferings come from either the direct or the permissive Will of God. God has two kinds of medicines, bitter and sweet. Job asks if God gives good things why can He not also give us trials. St. Paul suffered during his whole apostolic life from what some translations call "a thorn in the flesh." The original Greek word is *skolops,* which means a stake. No one knows precisely what it was and though St. Paul prayed to have it removed, the Lord refused to do so, as He refused to remove stuttering from the speech of Moses.

It is easier to see pure pain as coming from God than it is to see impure pain as the work of His Mind. Despite all rational acknowledgment that there are no accidents in life, I found there were some corners of my soul that were not swept clean of atheism. The intermittent cry of *Domine, usque quoque* (How long, O Lord, how long) is impatience that belies what the tongue confesses that every trial is in the Hand of God. The keeping of the scorecard of past wrongs, the chewing of a cud of resentment, licking of the wound, and the memories of how we received them, the playing of the tapes of injustices real or imagined, were so many proofs that I had not thoroughly digested what my Faith taught me and my lips confessed, that all trials come from the Hands of the Loving God.

Another reflection on pain and suffering leads me to its quality of *transferability*. Seventy pints of blood were poured into my body after open-heart surgery because for a long time the body refused to circulate the blood. This blood came from those who poured their own blood into the blood bank of Lenox Hill Hospital. What the transference of blood is in the physical order becomes the transference of merit, prayer and sacrifice in the spiritual realm. God told Abraham that ten just men would have saved Sodom and Gomorrah. St. Paul applies transference to marriage: "The believing wife sanctifies the unbelieving husband; the believing husband sanctifies the unbelieving wife."

I had been ordained only about three or four years when that lesson was forcibly driven home to me by my retreat master, Dr. Leseur, a Dominican of Belgium. He had, as a young doctor, married a woman who was a mediocre Catholic; but while he practiced medicine he became interested in atheism and edited an atheistic newspaper. His wife, Elizabeth, tossed on a bed of constant pain for ten years. When she was dying she said: "Felix, when I am dead, you will become a Catholic and a Dominican priest." He answered: "Elizabeth, you know my sentiments. I've sworn hatred of God. I shall live in that hatred and die in it." She repeated her words and passed away. He found her will, in which the wife wrote: "In 1904 I asked Almighty God to send me sufficient sufferings to purchase your soul. On the day that I die you will have been bought and paid for. Greater love than this no woman hath." She died in 1914. Dr. Leseur, who had written a book against Lourdes showing that it was a fraud and a superstition, was finally converted by a sudden light of the Holy Spirit, and later on became a Dominican priest.

Only two or three times in my life, at the most, did I ever take on extra and rather extreme penances in order to save a soul. Once, a week of fasting to reconcile a daughter and a father who had not spoken in years. Another time was at Lourdes, as I recounted elsewhere in this book. On lesser occasions the offering of intense physical suffering in the hospital did show the immediate effects of transference. On one occasion as I was at the point of death, a young woman doctor thought I was going into despair and she sent for a priest psychiatrist to use his techniques to lift me out of what she thought was a depression but was really only agony. I have the vaguest recollections of anger at being asked Freudian questions as I was dying. I do recall what was going through my mind at the time. I was in intensive care and I overheard a nurse say: "Mr. So-and-So is dying." She was referring to another patient in a nearby bed. I remember offering my sufferings at that moment for the salvation of his soul and the souls of priests and religious. I had no strength to lift my hand so I only raised my finger and gave him conditional absolution and at that moment he died. A few months later when I was on the way to recovery, his wife came to see me and said: "Did you give my husband absolution from his sins as he was dying? I saw you make a little sign of the Cross

with your finger. I thought that is what you were doing."
When I assured her that I had done so, she told me her loss
was softened. She gave me a little Jewish long-life medal in
gratitude for even thinking of her husband while I was in intensive care.

On the way to recovery a Jewish gentleman came to visit
me every day over a period of two or three months. After an
absence of four days, on one occasion, he said: "I missed
coming to see you because my wife is to be operated on for
cancer. She has been under treatment all week in this hospital and tomorrow is the day when the last test will be made
before the operation." I gave him a small silver crucifix which
had been blessed by John XXIII and explained: "I am going
to give you something which is Jewish and for that reason
I know that you will revere it. It is the death of Christ on
the Cross. I will only tell you that He was Jewish on His
Mother's side. Who was His Father, you will have to find out
from Heaven. But if you throw your trust with the well-
being of your wife into His Hands, you may one day discover who His Father is." He came back a few days later and
told me there was to be no operation, for it was found un-
necessary. But he said: "I found out Who Christ's Father
was." Then, opening his shirt, he showed me the silver crucifix about his neck.

A year later when I had to return to the hospital for treatment a nurse announced to me that a man down the corridor had tried to commit suicide. She went into his room and
found the sheets pressed against his ear; pulling them away
the blood burst out from the veins in his neck. He had taken
a knife and slit his throat, just missing a vein that would have
meant death. I asked the nurse to get his permission for a

In the pulpit of St. Basil's Church, Los Angeles, Good Friday 1978.
*(Thelner Hoover Photo)*

visit, which was granted. In the afternoon the nurse wheeled
him alongside my bed with all the bottles over his head with
which hospital patients are so familiar. I asked him if he was
ever a Catholic. He answered in the affirmative but also
added that he did not believe in the Divinity of Christ or in
the Church.

I began the conversation hoping that the hospital bill
would not be too great a burden for him. He answered in the
negative. Then I inquired about other debts which might
have worried him, and he told me that after seventy-seven
years of life he had prepared himself for such eventualities. I
pressed the point, asking: "Are you sure you've paid all your
debts: have you ever injured another's character, have you ever
committed adultery, have you ever cursed or blasphemed?
Who paid those debts?" Pulling a rather large silver crucifix
from my pocket I said: "He paid your debts—every one of
them." I then went into a simple explanation of Our Lord

Who came not to teach but to redeem us from our sins. A few hours later I offered the Holy Eucharist from my bed, heard his confession and gave him his first Communion in forty-five years. I had asked the Lord to let my sufferings do some good for some soul and He had answered the prayer.

The third observation which comes to mind as one feels the chisel of the Divine Sculptor is that the trials and burdens of life are not merely for the expiation of our own sins but also to fill up the *quota assigned to the Church*. Our Blessed Lord on the Cross said: "It is finished," meaning that the salvation of the world was complete. He had drunk the dregs from the chalice filled with the iniquity of the world's sin, and no other price for redemption could ever be paid. But curiously, we read that St. Paul, reflecting on his imprisonment and other tortures, wrote to the Colossians that he was helping to *finish* the sufferings of Christ: "It is now my happiness to suffer for you. This is my way of helping to finish, in my poor human flesh, the full tale of Christ's affliction still to be endured, for the sake of His Body which is the Church."

Evidently, there is a *quota* of suffering that is assigned to the Church. Christ as the Head of the Church had fulfilled His mission, but the Church as His Mystical Body has not finished its mission. The prolonged victimhood of Christ manifests itself in two ways: first in a conscious continuation of those who by an act of will offer their frustrations and fears and loneliness with the Cross; "I have been crucified with Christ," as Paul told the Galatians. The unconscious continuation of the Passion of Christ is in the hunger, destitution and loneliness of much of our humanity. Christ is present when people are crowded into the foul stench of the slums, when a race or color is persecuted because it comes from lowly Nazareth and whenever truth is crucified by a court that penalizes prayer. In the course of history, the marks of Calvary will be found on many hands and feet and sides of humans who never heard of Christ or Calvary; but they, too, are adding to the quota assigned to the Church to perfect the work of salvation.

Now in the era of the Second Look, *I consider everything a waste except knowing Christ. Anything that is done or read or spoken or enjoyed or suffered that does not bring me closer to Him makes me ask myself: why all this waste?*

> *Si Christum discis*
> *Satis est si cetera nescis;*
> *Christum si nescis,*
> *Nihil est in cetera discis.*

"If you know Christ, it does not matter if you know nothing else; but if you know not Christ, it is as nothing to know everything else."

Any spirituality that I have revolves around the crucifix and the price of my redemption and the assurance of my resurrection. The pectoral cross which I carry is a crucifix. In my bedroom is a large crucifix about six feet high which, in my long confinement to bed, is the panorama of salvation which I gaze on during the day, and at night when waking. In my chapel is a painting done by the cardiologist who saved my life, Dr. Simon Stertzer. It is a painting of Christ on the Cross with a concentration on the eyes which look out both in pity and in love, as did the Second Look on Peter. The crucifix, to me, is not just something that happened; it is something that *is* happening, for Christ is crucified in every age by every one of us who sin. But it is also a Promise, for Our Lord never once spoke of His Death without speaking of His Resurrection. The very wounds He received He now carries as Scars. He carried Scars so that Thomas, touching them, could be cured of his doubt; Scars that He will make appear on the Last Day when He comes to judge; Scars that will make us rejoice that He gave us a "thorn in the flesh."

The second year after the open-heart surgery, because of overwork, I was confined to my bed again for many months. During that time I instructed four converts and validated two marriages. The horizontal apostolate may sometimes be just as effective as the vertical.

It could very well be that the goodness of God in my behalf has been manifested not only in the gift of Christian parents, unusual opportunities for education and on and on; the greatest gift of all may have been His summons to the Cross, where I found His continuing self-disclosure.

# "BYE NOW, FULTON SHEEN, AND GOD LOVE YOU FOREVER"

*Homily Delivered at the Funeral Liturgy of
Archbishop Fulton J. Sheen*

My dear friends:

A voice is silent in the midst of the Church and in our land, the like of which will not be heard again in our day. The vocation of Fulton Sheen is consummated; he has responded with one final "yes" to the call of God, a "yes" so final that human frailty and infirmity can never reverse it.

On September the twentieth of this year, with five of his friends, I listened to Arch-

bishop Sheen review his life during the celebration of the
Eucharist which was his thanksgiving to God for sixty years
in the priesthood. His own division of his life into three pe-
riods will serve us well on this occasion.

First there was the period of vocation, the call from God.
That call was as clear to him as was God's call to Jeremiah
the Prophet in the Old Testament passage we have just heard,
and as the "come and see" of Jesus Himself to John's disciples in the Gospel passage. Never was there a time in his life
when he did not want to be a priest; never was there a time
in his life when he wished he had pursued another career.

Part of his response to that call from God was a practice
he started in the year of his ordination to the priesthood.
Every day began with the very first hour, the freshest and
therefore the best hour—he was a morning person—given
to God in prayer. This was his Holy Hour, and it was always
made in the presence of the Blessed Sacrament. The practice
continued without interruption for the next sixty years. As
surely as we are here in St. Patrick's Cathedral this afternoon,
he made his Holy Hour last Sunday morning, the day of his
passing.

Whenever he chose to respond to those who asked him
the secret of his ability to touch minds and hearts, his answer
was always—"the Holy Hour"—when he spoke to God, and
listened to God speaking to him. Here his conflicts were reconciled, for he held no opinions lightly; here his anxieties and
insecurities were calmed, for he was the most human of men;
here his heart was literally set on fire with the drive that made
him ever restless to respond totally to God's call.

This period of his life marked also the expanding of his
intellect and the growth of his constant pursuit of excellence

and quality. He used to say frequently how grateful he was to the Church for the marvelous education he received, which opened his mind to an intellectual curiosity that never deserted him. He always had to have new books, he loved meeting interesting and informed people, the latest scientific discoveries and technological devices fascinated him.

On the twentieth of September, Archbishop Sheen spoke of the second period of his life as the Period of Proclamation. Returning from Europe in 1925, the amazing career of oratory, teaching and preaching began. He was the first to have an ongoing series of religious radio broadcasts, the first churchman to have a regular television program. The pulpit of this great cathedral became his over the years as throngs came to hear his sermons, and therein lies the touchingly beautiful significance of his burial in the crypt under the High Altar. His pen produced over sixty books, as well as articles and letters that will never be numbered. Always he addressed himself to the thought of the times, and insisted that a speaker must begin his message from where his hearers are, not where he is.

It was during this time of his life that the Church asked him to direct the Society for the Propagation of the Faith in the United States. By that time his reputation was solidly established as a professor at the Catholic University of America. Many asked him how he could leave such a position for this seemingly narrower apostolate . . . to which he replied: "I have pushed out the classroom walls, and now I can embrace the whole world." In this role he would be expected to intensify missionary enthusiasm within the Church and to gather financial help for missionary needs.

The Church throughout the world is his eternal debtor

for the way he discharged this responsibility. He gave missionaries all over the world a new sense of the dignity of their vocation. He capsulated missionary ideals in short, unforgettable phrases:

"It was a pagan Latin poet who said that charity begins at home. On a dry and rocky roadside between Jerusalem and Jericho, a certain Samaritan taught us that with Christ charity begins away from home, and with the most unattractive of our neighbors."

Again: "Our charity to the poor of the world is measured by God, not so much by what we give, but by how much we have kept for ourselves after our giving. That is why the widow's mite was such a large gift; she gave all that she had."

Again, talking to people like myself: "We can say that to dig we are not able, but let us never say that to beg we are ashamed."

His love for the Society for the Propagation of the Faith endured in life and in death, and surely you are not surprised that both in life and in death he gave it his every earthly possession.

Many came to faith in Christ and the Church through his words, and for every famous name he instructed, there were hundreds of others who were just as important to him as those in the public eye. His presentation of the fullness of the Catholic faith was powerful and convincing. One of his converts spoke for all of them and summed up this gift of his at the finish of an instruction by leaping to her feet and, with clenched fists, shouting heavenward: "O God, what a protagonist you have in this man!"

On the twentieth of September, Archbishop Sheen spoke also of a third period in his life. It was the one wherein he began to know Christ as never before, to love Him with ever greater intensity, and to experience unspeakable peace. In retrospect, this period seemed to me to begin with the writing of his monumental *Life of Christ* in the late 1950s. Gradually he divested himself of his possessions; he was a man who loved beautiful things. But they became less and less important to him as Christ became more and more important, and as his comprehension of the mystery of the Cross increased.

Frequently he spoke of his death to the amazement and oftentimes the consternation of his hearers and friends. But he said: "It is not that I do not love life; I do. It is just that I want to see the Lord. I have spent hours before Him in the Blessed Sacrament. I have spoken to Him in prayer, and about Him to everyone who would listen, and now I want to see Him face to face."

If we could ask him now, I am sure he would say that the apex of his career took place here in the Sanctuary of St. Patrick's Cathedral on this year's October second, when Pope John Paul II enveloped him in a brotherly embrace. Later, I asked him what the Holy Father said as the two stood there. "He told me that I had written and spoken well of the Lord Jesus, and that I was a loyal son of the Church."

Last Sunday at 7:15 P.M. God called Archbishop Fulton Sheen to himself by name. It was a moment known to God, and fixed by Him from all eternity, a call to perfect life and truth and love, a call to a life he will never tire of, that can never be improved, and which he can never lose.

Dear friend, Archbishop Sheen, we are all better because you were in our midst and were our friend. We trust you to the care of your "Lovely Lady dressed in blue." We pray that Jesus has already said: "I've heard My Mother speak of you."

A touching moment at St. Patrick's Cathedral, October 2, 1979, when the visiting Pope John Paul II embraced Archbishop Sheen and said: "You have written and spoken well of the Lord Jesus. You are a loyal son of the Church." (*The New York News*)

Bye now, Fulton Sheen, and God Love You Forever!

Archbishop Edward T. O'Meara, S.T.D.
*St. Patrick's Cathedral*
*New York City*
*December 13, 1979*

# VITA:

# ARCHBISHOP
# FULTON J. SHEEN

The Archbishop was born in El Paso, Illinois, May 8, 1895, one of four sons of Newton Morris and Delia (Fulton) Sheen. Baptized Peter, he took the name of John at Confirmation and later adopted his mother's maiden name. His father, of Irish ancestry, was a farmer "with an inventive turn of mind." While Fulton Sheen was still a small child, the family moved to Peoria, Illinois, where his uncle, Daniel Sheen, a law partner of Robert G. Ingersoll, the famous agnostic, had served as representative in the State Congress.

After attending St. Mary's School, he entered the Spalding Institute, a secondary school in Peoria conducted by the Brothers of Mary, from which he graduated in 1913. For his A.B. and M.A. degrees, he went to St. Viator College, Bourbonnais, Illinois, where he was on the debating team (which defeated Notre Dame for the first time) and the editorial staff of the college newspaper. Having completed his theological studies, both at St. Viator and at St. Paul's Seminary, St. Paul, Minnesota, he was ordained to the priesthood for the Diocese of Peoria, September 20, 1919.

Obtaining both his S.T.L. and J.C.B. degrees from the Catholic University of America in 1920, he went to the University of Louvain, Belgium, which awarded him the Ph.D. degree three years later. He also attended the Sorbonne in Paris and the Collegio Angelico in Rome. In 1924, he received his S.T.D. in Rome. In 1925, while a teacher of dogmatic theology at St. Edmund's College near Ware, England, he was made Agrégé en philosophie by Louvain and given the university's Cardinal Mercier International Philosophy Award.

Returning to the United States, he served as a curate at St. Patrick's Church in Peoria; but by the end of 1926 he had joined the Catholic University of America faculty as a philosophy of religion instructor, later being promoted to Associate and full Professor of Philosophy.

He preached at the summer conference held at Westminster Cathedral in London in 1925 and again from 1928 to 1931; he lectured at the Catholic Summer School at Cambridge University in 1930 and 1931. For five Lenten seasons he preached Sunday evenings at the Paulist Church, New York City, and for many years was annual Lenten preacher at New York's St. Patrick's Cathedral.

In June 1934 he was appointed Papal Chamberlain—Very Reverend Monsignor, elevated the following year to Domestic Prelate—Right Reverend Monsignor, and on June 11, 1951, he was consecrated Bishop in the Church of Sts. John and Paul in Rome by His Eminence, Adeodato Giovanni Cardinal Piazza, Secretary of the Sacred Consistorial Congregation.

On October 26, 1966, Pope Paul VI appointed Bishop Sheen Ordinary of the Diocese of Rochester, New York. The Bishop was installed as Bishop of that see on December 15, 1966. From 1950 until that time the Bishop was National Director of the Society for the Propagation of the Faith, which, according to Vatican Council II, is the Church's principal mission organization. Bishop Sheen resigned as Bishop of Rochester in 1969 and was appointed by the Holy Father Titular Archbishop of Newport (Wales).

RADIO AND TV: When the National Council of Catholic Men decided to sponsor the "Catholic Hour" Sunday evening broadcasts in cooperation with the National Broadcasting Company, Bishop Sheen became the first regular speaker on the program following the inaugural broadcast, March 2, 1930.

The program, which began on a 17-station network, was carried in 1950 by 118 NBC affiliates and by short wave around the world, with an average weekly listening audience estimated at 4 million persons in the United States alone. The Bishop frequently received as many as six thousand letters a day from listeners, about a third of them non-Catholics. Several million of his radio talks were distributed.

In 1940 Bishop Sheen conducted the first religious service ever to be telecast; the next year he served as narrator of the "March of Time" film *The Story of the Vatican.*

In the fall of 1951, Bishop Sheen began a television series entitled "Life Is Worth Living." By 1956 the Bishop was appearing on 123 ABC television stations in the United States alone (not counting Canada) and 300 radio stations. It was estimated that he reached 30 million people each week. "Life Is Worth Living" telecasts had an audience embracing people of all faiths. Bishop Sheen received as many as thirty thousand letters in one delivery, though normally he averaged from eight thousand to ten thousand letters per day.

He reached millions of others through his writings, including the "God Love You" column, which appeared in the Catholic press throughout the nation, and the "Bishop Sheen Writes" syndicated column for the secular press by George Matthew Adams Service, Inc. In addition he was the editor of the *World Mission*, a quarterly review, and *Mission*, a bimonthly, which is the most widely circulated Catholic magazine.

On Labor Day, 1955, he became the first Latin rite bishop in history to offer a Solemn Byzantine Rite Mass in English. This he did at Uniontown, Pennsylvania, where more than 150,000 pilgrims joined him in praying for "Holy Russia." This event was beamed abroad by the Voice of America.

Bishop Sheen's "Life Is Worth Living" TV series terminated in 1957. His subsequent series on the life of Christ and a second TV series produced in 1964—"Quo Vadis America?"—were shown throughout the United States, until the appearance throughout the country in 1966 of "The Bishop Sheen Program" in color.

VATICAN COUNCIL II: Bishop Sheen was appointed originally to the conciliar Commission on the Lay Apostolate for Vatican Council II. When the first session opened on October 11, 1962, he was chosen to be a member of the Commission on the Missions. He was the only American on the commission for the duration of Vatican Council II. He delivered an address in St. Peter's on the topic of the missions on November 9, 1964 (during the third session). In October 1965, he returned briefly to the United States from Rome while attending the fourth session of Vatican Council II at the request of the CBS network, to be special narrator of Pope Paul VI's visit to the United Nations, the first visit of a Pope to the United States. Pope Paul VI reappointed him to the post-conciliar Commission on the Missions in 1965.

CONVERT INSTRUCTION: Bishop Sheen has spent more than forty years instructing every type of convert. In 1965, he prepared twenty-five records on the Christian philosophy of life which have been issued under the same title as his television series, *Life Is Worth Living*. Each of the fifty talks runs about thirty minutes.

THE SOCIETY FOR THE PROPAGATION OF THE FAITH: It was announced on September 12, 1950, that Pope Pius XII had appointed Bishop Sheen National Director of the Society for the Propagation of the Faith, with the National Office at 366 Fifth Avenue, New York, N.Y. 10001. His work as National Director, for sixteen years, spanned the reign of three Popes. Under his direction the United States was responsible for two thirds of the General Fund of the Society for the Propagation of the Faith collected from the entire world.

ORGANIZATIONS: Archbishop Sheen was a member in such organizations as the American Catholic Philosophical Asso-

ciation, the Medieval Academy, the Catholic Literary Guild
and the American Geographical Association.

AWARDS: Honorary LL.D. degrees have been conferred upon
him by St. Viator College and Loyola University (Chicago)
in 1929, St. Bonaventure College (New York) in 1939, and
Notre Dame University in 1934; and that of Litt.D. by
Marquette University in 1934; and that of L.H.D. by St.
John's University (Brooklyn) in 1941. Georgetown University awarded him the Cardinal Mazzella Philosophy Medal
in 1936. In 1952, he received the Tau Kappa Award, the
Forensic Honor Society with headquarters at Purdue University, for "outstanding speaker in the field of religion."

Among the many awards received were the Emmy Award
in 1952 and the Look Television Award, received for three
successive years. The University of Notre Dame conferred
the Patriotism Award on His Excellency; and the American
Legion gave him the Golden Mike Award. For "outstanding
achievement in bringing about a better understanding of the
American way of life," he received the Freedoms Foundation
Valley Forge Award. For "outstanding achievement for the
State, Church and University," he was awarded the Cardinal
Gibbons Award of Catholic University, Washington, D.C. He
was the recipient also of the Catholic War Veterans Medal.
He was made a commander of the Order of the Crown of
Belgium by King Baudouin in 1959. In 1964 he was pre-
sented the Order of Lafayette Freedom Award "for distin-
guished leadership in combating communism."

In 1968 the Catholic Radio and Television Association
conferred its coveted annual award to Archbishop Sheen for
his outstanding contributions to these media.

# CHRONOLOGY

## BASIC INFORMATION

| | |
|---|---|
| Born El Paso, Illinois, May 8 | 1895 |
| Ordained, September 20 | 1919 |
| Papal Chamberlain | 1934 |
| Domestic Prelate | 1935 |
| National Director, SPOF | 1950–66 |
| Appointed Bishop: Pius XII | 1951 |
| Auxiliary Bishop of New York | 1951–66 |
| Appointed to Vatican Council II<br>Commission on the Missions<br>by Pope John XXIII | 1962 |
| Appointed to post-conciliar<br>Commission on the Missions<br>by Pope Paul VI | 1965 |

Consecrated missionary bishops
   with Pope John XXIII in
   St. Peter's, Rome                May 1960–May 1961
Appointed Bishop of Rochester,
   New York, by Pope Paul VI              1966
Elected by the American Episcopacy
   Chairman of Committee for the
   Propagation of the Faith                1966
Elected by the American Episcopacy to
   the Administrative Board of the National
   Council of Catholic Bishops            1966
Appointed to the Papal Commission for
   Non-Believers by Pope Paul VI          1969
Named Archbishop of the Titular See of
   Newport (Wales) by Pope Paul VI        1969
Named Assistant at the Pontifical Throne
   by Pope Paul VI                  July 1976

## DEGREES

J.C.B., Catholic University of America,     1920
Ph.D., Louvain, Belgium,                1923
S.T.D., Rome,                        1924
Agrégé en philosophie, Louvain,        1925
Honorary: LL.D., Litt.D., L.H.D.

# EDUCATOR

Dogmatic theology professor, St. Edmund's
  College, Ware, England,                    1925
Philosophy professor, Catholic University
  of America,                              1926–50

# PREACHER

Summer Conferences, Westminster,
  London,                        1925, 1928, 1931
Catholic Summer School, Cambridge
  University,                              1930–31
Annual Broadcasts, "The Catholic Hour,"   1930–52

# EDITOR

*World Mission* and *Mission* magazines

# COLUMNIST

"God Love You," Catholic press; "Bishop Sheen Writes," secular press

# AUTHOR

| | |
|---|---|
| *God and Intelligence,* | 1925 |
| *Religion Without God,* | 1928 |
| *The Life of All Living,* 1929; Rev. Ed. | 1979 |
| *The Divine Romance,* | 1930 |
| *Old Errors and New Labels,* | 1931 |
| *Moods and Truths,* | 1932 |
| *Way of the Cross,* | 1932 |
| *Seven Last Words,* | 1933 |
| *Hymn of the Conquered,* | 1933 |
| *The Eternal Galilean,* | 1934 |
| *Philosophy of Science,* | 1934 |
| *The Mystical Body of Christ,* | 1935 |
| *Calvary and the Mass,* | 1936 |
| *The Moral Universe,* | 1936 |
| *The Cross and the Beatitudes,* | 1937 |
| *The Cross and the Crisis,* | 1938 |
| *Liberty, Equality and Fraternity,* | 1938 |
| *The Rainbow of Sorrow,* | 1938 |
| *Victory over Vice,* | 1939 |
| *Whence Come Wars,* | 1940 |
| *The Seven Virtues,* | 1940 |
| *For God and Country,* | 1941 |
| *A Declaration of Dependence,* | 1941 |
| *God and War and Peace,* | 1942 |
| *The Divine Verdict,* | 1943 |
| *The Armor of God,* | 1943 |
| *Philosophies at War,* | 1943 |
| *Seven Words to the Cross,* | 1944 |
| *Seven Pillars of Peace,* | 1944 |

*Love One Another,*                                            1944
*Seven Words of Jesus and Mary,*                              1945
*Preface to Religion,*                                         1946
*Characters of the Passion,*                                   1946
*Jesus, Son of Mary,*                                          1947
*Communism and the Conscience of the West,*                   1948
*Philosophy of Religion,*                                      1948
*Peace of Soul,*                                               1949
*Lift Up Your Heart,*                                          1950
*Three to Get Married,*                                        1951
*The World's First Love,*                                      1952
*Life Is Worth Living,* Vol. I,                               1953
*Life Is Worth Living,* Vol. II,                             1954
*The Life of Christ,*                                         1954
*Way to Happiness,*                                           1954
*Way to Inner Peace,*                                         1954
*God Loves You,*                                              1955
*Thinking Life Through,*                                      1955
*Thoughts for Daily Living,*                                  1955
*Life Is Worth Living,* Vol. III,                            1955
*Life Is Worth Living,* Vol. IV,                             1956
*Life Is Worth Living,* Vol. V,                              1957
*Life of Christ,* 1958; Rev. Ed.                             1977
*This Is the Mass,* 1958; Rev. Ed.                           1965
*This Is Rome,*                                               1960
*Go to Heaven,*                                               1960
*This Is the Holy Land,*                                      1961
*These Are the Sacraments,*                                   1962
*The Priest Is Not His Own,*                                  1963
*Missions and the World Crisis,*                              1964
*The Power of Love,*                                          1965

*Walk with God,*                                                    1965
*Christmas Inspirations,*                                           1966
*Footprints in a Darkened Forest,*                                 1966
*Guide to Contentment,*                                             1967
*Easter Inspirations,*                                             1967
*Those Mysterious Priests,*                                         1974
*Life Is Worth Living,* First and Second Series Abridged,          1978

## OTHER BOOKS OF INTEREST

*The Wit and Wisdom of Bishop Fulton J. Sheen,* ed. by Bill Adler
    (Image Books)
*The Electronic Christian* (Macmillan)
*A Fulton Sheen Reader* (Carillon Books)